The Armenian Prayers (Աղօթք) attributed to Ephrem the Syrian

Texts from Christian Late Antiquity

36

Series Editor

George Anton Kiraz

TeCLA (Texts from Christian Late Antiquity) is a series presenting ancient Christian texts both in their original languages and with accompanying contemporary English translations.

The Armenian Prayers (Աղօթք) attributed to Ephrem the Syrian

Edited and Translated by
Edward G. Mathews Jr.

gorgias press
2014

Gorgias Press LLC, 954 River Road, Piscataway, NJ, 08854, USA

www.gorgiaspress.com

Copyright © 2014 by Gorgias Press LLC

All rights reserved under International and Pan-American Copyright Conventions. No part of this publication may be reproduced, stored in a retrieval system or transmitted in any form or by any means, electronic, mechanical, photocopying, recording, scanning or otherwise without the prior written permission of Gorgias Press LLC.

2014

ISBN 978-1-4632-0262-0

ISSN 1935-6846

Library of Congress Cataloging-in-Publication Data

Aghot'k' zorawor srboc' horn Ep'remi Khorin Asorwoy asats'eal. English.
  The Armenian prayers attributed to Ephrem the Syrian / edited and translated by Edward G. Mathews, Jr.
      pages cm. -- (Texts from Christian late antiquity, ISSN 1935-6846 ; 36)
  Text in Armenian and English translation; with introductory material in English.
  Includes bibliographical references and index.
   ISBN 978-1-4632-0262-0
 1. Prayers, Early Christian--History and criticism. 2. Armenian Church--Prayers and devotions. 3. Ephraem, Syrus, Saint, 303-373. I. Ephraem, Syrus, Saint, 303-373. II. Mathews, Edward G., 1954- translator. III. Aghot'k' zorawor srboc' horn Ep'remi khorin Asorwoy asats'eal. IV. Title.
  BR65.E634A7 2014
  264'.01401--dc23

2014011898

Printed in the United States of America

*The publication of this volume was made possible
by a generous grant
from the Dolores Zohrab Liebmann Fund*

TABLE OF CONTENTS

Table of Contents vii
Introduction: The Armenian Prayers (Աղօթք) Attributed to Ephrem the Syrian 1
    About the Reputed Author 1
    Life 1
    Writings 3
    Ephrem Armeniacus/Ephrem in Armenian 4
        Tradition 4
        Armenian Writings 6
    The Book of Prayers 9
        Authorship and Date 11
        Note on the Text and Translation 13
A *Sharakan* composed by St. Nersēs Shnorhali (†1173) for the feast of
    St. Ephrem Asori 15
Text and Translation 17
    Part I: The Prayers of the Mighty and Holy Ephrem, Our Father
        from Lower Syria 19
    Part II: More Prayers from Saint Ephrem 95
    Part III: More Prayers from [Ephrem] 105
    Part IV: More Prayers from [Ephrem] on Repentance 111
    Part V: More Prayers from [Ephrem] 129
    Part VI: More Prayers from [Ephrem] 133
    Part VII: More Prayers from [Ephrem] 159
    Part VIII: More Prayers from [Ephrem] 163
Select Bibliography 165
    Collected Works 165
        Armenian 165
        Syriac 165
        Greek 165
    The Prayers 165
    Other Edited Works and Translations 166
    Secondary Studies 168
Index 173
    Names and Terms 173
    Biblical Citations and Allusions 174

Introduction: The Armenian Prayers (Աղօթք) Attributed to Ephrem the Syrian

About the Reputed Author

St. Ephrem the Syrian is beyond any shadow of a doubt one of the giants of the early church. His renown spread far beyond the borders of his native country. Within a relatively short time after his death, he was already being lauded by such disparate figures as Palladius, Sozomen, Epiphanius, Jerome, Narsai, Philoxenos, Severus of Antioch, Jacob of Sarug, and others.[1] Theodoret of Cyr dubbed him "The Harp of the Holy Spirit,"[2] primarily for the beauty and the spiritual depth of the vast number of his hymns, which are considered by many modern scholars to be among the most beautiful of all religious poetry.[3] Many of these works were soon translated — some even during his lifetime — into nearly every language of the Christian Mediterranean world: Greek, Latin, Armenian, Arabic, Coptic, Ethiopic, Georgian, Old Slavonic, and Syro-Palestinian.[4] Ephrem is often remembered in a number of these Christian traditions not only as the author of such beautiful and edifying works, but even as native son and pillar of that particular tradition. Thus, in addition to his genuine compositions, Ephrem became the traditional — or reputed — author of numerous homilies, biblical commentaries, anti-heretical tracts, and prayers, many of which survive only in translation.

Life

Very little is known of Ephrem's life, and most of the later traditions about him are simply unsupported legends told by later hagiographers. What we do know is that he was born in Nisibis (Arm., *Mcbin*), around 306, into a Christian family. Ephrem spent

---

[1] For general introductions to Ephrem, see especially S.P. Brock, *The Luminous Eye*, and E.G. Mathews, Jr., "General Introduction," in E.G. Mathews, Jr. and J.P. Amar, *St. Ephrem the Syrian*, 3–56.

[2] Theodoret, *Epistle* 145; see Y. Azema ed., *Théodoret de Cyr, Correspondance III*, 190; Eng. tr. in LNPF II, vol. 3, 315.

[3] In a now oft-quoted phrase, Robert Murray, *Symbols of Church and Kingdom*, 31, calls Ephrem "the greatest poet of the patristic age and, perhaps, the only theologian-poet to rank beside Dante."

[4] The works in these languages, many of which are translations of Greek works, were first set out in E. Beck, et al., "Ephrem le Syrien". This material has now been updated in the relevant sections of K. den Biesen, *Annotated Bibliography of Ephrem the Syrian*.

most of his life there in the service of four bishops whose praises he continually sang.[5] He remained in Nisibis until he was about fifty years old, at which time the Persian Shapur II defeated and killed the Roman Emperor Julian, known as the Apostate. The newly elected Emperor Jovian was compelled to cede Nisibis, along with other important border regions, to the Persians in 363. According to the terms of the ensuing peace treaty all the Christian inhabitants of Nisibis and the surrounding territories were forced under threat of death to depart Persian territory. Ephrem, therefore, along with his fellow Nisibene Christians, packed up his belongings and began his journey eastward.[6] Eventually he made his way to Edessa (Arm., *Urhay*), then the center of Syrian Christianity, where he spent the last years of his life.

Later hagiographical tradition, full of standard literary *topoi*, portrays Ephrem as a child of pagan parents who fled from the ways of his parents and became a solitary recluse on a mountain outside of Edessa. This same tradition also recounts the tale that Ephrem accompanied his bishop Jacob of Nisibis to the Council of Nicaea in 325. While the chronology is correct, this story is no doubt apocryphal, perhaps even a deliberate attempt to mimic the same story preserved concerning his contemporary, the young Athanasius. Other apocryphal tales, such as his feigning madness to avoid ordination, his lengthy sojourn among the monasteries of Egypt, and his meeting with Basil the Great are also products of this same pseudo-historical hagiographical tradition.[7]

There is no evidence concerning the concrete details of Ephrem's daily life, but it is more than clear that he must have spent a lot of time teaching and preaching. He did at some point attain the rank of deacon[8] in which position, according to Jacob of Sarug (known in Syriac tradition as the "Flute of the Holy Spirit"), Ephrem may even have taught many of his hymns to a group of women called the *b'nāt q'yamâ*, the daughters of the covenant.[9] It is also clear from his writings that Ephrem spent a great deal of his time in prayer and study of the Bible.

---

[5] The first of these was Jacob of Nisibis (Arm., Hakob Mcbin) who has his own history in Armenian tradition, where he is remembered as the one who found Noah's Ark; cf. N.G. Garsoïan, *The Epic Histories attributed to P'awstos Buzand*, 77–80. In some later Armenian texts, he is remembered as the nephew of St. Gregory the Illuminator; cf. L. Avdoyan, *Pseudo-Yovhannēs Mamikonean, The History of Tarōn*, 72. The Armenian translation of the works of the Syrian author Aphrahat is also attributed to Jacob of Nisibis; for bibliography see R.W. Thomson, *A Bibliography of Classical Armenian Literature to 1500 AD*, 30, 62.

[6] The account of this evacuation is recorded by the Roman historian, Ammianus Marcellinus; see J.C. Rolfe, *Ammianus Marcellinus*, XXV.9.

[7] These tales were first analyzed in B. Outtier, "Saint Ephrem d'après ses biographies et ses oeuvres"; cf. also E.G. Mathews, Jr., "The Vita Tradition of Ephrem the Syrian, the Deacon of Edessa", and *idem*, "General Introduction," in E.G. Mathews, Jr. and J.P. Amar, *Selected Prose Works of Ephrem the Syrian*, 12–37.

[8] First recorded in R.T. Meyer, *Palladius, The Lausiac History*, XL. There do exist traditions that Ephrem had been ordained a priest, but these too are late and apocryphal.

[9] A tradition recorded in Jacob of Sarug's *Panegyric on Ephrem*, cf. P. Bedjan, ed., *Acta Martyrum et Sanctorum Syriace*, III.668; see now J.P. Amar, ed., *Jacob of Serug: A Metrical Homily on Holy Mar Ephrem*, 34/35.

Although he lived in Edessa for less than a decade, it seems to have been the most productive literary period of his life as he wrote on various aspects of the faith, and against the heretical groups that were then entrenched in that city and its environs. What may have been the very last event of Ephrem's life is first told in the collection of early monks' lives known as *The Lausiac History*.[10] According to this report it was solely through the efforts of Ephrem that the citizens of Edessa were saved from a severe famine in 373. Ephrem secured the aid of the wealthier townspeople, getting them to agree to provide sufficient funding to procure space as well as food and drink for those many citizens who were struck down by the famine. It must have been very shortly after this act of mercy that Ephrem passed on to his heavenly reward. The date of Ephrem's death is generally held, following the *Chronicle of Edessa*, to be 9 June 373.[11]

WRITINGS

While Ephrem composed biblical commentaries and apologetic treatises, he was most famous for his poetry, which the church historian Sozomen numbered at over three million verses. Ephrem wrote these poems in two styles: *mêmrê* and *madrāšê*, often translated as "metrical homilies," and "hymns," respectively. The *madrāšê* were written in a great variety of musical tones, whereas the *mêmrê* were composed in a standard 7x7 syllable line, later referred to as the "meter of Ephrem". Judging from the great quantity that has survived, the *madrāšê* were Ephrem's favorite style of composition; they have come down to us in over fifteen collections, which were later collected together by his disciples and successors. These include 87 *Hymns on Faith*, 56 *Hymns against Heresies*, 52 *Hymns on the Church*, another 52 *Hymns on Virginity*, 77 *Hymns on Nisibis*, 28 *Hymns on the Nativity*, as well as smaller collections *On Fasting*, *On Unleavened Bread*, *On the Crucifixion*, *On the Epiphany*, *On the Resurrection*, and *On Paradise*. He also composed other hymns on the subject of such contemporary figures as the Emperor Julian, the monks Julian Saba and Abraham Kidunaya, and a small collection on the Martyrs. The *mêmrê*, or metrical homilies, attributed to Ephrem include six *On Faith*, several *Against Bardaisan*, and over twenty homilies on a variety of themes, not all of which are genuine.

He also composed a number of discourses in prose, known as the *Prose Refutations*, against the false teachings of Bardaisan, Marcion, Mani, Hypatius, etc., and a discourse *On Virginity*. There also survive three biblical commentaries. Of these only one, the *Commentary on Genesis*, has survived in a complete version; the commentaries *On Exodus* and *On the Diatessaron*, the second-century compilation of the gospels generally attributed to Justin the Martyr, have both survived nearly complete; the latter has survived completely only in Armenian translation. Included among his prose works are several works that are in such a florid literary style that they have often been referred to as *Kunstprosa*, or Artistic Prose; these include a *Homily on Our Lord*, and a *Letter to Publius*,

---

[10] Palladius, *The Lausiac History*, XL.
[11] L. Hallier, *Untersuchungen über die Edessenische Chronik*, 149; in other ancient accounts, 378 appears as the year of Ephrem's death, see P. Peeters, *Bibliotheca Hagiographica Orientalis*, 63.

of which only two long extracts have survived. There exist also a number of works that are attributed to Ephrem but are almost certainly the work of other writers.[12]

Ephrem was a prolific author who was most widely known for his poetry, which was not only lyrically beautiful but astonishing in the depths of its meditations on the mystery of the divine, and especially on the Incarnation.[13] Due at least in part to this popularity, there were many works attributed to Ephrem that were not actually composed by Ephrem himself. A very striking element of Ephrem's legacy is the size of the three main components of his corpus: the Syriac, the Armenian, and the Greek. Each of these three corpora comprises several large volumes. But the most striking characteristic of all, even beyond their sheer volume, is the fact that these three huge corpora are, for all intents and purposes, entirely separate and distinct collections; there is very little correspondence between any of them! The Greek corpus of his works, which is the largest of all collections of Greek patristic writers with the sole exception of the works of John Chrysostom, includes almost exclusively ascetic treatises — neither poetry nor biblical commentaries — with only a few thematic or periphrastic connections to the genuine Syriac corpus.[14] The collection of works that go under the name of Ephrem in the Armenian language have their own history and tradition.

EPHREM ARMENIACUS/EPHREM IN ARMENIAN

Tradition

When an outsider thinks of the Armenian Church, it is not likely that Ephrem the Syrian (Arm., *Sourb Yeprem Asori*), would be the first one figure to come to mind. As even his name in Armenian makes clear, he was not a native Armenian; he was from Syria, which lay to the southwest of Armenia.[15] So far as we know he never went to Armenia, never spoke Armenian, nor even knew a single person who was Armenian, yet the Ar-

---

[12] Further information and bibliography on all these works can be found in S.P. Brock, "A Brief Guide to the Main Editions and Translations of the Works of St. Ephrem", and, in greater detail, K. den Biesen, *Annotated Bibliography of Ephrem the Syrian*.

[13] For the beauty and profundity of Ephrem's genuine works see, above all, R. Murray, "The Theory of Symbolism in St. Ephrem's Theology"; S.P. Brock, *The Luminous Eye*; T. Bou Mansour, *La pensée symbolique de Saint Ephrem le Syrien*; and K. den Biesen, *Simple and Bold: Ephrem's Art of Symbolic Thought*.

[14] These works are all listed in "Ephraem Graecus," in M. Geerard, *Clavis Patrum Graecorum*, II.366–468. See also, D. Hemmerdinger-Iliadou and J. Kirchmeyer, "Ephrem grec et latin," in *DS* IV.800–822; D. Hemmerdinger-Iliadou, "Ephrem: versions grecque, latine et slave. Addenda et corrigenda". The best evaluation of this Greek corpus is still A. de Halleux, "Ephrem le Syrien".

[15] Early Armenian texts remember him as St. Ephrem of Lower Syria (Arm., *Xorin Asorwoy*), the Roman geographical province known in Greek as Κοίλη Συρία, Latin as *Coele Syria*, or *Syria Profunda*, which had its metropolitan seat in Antioch. The Armenian word Xor was later corrupted into Xour, thus Xourin Asorwoy, "the Syrian priest", derived from the similarly sounding word in Arabic, meaning 'parish priest'.

menian Church, which was evangelized, according to tradition, by the Syrian disciple Addai who was sent there by the Apostle Thomas, has always held Ephrem in the highest regard, and even holds him as a native son. Ephrem is annually celebrated by the Armenian Church during the Advent season, usually in December, and St. Nersēs Shnorhali composed a *sharakan* specifically for Ephrem's feast day (see translation at the end of this introduction).

What might be even more surprising is just how popular — even of what fundamental importance — Ephrem is to the Armenian Church. He seems to have exerted such an influence on the development of various facets of the theology and life of the Armenian Church that he is held to be a pillar of the church there just as he is in his own native Syria. Even with the study of Ephrem's influence on the Armenian Church still in its embryonic stage and much of Armenian literature, especially many important medieval biblical commentaries still unedited — and, in a few cases, even inaccessible in manuscript vaults around the world — certain details can nonetheless be brought forward, even if they cannot paint for us the entire picture.

In Armenian tradition, the works of Ephrem constitute such a significant collection of materials that they have been referred to as "the greatest contributions to the field of patristics."[16] But the sheer quantity of these translated works, however impressive they might be, are still not the measure of the popularity of Ephrem in Armenian tradition. A much more significant indication is how often Ephrem is quoted as an authority in all types of theological literature. He is quoted rather extensively in such ecclesiastical collections as the *Knikʿ Hawatoy* (*Seal of Faith*), the eighth-century compilation of orthodox doctrine, as well as in a later collection entitled the *Armat Hawatoy* (*Root of Faith*). His works are constantly referred to by such great medieval Armenian theologians as Yovhannēs Ōjnetsʿi and his contemporaries Stepʿanos Siwnetsʿi and Grigor Artsruni. Vardan Areweltsʿi cites Ephrem so often that it can sometimes seem as if he is commenting on Ephrem's commentary rather than the biblical book in question. Vanakan Vardapet, in his questions and responses on biblical matters, often simply begins his response with "*Ephrem ases*, Ephrem says". Ephrem is clearly a major source for nearly every medieval Armenian biblical commentary. In one of his epistles, written while briefly imprisoned, Grigor Magistros made a single request, for a work of Ephrem.[17] It was even once suggested that it was the Armenian *Commentary on Genesis* attributed to Ephrem that influenced the famous frescoes on the island church of Aghtamar. The long penitential prayer that is recited at every Armenian Liturgy (now usually recited in an abbreviated form) is traditionally ascribed to Ephrem.

Ephrem's writings were nearly as influential as those of St. John Chrysostom on the development of Armenian theological literature. In fact, the writings of these two constituted the foundation of Armenian theology, especially her biblical exegesis and her early Mariology. One recent scholar has stated unequivocally that: "Ephraem …

---

[16] L. Ter Petrossian, *Ancient Armenian Translations*, 30.
[17] Grigor Magistros, *Epistles*, 3.

and Chrysostom … must be considered the founding fathers of Armenian Gospel exegesis."[18] He further qualifies this statement:

> "while both the practical literal method of Chrysostom and the symbolic synecdoche of Ephraem were enthusiastically received in Armenia, it is Ephraem's approach that seems to prove more decisive for the development of native Armenian exegesis … How much of [Yovhannês] Erznkats'i's (c.1260-c.1335) *Commentary* [*on Matthew*] is original it is difficult to say, since the other Armenian commentators of the Middle Ages remain unpublished. But his wholesale dependence upon Chrysostom and Ephraem is striking; perhaps as much as a half of his commentary can be traced to these two sources, either in paraphrase or in verbatim quotations. It is important to notice too that when he voices a line of exegesis independent of these two sources he tends to prefer Ephraem's method of symbolic synecdoche."[19]

It also seems clear that the identification of the Blessed Virgin as the Church and the mother of the faithful entered the Armenian tradition with Ephrem, perhaps from his *Commentary on the Diatessaron*.

Another, relatively minor but not insignificant, indicator of Ephrem's popularity in Armenia is the number of important figures in Armenian tradition who were given the name of Ephrem. Hratch Acharyan's *Dictionary of Personal Names* lists nearly twenty important figures with the name of Ep'rem, including the 119th Catholicos, Ep'rem of Tzoragueh who was in office 26 December 1809–6 March 1831, and who seems to have overseen the renovation of a number of monasteries, a fitting tribute to the traditional legacy of his namesake.[20] Ep'rem Ssnec'i was a major theological figure of the 18th century whose works were occasionally mistakenly included among the Armenian works of Ephrem the Syrian. Another Ephrem figures among the correspondents of Grigor Magistros.

Armenian Writings

The question of just what works of Ephrem were translated into Armenian or, more accurately, what works attributed to Ephrem in Armenian were actually composed by the fourth-century poet is one that is now "under reassessment". Levon Tēr Petrosyan, who devoted many years to the study of Ephrem, presumes that the Armenian translations of Ephrem's works are all genuine and were completed in the fifth century by the Holy Translators, Mashtots', Sahak and companions.[21] One is indeed struck by the vast extent of the Armenian works attributed to Ephrem; as already noted above, there are nearly as many texts in Armenian attributed to Ephrem as there are extant genuine Syr-

---

[18] T.F. Mathews and A.K. Sanjian, *Armenian Gospel Iconography*, 81.

[19] Ibid., pp. 82–86, and see pp. 91, 92–94, 107, 114, 115, 121, 123, 149, 162 for specific citations.

[20] Among others, he ordered the reconstruction of St. Thaddeus Monastery, now in NW Iran; he is also remembered in inscriptions *in situ* for his restoration of the Monastery of St. Step'anos, located in present day Azerbaijan.

[21] L. Ter Petrossian, *Ancient Armenian Translations*, 30.

iac works; likewise, there are nearly as many Armenian works as there are Greek works attributed to Ephrem. In fact, of all Greek patristic literature, the number of works attributed to Ephrem are second only to the works attributed to John Chrysostom, the most popular of the Greek fathers in eastern traditions.[22] Also — again like the corpus of Greek works attributed to Ephrem — these Armenian works attributed to Ephrem have little — though slightly more than the Greek — correspondence to the genuine extant Syriac works of Ephrem.

It was in 1836 that the Mekhitarist Fathers in Venice published four volumes, over thirteen hundred pages, of the works of St. Ephrem printed from single manuscripts found in their own library.[23] Of these four volumes, the first three contained nothing but biblical commentaries, whereas in Syriac only three commentaries have survived, and then only one in a complete version (see above). The contents of the entire four volumes are as follows:

I: Commentaries on Genesis, Exodus, Leviticus, Numbers, Deuteronomy, Joshua, Judges, 1-2 Samuel and 1-2 Kings (as I-IV Kings), 1-2 Chronicles

II: Commentary on the Diatessaron, An Exposition of the Gospel

III: Commentaries on the Letters of Paul[24]

IV: Assorted Homilies and Treatises, Book of Prayers

Nearly half of the commentaries in volume I and all of those in volume II have now been re-edited in modern critical editions, with modern translations.[25] Fragments of other Old Testament commentaries attributed to Ephrem have also survived: on Job,[26]

---

[22] The skimpy notices in the standard histories of Armenian literature are woefully inadequate. G. Zarbhanalian, *Matenadaran Haykakan T'argmanut'eants' Nakheats'*, although considerably out of date, gives a generally reliable catalogue of the works in this corpus. J. Torossian, "Aknark mě S. Ep'remi Hin Ktakaranin Meknut'eants' Hay t'argmanut'ean vray," is out-of-date and even more inadequate. See now E.G. Mathews, Jr., "The Armenian Literary Corpus attributed to Ephrem the Syrian".

[23] *Srboyn Ep'remi Matenagrut'iwnk'*. For a brief resume of this edition and its contents, see M. Djanachian, "Les Arménistes et les Mékhitaristes," 403–409. See also, K. den Biessen, *Annotated Bibliography of Ephrem the Syrian*, and the brief list of contents below.

[24] These commentaries do not include the letter to Philemon, but do include a commentary on III Corinthians, which reflects the canon in the early Syrian, as well as the Armenian, Church.

[25] L. Leloir, ed., Saint Ephrem. *Commentaire de l'évangile concordant, version arménienne*; G. Egan, ed., *An Exposition of the Gospel by Saint Ephraem*; E.G. Mathews, Jr., ed. and tr., *The Armenian Commentary on the Book of Genesis attributed to Ephrem the Syrian*, and idem., ed. and tr., *The Armenian Commentaries on Exodus-Deuteronomy attributed to Ephrem the Syrian*. New editions and translations of the Historical Books, Joshua – II Chronicles, are in preparation.

[26] A. Vardanean, "Srboyn Ep'remi Meknut'iwn ew skizbn Yobay"; C. Renoux, "Vers le commentaire de Job d'Ephrem de Nisibe," lists more than fifty manuscripts. See now L. Tēr Petrosyan, "Kts'urdk' S. Ep'remi Khorin Asorwoy. He has argued that Eznik knew of this work

the Psalms,[27] Isaiah,[28] Ezekiel,[29] the Twelve Prophets,[30] and Daniel,[31] but none of these has ever been edited or studied. In addition to the two Gospel commentaries edited by the Mekhitarists, a *Commentary on the Acts of the Apostles* was subsequently published by Fr. Nersēs Akinian.[32] Again, one finds in manuscript catalogues references to a *Commentary on the Gospel of Matthew* and to a *Commentary on the Gospel of John*,[33] but in other manuscripts they are attributed rather to Ephrem, the XVIIIth century Catholicos of Sis, already mentioned above, to whom they probably belong.

Most of the homilies contained in volume IV have still not received any serious scholarly attention. Two significant collections of poetical works, unknown to the Mekhitarist editors, have been subsequently been published, in critical editions with modern language translations: a collection of fifty-one Hymns (Arm., *kc'urdk'*) which, in style, are clearly translations of Syriac *madrāšē*;[34] and a large collection of hymns titled *On Nicomedia* which equally clearly correspond to Syriac *mêmrê*.[35]

The *Hymns* contain a varied collection of poetic pieces on an assortment of different subjects, such as Virginity and Eucharist; it also includes a number of dialogue poems and a short Hymn on the consecration of a daughter of the covenant (Syr., *bat q'yāmâ*). The *Hymns on Nicomedia* give to the reader a vivid contemporary account of, and theological reflection on, the great earthquake that struck the city of Nicomedia on

---

and therefore the *Commentary on Job* must have been translated in the first decades of the fifth century.

[27] Br. Lib. Add. 19279, is a *catena* on the Psalms from the works of Ephrem, Athanasius, Basil, Daniel, Dionysius, Epiphanius and John Chrysostom. See F.C. Conybeare, *A Catalogue of the Armenian Manuscripts in the British Museum*, 188–189.

[28] Ms. Matenadaran 4825, is a commentary by George Skewrats'i on Isaiah which contains many fragments from a commentary on Isaiah attributed to Ephrem. See D. Bundy, "The Sources of the Isaiah Commentary of Georg Skewrac'i," 401–402.

[29] Ms. Matenadaran 5906, is a commentary on Ezekiel culled from the commentaries of Ephrem, Esayi Nch'ets'i, and Cyril of Alexandria.

[30] Ms. Matenadaran 4042, is a commentary on the Twelve Prophets attributed to Ephrem.

[31] Vat. Arm. 14, contains a catenae on Daniel taken from the works of Ephrem and Hippolytus. See E. Tisserant, *Codices Armeni Bibliothecae Vaticanae Borgiani Vaticani Barberiniani Chisiani*, 245. Ms. Matenadaran 3606, is a commentary by Vardan Arawelts'i on Daniel which contains many fragments from works attributed to Ephrem, Hippolytus and Step'anos Siwnets'i.

[32] N. Akinian, Srboyn *Ep'remi Asorwoy Meknut'iwn Gortsots' Aṛak'elots'*.

[33] Fragments of a commentary on the Gospel of Matthew are found in Mss. Mat. 1138 (with commentaries of Ephrem on Samuel, Kings and the letters of Paul), 3791, 4676, and 4802. Fragments of a commentary on the Gospel of John are found in Mss. Mat. 1204, 4139, and 9372.

[34] L. Mariès and C. Mercier, eds., *Hymnes de S. Ephrem conservées en version arménienne*, with accompanying Latin translation; there is no surviving trace of their Syriac originals.

[35] C. Renoux, ed., *Ephrem de Nisibe Mêmrê sur Nicomedie*, Armenian text with Syriac fragments, accompanied by a French translation.

the 24th of August in the year 358, providing us with a substantial counter-witness to the *Oration* of the pagan orator Libanius on the same catastrophe.[36]

A few other texts, categorized under the heading 'homily', have also been published in Western journals in the last half century.[37] These seem to be mostly prose texts in Armenian, whatever their original format was. Manuscript catalogues provide titles of more than two dozen additional homilies, but little more can be said about them until we have reliable editions. To complete the inventory, note might also be made here of Armenian translations of most of the standard biographical works about Ephrem, the *Life of Ephrem*, the *Testament of Ephrem* and an *Encomium on Ephrem* attributed to Gregory of Nyssa, as well as a number of *Synaxaria* entries, which are also now available in critical editions, with modern translations.[38]

THE BOOK OF PRAYERS

In addition to all those works just enumerated, there also exists a significant collection of prayers (Arm., *aghōt'k'*) attributed to Ephrem that must have been immensely popular among Armenians, since they have been preserved in over seventy manuscripts. Three of the manuscripts, currently found in the Matenadaran in Erevan (nn. 5115, 5453, and 10062), dated to the thirteenth century, are the oldest that have survived. Manuscripts that contain only the *Prayers of Ephrem* do not seem to appear before the seventeenth century; the earliest of these, Jerusalem 1525, which is almost certainly the basis for the Jerusalem printed edition (see below), is dated 1619.[39] Just as the large quantity of these manuscripts indicate the great popularity of these *Prayers* so too do the printed editions. The first printed collection was published in Constantinople in 1734, reprinted several times, and there have been a number of subsequent editions.[40] It seems likely that these prayers were as popular to Armenians as — if not more than — such prayers as those of Gregory Lusaworich' or of Yovhannēs of Garni, with

---

[36] Libanius, "Monody on Nicomedia," in R. Foerster, ed., *Libanii Opera*, vol. 4, 322–341; Eng. tr., in J. Duncombe, *Select Works of the Emperor Julian and Some Pieces of the Sophist Libanius*, II. 227–242.

[37] See, for example, G. Garitte, "La version arménienne du sermon de saint Ephrem sur Jonas"; A. Srjuni, "Srboyn Ep'remi i Yusēp' ewt'n Vahangi"; B. Outtier, "Un discours sur les ruses de Satan attribué à Ephrem: texte arménien inédit".

[38] These texts have been conveniently gathered together, with French translations, in L. Ter Petrossian, ed., and B. Outtier, tr., *Textes arméniens relatifs à S. Ephrem*.

[39] The others are Matenadaran mss. 8418, 9453, 9576, 9687, and 9848.

[40] *Girk' Aghōt'its'*. Subsequently, the collection has been printed in *Srboyn Ep'remi Matenagrut'iwnk'*, IV. 227–276, and in *Girk' Aghōt'its' asats'eal Srboyn Ep'remi Khurin Asorwoy*, 43–233. There have also been numerous other editions of this popular collection, many based on that first Constantinople collection; M. Djanachian, "Les Arménistes et les Mékhitaristes," 404, n. 62, lists nine editions from the eighteenth and nineteenth centuries, along with others "de peu d'importance".

which they are often paired together in the manuscript tradition.[41] The number of recent translations into modern Armenian — both Eastern[42] and Western[43] — attests to a substantial renewed interest in, and appreciation for, these *Prayers*. Nonetheless, it remains the case that these *Prayers* attributed to Ephrem never reached the height of popularity as those composed by Grigor Narekatsʻi which are often accorded mystical, even almost biblical, status — even though they are sometimes combined together in a single manuscript.[44]

As with nearly all the other works in Armenian attributed to Ephrem, these *Prayers* too are unique among all the many works that go under his name. There are many prayers attributed to Ephrem in his native Syriac, but they seem never to have been collected together. And Ortiz de Urbina has already noted that these prayers are found only in very late manuscripts.[45] Other Christian traditions also preserve prayers attributed to Ephrem, for example, the famous *Prayer of St. Ephrem* used in the Byzantine Paschal Liturgy.[46] In Russian there exists a collection of prayers attributed to Ephrem but these are, in fact, translations of some of the non-genuine Greek ascetic works, that were extracted and compiled in the nineteenth century by Theophan the Recluse in the form of prayers.[47] Thus, with this Armenian collection of prayers we seem to have a very similar situation, in microcosm, as we have with the entire literary legacy of Ephrem, described above; there are prayers attributed to Ephrem in these same Syriac, Greek, Armenian traditions, but there is no discernible correspondence between any of them. This particular collection of prayers attributed to St. Ephrem exists only in Armenian and has been the exclusive treasure of the Armenian Church for centuries.

---

[41] Other authors whose prayers are also often grouped with those of Ephrem are the Greeks Athanasius, Cyril of Alexandria, and John Chrysostom.

[42] A. Arabajyan, "Surb Eprem Xuri Asori (306–379)," translated 18 select prayers. T. Xachʻatryan translated the first 140 prayers in "Surb Epʻrem Asori". The same prayers were reprinted, along with a homily on repentance, in T. Xachʻatryan, *Sourb Epʻrem Asori, Hordorak Apashxarutʻyan Zorawor Aghōtʻkʻ*.

[43] Prayers 1–141 were translated by Anoushavan Srpazan Tanielian [as Anoushvard], in "Yogewor Margritner". The same 141 prayers were translated, along with a homily on repentance, in V. Ohanean, *Surb Epʻrem Asori, Yordorak Apashxarutʻean Zorawor Aghōtʻkʻ*. There exist, to my knowledge, no other translations of these prayers into any modern language.

[44] At least two manuscripts, Matenadaran 5666 (xiv century) and 6064 (xvii century), contain only the prayers of Ephrem and the *Book of Lamentations* of Grigor Narekatsʻi.

[45] I. Ortiz de Urbina, *Patrologia Syriaca*, 75. Some of these prayers can be found in T.J. Lamy, ed., *Sancti Ephraem Syri Hymni et Sermones*, III.211–230. Other unedited prayers are listed in A. Baumstark, *Geschichte der syrischen Literatur*, 51, n. 6.

[46] On this prayer, see A. Schmemann, *Great Lent*, 36–41, O. Clément, *Three Prayers*, 71–84, and W.C. Mills, *The Prayer of St. Ephrem the Syrian*.

[47] For some of these Russian prayers attributed to Ephrem, see A. Janda, *A Spiritual Psalter or Reflections on God excerpted by Bishop Theophan from the Works of our Holy Father Ephraim the Syrian*.

Authorship and Date

These very beautiful and inspiring Armenian *Prayers* are unanimously attributed to Ephrem the Syrian in the manuscript tradition, but there are a number of factors that militate against this attribution. As I have attempted to demonstrate elsewhere, these prayers betray a rigid type of asceticism and a remarkably preponderant tone of an individualistic type of repentance that are essentially foreign to the genuine works of Ephrem. Whereas in his genuine works Ephrem is far more interested in the awe and the grandeur of God that provokes prayer and praise in the beholder, the Armenian *Prayers* are almost entirely centered on the author, his sinfulness and his personal need for God's mercy. One also finds in these *Prayers* a liberal use of titles for Christ, just as one finds in the genuine Syriac works of Ephrem. However, apart from those titles that can be traced back to biblical antecedents none of the titles in these Armenian *Prayers* is identical to any of those found in Ephrem's genuine works.[48]

In addition to these observations, there are no discernible traces of a Syriac original to these *Prayers*. They flow so nicely and freely that any hint of "translationese" can no longer be detected, unlike the *Hymns* or the *Hymns on Nicomedia* which both betray their underlying Syriac and also contain all the general features of Ephrem's literary style and theological outlook.

Whenever the author of the *Prayers* actually cites, rather than simply alludes to, a biblical verse, the text nearly always corresponds to the text as found in the Zohrab bible which, albeit having older roots, is generally associated with the revision of Gēorg Skewṙatsʻi, who flourished in the thirteenth century.

Then, one also finds certain phrases that seem to betray an original composition in Armenian. For example, the author, in *Prayer* 136 of Book I, invokes the intercession of St. Gregory the Illuminator who first established Christianity in Armenia. This invocation is not at all out of place — actually, it would be expected in an Armenian composition — but this Gregory, although chronologically prior to Ephrem, is utterly unknown in the genuine Syriac works of Ephrem.

Lastly, one finds a suspiciously large number of occurrences in the *Prayers* of two words that might also be more indicative of a later than an early composition. The first is *bazmamegh* ("of many sins"). While this compound can be found in early Armenian texts, it is much more common in later texts, and is especially associated with the refrain of the famous prayer, *In Faith I Confess*, composed by Nersēs Shnorhali and still recited by faithful Armenians. The other term, *mardasēr* ("Lover of mankind"), can again be found in some early texts but is a phrase that seems to have become popular in Armenia through its usage in the later Byzantine Church. In any case, the Syriac equivalent of neither of these two words (though the idea can certainly be found) is found in the genuine works of St. Ephrem.

Just as these indications are not precise, no precision of date or authorship can be offered here, but all the above factors seem to point to an Armenian environment perhaps closer in time to the early second millennium rather than to the fifth century

---

[48] E.G. Mathews, Jr., "A First Glance at the Armenian *Prayers* attributed to Surb Epʻrem Xorin Asorwoy".

when the first translators were so active. It may even not perhaps be too far beyond the realm of possibility to suggest that these *Prayers* came out of the activity of the Cilician translators, Grigor Vkayasēr, Nersēs Shnorhali and Gēorg Kesuntsʻi et al., all of whom are known to have been far more involved in the translation of the extant Armenian works of Ephrem than heretofore realized.[49]

This collection of Armenian *Prayers*, as it now exists, is divided into eight sections of very different formats and lengths. The first section, by far the longest, is further divided into 141 individual prayers that vary from a few lines to several pages in length. The remaining seven sections are essentially single prayers varying in length from less than two to more than thirty-six pages in the pocket-size Jerusalem edition.

As the reader, or pray-er, sees very quickly, these *Prayers* are filled with a very deep spirituality and with a very profound foundation in the biblical text — almost every line evokes a phrase or an event from the Bible. Ephrem's many titles for God are all grounded in biblical images: Fount of Life and Immortality, Treasury of all Goodness, True Light, etc. If one does not simply read these prayers, but instead really prays with the author, one can almost feel filled with the same love of the author for that Christian God who is all-good and all-loving. His soul pours out all his weaknesses, laying them at the feet of the Almighty depending on and begging for His deep and infinite Mercy. It is not stretching the truth to say that the ascetical nature of these poems shares more than a little in common with the much more famous prayers of St. Grigor Narekatsʻi, as James Russell already pointed out more than a quarter century ago.[50]

These prayers are sometimes categorized as dark, dwelling on the sinfulness of man, but this is to miss the point of these *Prayers*, just as it would be to make the same categorization of the *Lamentations* of Narekatsʻi. Such an interpretation misses both the reality of the infinite distance between man, here in the person of the author, and God and the great trust that the author constantly places on the grace and mercy of God in whom he clearly trusts completely to forgive him, to cleanse him from all his sins and to bring him into eternal communion with Him. Any "darkness" is rather an honest acknowledgement of man's sinfulness and that he is incapable on his own power to attain the divine. The author recognizes that it is God alone who can bridge that chasm between God and man, between heaven and earth; he constantly begs God to grant him the strength to keep him on His path and to grant him the strength to love God's commandments as revealed in scripture and to follow them at all times despite his great weaknesses; there is nothing that he himself can do (cf. John 15:5).

All this, however, is not to suggest that this collection of *Prayers* is not worthy to be read and prayed. While these prayers may not be from the pen of the fourth-century Syrian poet, they bring to the fore the sinfulness of human beings and their utter dependency on the grace of an all-loving and merciful God. This alone makes them im-

---

[49] For the activity of these translators see, most recently, J.J.S. Weitenberg, "Armeno-Syrian Cultural Relations in the Cilician Period (12th – 14th c.)"; E.G. Mathews, Jr., "Syriac into Armenian: The Translations and their Translators"; R. Thomson, "Literary Interactions between Syriac and Armenian".

[50] J.R. Russell, "On St. Grigor Narekatsi, His Sources and His Contemporaries," 62–63.

portant for helping the contemporary Christian in turning back to that merciful God and away from the all too prevalent contemporary culture of greed and material possession, which has wrought such great harm not only to those souls so obsessed, but also to society in general. So, while these Armenian *Prayers* may not be from the pen of Ephrem the Syrian, they are genuine, deep and profound Christian pleas offered up to God, and Christians everywhere ought to be grateful to the Armenians for having preserved them, whoever their now anonymous author might have been. And, at the very least, these treasures are worthy not only of preserving, but also of sharing.

Note on the Text and Translation

The text reproduced here is from the edition published by St. James Press in Jerusalem in 1933. I have, however, not hesitated to tacitly correct a few inadvertent misprints. As the reader will notice immediately, I have also taken the liberty of setting out the original prose text in something akin to poetic lines in order to highlight the rhythmic prose of the *Prayers*. I believe it also aids in the reading —or praying — of the text but it is not in any way to be interpreted as indicating my position on the original format of the *Prayers*.

As for the translation, I have tried to stay as literal to the original as English syntax allows. Nonetheless, in order to try to make these *Prayers* flow smoothly in English (I indulge the reader's patience here) I have here too taken the occasional liberty of altering the literal construction for the sake of the English, such as changing a passive voice to an active, or a genitive noun construction into an adjective. While I normally indicate with brackets any additional words not actually in the original text, I have added a few obvious possessive adjectives, not expressed in the text, without the intrusion of the brackets.

This is the first non-Armenian translation of Book I of these *Prayers* and, to my knowledge, the first ever translation from the Classical Armenian text of the remaining seven books. If these translations do anything at all to bring these *Prayers* into use in the Western world, I will consider my task more than rewarded. May that ever merciful God shower His great mercy on all those who take them up and pray in true humility and service.

A *SHARAKAN* COMPOSED BY ST. NERSĒS SHNORHALI (†1173) FOR THE FEAST OF ST. EPHREM ASORI

You who have dwelt in the desert like the great Elijah
    and John the Baptist toiling in the angelic life,
    a rose flower among the thorns of the hills,
    smelling the sweetness of Christ,
    of the lives of those being saved for life.

O blessed Saint Ephrem,
    intercede with Christ on behalf of those who celebrate your feast-day,
    you who have drunk the flowing waters of grace
    from the heavenly spiritual streams,
    just as the ranks of the Apostles in the upper room
    from the fiery tongues which you poured out abundantly
    and distributed throughout the world for thirsty souls to drink,
O blessed Saint Ephrem.

O divinely planted wise servant of life,
a grape bunch has come forth from you,
    from which you have given to eat
    and give to eat always to the young people of the church,
O scribe of the heavenly kingdom and learned doctor of the Old and New Testaments,
O blessed Saint Ephrem.
Come, learn O children of the desert,
    students with hunger for the word of truth.

With exultation, let us complete the memorial of [this] teacher of the church,
    who completed his course [of life] today
    and was transported to that divinely built Tabernacle
        among the ranks of the spiritual first-born.
On our behalf, intercede always before the Lord,
    and make atonement for our transgressions.
With thanksgiving, let us glorify you, O Christ, King of Glory,
    who have chosen as the herald of your divine law Saint Ephrem,
    who has placed the true silver of the word from You
    for interest for the spiritual children of mankind.
By his supplication, make us worthy to glorify the holy Trinity forever. Amen.

TEXT AND TRANSLATION

ԱՂՕԹՔ ՁՈՐԱԽՈՐ ՍՐԲՈՑ ՀՕՐՆ
ԵՓՐԵՄԻ ԽՈՐԻՆ ԱՍՈՐԻՈՅ ԱՍԱՑԵԱԼ

Ա

1 Տես Տէր՝ զտառապանս իմ եւ զցաւս Հոգւոյ իմոյ
  բազմամեղիս.
  դարձ՝ ներեա՛ եւ ի քեզ առաջնորդեա՛, որ ասացեր՝
  «դարձարուք առ իս, եւ ես դառնամ առ ձեզ»։
  Ինձ լքելոյս ողորմեա՛.
  ինձ եղկելոյս օգնեա՛.
  ինձ խաւարելոյս ճառագայթեա՛,
  ինձ մոլորելոյս առաջնորդեա՛,
      որ լի եմ մեղօք եւ անբաւ յանցանօք,
      եւ ի յորձանս անօրէնութեան տարաբերեալ ծփիմ,
  եւ առ քեզ ապաւինիմ,
  որպէս Պետրոսին՝ ձեռնարկեա ինձ։
  Գոչեմ որպէս զմաքսաւորն արդարանալ.
  ճնորհեմ դյանցանս իմ որպէս զաւազակին.
  բաց եւ ինձ զդուռն կենաց ճանապարհին,
  եւ մոյծ դիս յարքունական առագաստն։

2 Ո՛վ խորք մեծութեան եւ իմաստութեան,
  փրկեա՛ զըմբռնեալս՝
      որ ի խորս մեղաց ծովուն անկեալ եմ.
  զերծմ եւ զօրացմ դիս առնել զկամս քո,
  սպալ եւ լալ անդադար ի տուէ եւ ի գիշերի
      զամենայն անօրէնութին եւ զեղգութինս իմ։

PART I:

THE PRAYERS OF THE MIGHTY AND HOLY EPHREM, OUR FATHER FROM LOWER SYRIA

1. See, O Lord, my tribulations and the afflictions of my soul,
   for I am burdened by my many sins.
   Return, grant pardon and lead me back to You, for You said,
   "Return to Me and I will return to you."[1]
   Have mercy on me for I am languishing;
   Help me for I am so wretched,
   Shine on me for I am so dark
   Guide me for I have gone astray;
   I am filled with sins and uncountable transgressions,
   I am floundering and tossed about in torrents of iniquity.
   But I take refuge in You,
   Reach out Your hand to me as You did to Peter.[2]
   I call upon You to justify me as You did that tax-collector;[3]
   Pardon my transgressions as You did those of the thief.[4]
   Open to me the gate to the Way of Life,[5]
   and bring me into the royal bridal-chamber.[6]

2. O depths of majesty and of wisdom,
   Deliver me for I am trapped,
   and I have fallen into the depths of the sea of sin.
   Free me and give me the strength to do Your will,
   That day and night without ceasing I may weep and lament
   all my iniquity and my slothfulness.

---

[1] Zechariah 1:3.
[2] Cf. Matthew 14:31.
[3] Cf. Luke 18:9–14.
[4] Cf. Luke 23:39–43.
[5] Cf. John 14:6.
[6] Cf. Matthew 22:10.

3 Աղբիւր կենդանութեան եւ անմահութեան՝
   արբո՛ գծարաւեալ Հոգի իմ յառատաբուղխ վտակէ քումէ,
      որ պատքեալ տողորիմ ի բագում անօրէնութեանց իմոց.
   խթեա՛ ի քարացեալ սիրտ իմ,
   եւ Հա՛ն ինձ արտասուս ապաշխարութեան։

4 Գանձդ ամենայն բարութեանց՝ շնորհեա՛ ինձ դանկի միոյ չափ
      ի քո բագում առատ բարեացդ,
   որ չարաչարս եմ աղքատացեալ եւ քաղցեալ.
   զգեցո՛ եւ կերակրեա՛ զիս արտասուօք ապաշխարութեան։

5 Լոյս ճշմարիտ Քրիստոս՝ որ լուսաւորես զամենայն մարդ,
   լուսաւորեա՛ զիս զխաւարեալս մեղօք.
   բա՛ց դաչս սրտի իմոյ, եւ Հաստատեա՛
      յերկիւղ եւ ի սէր պատուիրանաց քոց։

6 Մի՛ դատեր եւ մի՛ դատապարտեր զիս Տէ՛ր՝
      ըստ անբաւ գազիր գործոց իմոց,
   եւ մի՛ կացուցես զիս ընդ այլսն որք գայրացուցին զքեզ.
   այլ ընդ փառաւորեալսն փառաւորեա՛,
   եւ ընդ պսակեալսն պսակեա՛,
   եւ ընդ բերկրեալսն ուրախացո՛։

3   O Font of Life and of Immortality,
    Give my thirsting soul drink from Your copiously-flowing streams,
        for I am burning and parched from the multitude of my iniquities.
    Strike my stony heart
    and draw out for me tears of repentance.[7]

4   O Treasury of all Goodness, grant the measure of a single penny[8]
        from the superabundance of Your goods
    to me who am so miserably impoverished and starving.
    Clothe me[9] and nourish me with tears of repentance.

5   O Christ, the True Light, who enlightens everyone,[10]
    Give Your light to me for I am so darkened by my sin.
    Open the eyes of my heart and restore it
        to fear and to love Your commandments.[11]

6   Do not condemn me and do not damn me, O Lord,
        on account of my countless impure deeds,
    and do not set me among those goats who provoked You.[12]
    But glorify me along with those who have been glorified,
    Crown me along with those who have been crowned,
    and give me joy along with those who rejoice.

---

[7] The author here seems to be playing on the combined images of the stony heart of Ezekiel 11:19, and the rock that Moses struck in the desert, Exodus 17:6 (longer version in Numbers 20:2–13).

[8] Cf. Mark 12:42, and parallels.

[9] Perhaps an allusion to Genesis 3:21.

[10] Cf. John 1:9, 8:12.

[11] This last phrase, which even occurs exactly in stanza 14, et al., is the first occurrence of a very important theme running throughout these prayers, following an injunction found nearly everywhere in the bible. While the injunction pervades the bible, the author seems to understand it in its Johannine formulation, cf. John 14:15, 21, 15:10, and 1 John 2:3–4, 3:22, 24, 5:2–3.

[12] Cf. Matthew 25:32–33, and parallels.

7   Շատ է ինձ Տէր. բայց յուսամ յողորմութիւնդ քո,
        դի եւ շունք կերակրին ի փշրանաց
        անկելոց ի սեղանոյ Տեառն իւրեանց.
    շուն կոչեմ զիս Տէր՝ դի գայցեմ զկնի քո:
    Հովիւ բարի՝ խնդրեաշ զիս գմոլորեալս.
    Նաւապետ բարի Յիսուս՝ փրկեաշ զիս
        ի բազմութենէ ալեաց մեղաց իմոց,
    եւ տուր ինձ նաւահանգիստ խաղաղութեան:

8   Տո՛ւր ինձ Տէր՝ սուգ եւ արտասուս,
    կարողացո՛ գմարմինս իմ. կակղացո՛ զքարացեալ սիրտ իմ,
    եւ ժողովեա՛ գմիտս իմ ի քեզ:
    Ձնջեա՛ զբազմութիւն յանցանաց իմոց,
    եւ շնորհեա՛ ինձ գոգուտն իմ.
    ընկա՛լ եւ մի՛ անտես առներ զՀառաչանս սրտի իմոյ:

9   Տո՛ւր ինձ իմաստութիւն, եւ տնկեա՛ Տէր՝
        գմահ եւ գերկիւղ քո ի սրտի իմում,
    լուսաւորեա՛ գխորհուրդս իմ. կարողացո՛ զմարմինս իմ՝
    ժուժկալութեամբ կալ ի պատուիրանի քում յամենայն ժամ:

10 Բա՛ց Տէր՝ դաշս սրտի իմոյ
    եւ լուսաւորեա՛ Հոգւովդ սրբով.
    պարգեւեա՛ ինձ առողջ խորհուրդս եւ առաքինի վարս՝
        ողբալ Հանապազ, աշխ եւ դողութեամբ
    կալ առաջի քո յամենայն ժամ անդրադ:

11 Ո՛վ բարերար եւ մարդասէր Տէր,
        առանց շարշարանաց եւ ժուժկալութեանց
    դիա՞րդ ազատեցայց ի բազմութենէ մեղաց իմոց.
    դի մարմնովս տկար եմ եւ Հոգւովս խաւար.
    օղորմեա՛ Տէր՝ եւ որպէս կամիս օգնեա՛ ինձ:

7   It is almost beyond me, my Lord, but I trust in Your mercy,
        for "even the dogs eat the crumbs
        that fall from their master's table".[13]
    Call me a "dog", O Lord, that I may walk along behind You.
    O Good Shepherd,[14] seek for me for I have gone astray.
    O Good Jesus, my Captain, save me
        from the abundant waves of my sins,
    and settle me in a peaceful harbor.

8   Give to me, O Lord, mourning and lamentation;
    Give strength to my flesh, soften my stony heart[15]
    and recollect my mind to You.
    Wash away the multitude of my transgressions
    and grant me what is beneficial to me.
    Receive me and do not despise the groans of my heart.

9   Give me wisdom, O Lord, and plant
        in my heart death and fear of You.
    Give light to my thoughts and give strength to my flesh
    That at every moment I may live steadfastly by Your command.

10 Open, O Lord, the eyes of my heart,
    and enlighten them with Your Holy Spirit.
    Bestow upon me wholesome thoughts and a virtuous life,
        that I may make constant lament and, at every moment,
        stand before You undistracted, in fear and trembling.

11 O Beneficent Lord and Lover of mankind,
    How am I to be set free from the multitude of my sins
        without suffering or patient endurance?
    In my flesh I am powerless and in my soul I am dark.
    Have mercy on me, O Lord and give me help just as You wish.

---

[13] Matthew 15:27.
[14] John 15:11.
[15] Cf. Ezekiel 11:19.

12 Անդխակալ Տէր՝
    մի՛ վասն բազում չարեաց իմոց անտես առներ զիս.
    այլ դարձիր լիս, եւ դարձո՛ զամենայն ցանկութիւնս իմ ի քեզ,
    սիրել զքեզ միայն ի բոլոր սրտէ իմմէ:
    Ի նուազ եւ յանպաճոյճ կերակրող ամբողջ պահեա՛ զմարմին իմ:

13 Պատկերացո՛ Տէր՝ զանհրաժեշտ գալուստ քո առաջի աչաց իմոց.
    եւ դողացո՛ զմարմին իմ
        սգալ եւ լալ անդադար յերկիւղէ անհեղ դատաստանաց քոց.
    եւ մի՛ փակեր զգութ արարչական սիրոյ քոյ
        ի ստեղծուածոյս քո՛ որ մեղօք եմ մեռեալ:

14 Աճեցո՛ Տէր՝ զբարիս գործել ինձ յամենայն ժամ,
        եւ խափանեա՛ զամենայն չարիս ի չար մտաց իմոց.
    ի պիղծ եւ յանուղղայ գնացից՝
        եւ ի չար սովորութենէ դարձարեցո՛ զիս,
    եւ Հաստատեա՛ յերկիւղ եւ ի սէր պատուիրանաց քոց:

15 Արեգակն արդարութեան՝ փրկիչ իմ եւ ազատիչդ Յիսուս Քրիստոս՝
        ի լոյս քո ապաւինիմ.
    լուսաւորեա՛ եւ ջերմացո՛ գսիրտ իմ,
    Հրակիզեա՛ զչար խորհուրդս իմ,
        եւ Հալեա՛ զստունմանխիա մեղաց իմոց:
    Շնորհեա՛ Տէր՝ զգարուն Հոգւոյ իմոյ՝
        ծաղկիլ եւ պտղաբերել զարդարութեան պտուղն:

16 Ազատիչդ Քրիստոս՝
    ազատեա՛ զիս ի դառնաշունչ օրոց մեղաց ձմերայնոյ.
    զխաւարեալ եւ զատուցեալ Հոգի իմ պայծառացո՛ եւ ջերմացո՛,
    եւ ցօղեա՛ զցօղ շնորհի ջերմութեան քո
        ի յանդաստանս մտաց սրտի իմոյ:

12   O Lord, who are free of malice,
Do not despise me on account of my many evil deeds;
Rather, turn back to me and turn all my desires towards You,
To love You alone with all my heart.
With plain and simple foods keep my body healthy.[16]

13   Paint, O Lord, the image of Your irrevocable coming before my eyes,
and make my flesh tremble,
> so that I mourn and weep ceaselessly in fear at Your
> terrible judgments.

Do not close up the tenderness of Your creative love
> for me, Your creation, who am dying in my sins.

14   Grant to me, O Lord, that I may perform good deeds at all times,
> and remove every evil from my evil mind.

Turn me away from impurity, from perverse paths,
> and from my evil habits.

Give me the strength to fear and to love Your commandments.

15   O Jesus Christ, Sun of Righteousness,[17] my Savior and Deliverer
> in Your light I take refuge.

Give light and warmth to my heart.
Burn away my evil thoughts
> and melt the ice of my sins.

Grant, O Lord, a springtime to my soul,
> that it may come to blossom and produce the fruit of righteousness.[18]

16   O Christ, You who are the Deliverer,
Deliver me from the violent winter winds of sin.
Make my dark and frigid soul full of life and fire,
and sprinkle the warming dew of Your grace
> upon the fields of the thoughts of my heart.

---

[16] Cf. Daniel 1:8–16.
[17] Malachi 4:2.
[18] Cf. Hebrews 12:11.

17 Շնչեա՛ Տէր՝ զՀարաւ քաղցրաշունչ Հոգւոյդ սրբոյ
 ի խստացեալ եւ ի թանձրացեալ սիրտ իմ,
 եւ զարթո՛ որոտնդոստ փայլատակմամբ քո
 զատնացեալ եւ զգամեքեալ միտս իմ:

18 Բա՛ց Տէր՝ զփակեալ դուռն սրտի իմոյ,
 եւ ծագեա՛ ի ներքս զլոյս արդարութեան ճառագայթից քոց:
 Սրբեա՛ եւ զազդ մեղաց իմոց,
 եւ զվէրս Հոգւոյ իմոյ բժշկեա՛,
 եւ ամրացո՛ երկիւղիւ քով,
 եւ գործցո՛ առնել զարդարութիւն յամենայն ժամ:

19 Ադբերացո՛ Տէր՝ զզղուխ իմ ի բղխումն արտասուաց.
 լուա՛ զԹարախ Հոգւոյ իմոյ, սրբեա՛ զզզայարանս իմ.
 եւ զգործողդս շարեաց փոխարկեա՛ ի դղձումն ջերմութեան սիրոյ քոյ՝
 զգաստ մարմնով կեալ ի պատուիրանս քո:

20 Զգեա՛ Տէր՝ զձեռն քո ի նաւթեկեալս՝
 որ ընկղմեալս եմ ի խոր շարեաց,
 եւ փրկեա՛ զիս ի սատիկ ծովածուփ բռնութենէ ալեաց մեղաց իմոց:
 Սանձեա՛ Տէր՝ եւ կարկեա՛ զխստերան միտս իմ
 ի զբաղմանց ունայնութեանց կենցաղոյս:

21 Արբո՛ Տէր՝ զծարաւ Հոգւոյ իմոյ
 յառատաբուխ շնորհաց քոց,
 եւ մի՛ անտես առներ գտողորումն սրտի իմոյ,
 որ պապակիմ ի տապոյ ասպի շարեաց իմոց.
 զովացո՛ եւ լուա՛ զապականեալ եւ զՀոտեալ չրթունս իմ
 ջրով ողորմութեան քոյ:

22 Մագեա՛ Տէր՝ զլուսաւորութիւն եւ զխաղաղութիւն շնորհաց քոց
 ի սրտի իմում.
 եւ զցաւագին գիշեր մեղաց ի մտաց իմոց Հալածեա՛.
 եւ մարմնոյ իմոյ շնորհեա՛ զարիական վարս՝
 առաքինութեամբ կեալ ի Հաճոյս կամաց քոց յամենայն ժամ:

17   Breathe, O Lord, the gently blowing south wind of Your Holy Spirit
        into my hard and obstinate heart,
    and with Your thunderous lightning bolts
        revive my frozen and languishing mind.[19]

18   Open, O Lord, the closed gate of my heart
    and shine into it the light of Your radiant righteousness.
    Cleanse also the stain of my sins,
    and heal the wounds of my soul.
    Sustain me by the fear of You,
    and give me the strength always to act righteously.

19   Make my head, O Lord, a fountain for a torrent of tears,
    Wash away the pus from my soul and purify my senses.
    In Your ardent love turn me, who have done evil, to contrition
        so that with vigilant flesh I may live by Your commandments.

20   Stretch forth, O Lord, Your hand to me for I am shipwrecked
        and I am drowning in the abyss of my evil deeds.
    Deliver [me] from the stormy and violent force of the waves of my sins.
    Bring, O Lord, my rebellious mind under control and give it calm
        from the distractions and the vanities of my life.

21   Give drink, O Lord, to my thirsty soul
        from the abundant flow of Your graces.[20]
    Do not ignore the parched state of my heart,
        for I am scorched due to the searing heat of my evil deeds.
    Cool down and wash my putrid and fetid lips
        with the waters of Your mercy.

22   Shine, O Lord, the light and the peace of Your grace
        into my heart,[21]
    and drive out from my mind the sorrowful night of sin.
    To my flesh grant a courageous life
        that with valor I may live always to please Your will.

---

[19] This image employed here may be allusion to the ancient notion that pearls were conceived when the oyster shell was struck by lightning.

[20] Cf. John 4:10.

[21] Cf. 2 Peter 1:2.

23 Հան Տէր՝ գփուշ մեղաց ի սրտէ իմմէ,
    զի զՀոգի իմ Հանապազ խոցոտէ եւ վիրաւորէ.
    եւ սերմանեա՛ սերմն բարի ի սրտի իմում՝
    աճեցուցանել եւ պտղաբերել զարդարութեան պտուղն:

24 Հայածեա՛ Տէր՝ զխաւար ի Հոգւոյ իմմէ,
    եւ զգեցո՛ զլոյս արդարութեան ճառագայթից քոց.
    զարդարեա՛ երկիւղիւ եւ դողմամբ արտասուաց զսիրտ իմ
        երկնչիլ ի դատաստանաց քոց,
    եւ պաՀել զամենայն պատուիրանս քո:

25 Զարթո՛ զիս Տէր՝ յաՀագին խորութենէ քնոյ մեղաց իմոց.
    եւ գտարակուսեալ մարմին իմ զգաստացո՛
        յամենայն գործս բարիս խորՀիլ միշտ՝
    մեծաւ երկիւղիւ առնել զՀաճոյս քո յամենայն ժամ:

26 Ազատեա՛ զիս Տէր՝ ի ճառայութենէ մեղաց
    եւ խառնեա՛ զիս ի թիւս ճառայից քոց՝
        որք սիրեցին զքեզ եւ զպատուիրանս քո պաՀեցին.
    տո՛ւր գերկիւղ նոցա ի սրտի իմում,
    եւ ուսո՛ զիս գնալ ի շաւիղս գնացից նոցա:

27 Թեթեւացո՛ Տէր՝ զկարիս մարմնոյ իմոյ,
    եւ յաճախեա՛ յիս գշնորՀս Հոգւոյդ սրբոյ
        լինիլ տաճար եւ բնակարան աստուածային կամաց քոց.
    եւ անյագ սիրով սիրել գքեզ
    եւ ատել գամենայն ցանկութիւն եւ գվէր աշխարՀիս այսորիկ,
        որով եղեւ կորուստ եւ յանցումն Հոգւոյ իմոյ:

28 Ողորմեա՛ Տէր՝ բնակողիս յանրնակ անապատիս,
    եւ ի ճեռն սրբին արժանաւորեա՛ զիս խառնիլ ընդ առաջին սուրբ
        Հարանցն՝
    արի եւ գգաստ ժուժկալութեամբ ժառանգել գլոստացեալ պարգեւն:

23 Prune, O Lord, the thorn of sin from my heart
    for it continually pricks and pierces my soul.
Sow the good seed[22] in my heart
    that it may produce and bear the fruit of righteousness.[23]

24 Drive out, O Lord, the darkness from my soul,
Clothe it in the light of Your radiant justice.
Adorn my heart with dread and tearful repentance
    to fear Your judgments
    and to keep all Your commandments.[24]

25 Wake me, O Lord, from the horribly deep sleep of my sins,
Rouse my weakened flesh
    that I may always meditate on [Your] every good deed[25]
    and with great fear do what is pleasing to You at every moment.[26]

26 Free me, O Lord, from my slavery to sin,
Join me to the number of Your servants
    who have loved You and kept Your commandments.
Put their fear into my heart
and teach me to walk on the paths that they have trodden.

27 Decrease, O Lord, the torments of my flesh
and increase in me the graces of Your Holy Spirit
    that I may become a temple and a dwelling place for Your divine will,[27]
    that I may love You with insatiable love
    and that I may hate every desire and love of this world
    through which transgression and corruption have come into my soul.

28 Have mercy, O Lord, on me who dwell in an uninhabitable desert,[28]
and thus make me worthy to be included among those first holy fathers,
and with valiant, steadfast endurance to inherit the honors promised to them.

---

[22] Cf. Matthew 13:37, and parallels.
[23] Cf. Hebrews 12:11, Philippians 1:11, et al.
[24] A common biblical injunction; cf. above, n. 11.
[25] Cf. Psalms 77:12, 119:27, 143:5, 145:5.
[26] Cf. Ephesians 5:8–10.
[27] Cf. 1 Corinthians 6:19, 2 Corinthians 6:16, et al.
[28] This phrase appears to situate Ephrem in his traditional role as a hermit, but see the discussion in the introduction, above, p. 2.

29 Առաջնորդեա՛ ինձ Տէր՝ ի քեզ եւ ի նուրբ ճանապարհն,
    որպէս առաջնորդեցեր սրբոց քոց.
    եւ զորացո՛ զտկարութիւնս իմ՝ ժուժկալութեամբ եւ համբերութեամբ
    գնալ ի ճանապարհս քո ջերմեռանդն սրտիւ։

30 Նայեա՛ Տէր՝ ի նեխեալ եւ ի թարախեալ հոգի իմ.
    եւ լուա՛ աստուածային ջրով քով.
    եւ հոգեւոր ադիդ համեմեա՛,
    եւ անուշահոտ իւղով սրբով օծեա՛,
    եւ կատարեալ առողջութիւն ընձեռեա՛։

31 Անսուրացո՛ Տէր՝ զքուն աչաց իմոց,
    եւ թօթափեա՛ զնիրհումն ի գլխոյ իմոյ,
    զի ծանրացեալ դանդաղանօք պաշարէ զմարմին իմ.
    արա՛ զիս Տէր՝ արթուոս եւ պատրաստ յամենայն ժամ,
    զի զգաստութեամբ եւ արդարութեամբ վարեցից զկեանս իմ։

32 Տէս Տէր՝ զլքումն որովայնի իմոյ՝
    որ գորացեալ է ի վերայ իմ,
    եւ հանապազ ցանկայ կերակրոց եւ ըմպելեաց
    եւ համեղութեան խորտկաց.
    այլ դու Տէր՝ յամենայնի կարող,
    կորեա՛ զցանկութիւն մարմնոյս տենչանաց։

33 Եւ քանզի միտք իմ ցնդեալ պղտորեալ բանդագուշեալ
    շրջի ի հոսանս երկրաւոր կենցաղոյս,
    այլ դու Տէր՝ լուսաւորեա՛ զայս հոգւոյս
    առանց զբաղմանց եւ երկմտութեանց
    արի եւ զգաստ ամենայորդոր փութով գալ
    զհետ աստուածային սիրոյ քոյ։

29   Lead me, O Lord, on the straight and narrow path,[29]
      just as You led Your holy ones.
  Give strength to my weakness that patiently and steadfastly
      I may walk on Your paths[30] with an ardent heart.

30   Look, O Lord, upon my fetid and putrid soul;
  Cleanse it with Your divine water,
  Flavor it with [Your] spiritual salt,
  Anoint it with Your sweet and holy oil,
  and bestow upon it perfect health.

31   Diminish, O Lord, the sleep from my eyes,
  Shake off that drowsiness from my head
      which slowly and oppressively besieges my flesh.
  Make me watchful, O Lord, and ready at every moment
      that I may conduct my life with vigilance and uprightness.

32   See, O Lord, the despondency of my belly
      that has gained power over me[31]
      that constantly craves food, drink,
          and the taste of cooked dishes.
  But You, O Lord, most powerful in all things,
  take away my desire for fleshly pleasures.

33   Because my mind is so inattentive, listless and unfocused,
      it drifts away on the streams of worldly concerns.
  But You, O Lord, give light to the eyes of my soul,
      that it may go without distraction or doubt,
      steadfastly and with all haste,
      after Your divine love.

---

[29] Cf. Matthew 7:14, and parallels.

[30] Like following the commandments, see n. 11, above, walking on the right path is another major theme found throughout these prayers, another theme of major importance found in the bible.

[31] Cf. Philippians 3:19.

34 Հայածեմ Տէր՝ զամենայն չար մտածմունս
  յերկրաքարշ խորհրդոց մտաց իմոց,
  արմատ բարեաց տնկեա՛ Հաստատութեամբ ի սրտի իմում,
  եւ պտուղ շնորհաց ի Հոգի իմ նկարեա՛:

35 Ազաչեմ բարերար եւ ողորմած Տէր՝
  արթունս եւ զուարթունս պատրաստեա՛ զիս.
  ուսո՛ ինձ գնալ ի ճանապարհս քո բարիս,
  զի արժանի եղէց մեծի փառաց քոց:

36 Եւ քանդի ցանկութիւն ճաշակման ամենայնիւ
  զբաղեցուցեալ զմիտս իմ խռովէ,
  արդ Հայածեա՛ գործկորստութիւն յինէն՝
  յորմէ խաբեցայ միշտ.
  եւ կերակրեա՛ զիս երկիւղիղ քով սրբով:

37 Առաքեա՛ Տէր՝ զմի ի սերովբէից քոց,
  զի բերելով զկայծակն Հրոյ
  մերձեցուսցէ ի շրթունս իմ,
  եւ Հանցէ ի բաց զանօրէնութիւնս, եւ զմեղս իմ սրբեսցէ,
  եւ զխորհուրդս իմ մաքրեսցէ,
  եւ ջնջեսցէ զանօրէնութիւն եւ զագտեղութիւնս իմ,
  եւ լուսաւորեսցէ զմիտս իմ ժառանգել նովաւ զկեանսն յաւիտենից:

38 Առաքեա՛ Տէր՝ զբաժակ ուրախարար Հոգւոյդ սրբոյ
  ի յեղկելիս՝ որ ծարաւիմն առ քեզ.
  արբո՛ եւ զուարթացո՛ գեռանդն սիրոյ քոյ ի սրտի իմում.
  լո՛յծ եւ ի բաց ջնջեա՛ զմրուր դառնութեան յանցանաց իմոց:

39 Առաքեա՛ Տէր՝ զլոյս քո լուսաւորեա՛ զմիտս իմ
  եւ զխորհուրդս իմ լուսով գիտութեան քոյ.
  զիսաւար մեղաց մտաց իմոց Հայածեա՛,
  եւ գտկարութիւն անճին իմոյ կարողացո՛
  ի ջանս եւ ի վաստակս Հոգւոյ իմոյ:

34 Chase away, O Lord, every evil consideration
        from the wordly thoughts of my mind.
    Plant a root of good [thoughts] firmly in my heart
    and form[32] the fruit of grace in my soul.

35 I beseech You, O beneficent and merciful Lord,
    Prepare me to be watchful and vigilant,
    Teach me to walk upon Your good paths[33]
        that I may become worthy of Your great glory.

36 Because desire for food continuously
        agitates my distracted mind,
    Chase away from me this gluttony
        by which I am constantly blinded
    and nourish me with holy fear of You.

37 Send, O Lord, one of Your seraphs,
        the one who bore the burning coal,[34]
    Let him touch it to my lips,
    and may it remove my impious deeds and cleanse my sins.
    May it purify my thoughts,
    Wipe away my iniquity and my impurities,
    and enlighten my mind that I might thereby inherit eternal life.

38 Send, O Lord, the cup of Your joyous Holy Spirit
        to my wretched self, for I am thirsting for You.
    Give drink and waken in my heart a fervor to love You.
    Wipe away and purge the bitter dregs of my transgressions.

39 Send, O Lord, Your light. Enlighten my mind
        and my thoughts with the light of Your knowledge.
    Dispel the darkness of sin from my mind
    and give strength to my weak spirit
        for the care and the profit of my soul.

---

[32] The word here, նկարել, literally means 'to paint, to depict', which was a favorite word of the genuine Ephrem; but a careful reader/imitator of Ephrem would certainly notice this. Its single usage here certainly does not prove that the author was indeed the fourth-century Syrian poet.

[33] Cf. Psalm 25:4, Micah 4:2.

[34] Cf. Isaiah 6:6.

40 Աղաքեա՛ Տէր՝ զՀրեշտակ խաղաղութեան քո
վերակացու եւ պաՀապան անձին իմոյ.
եւ որպէս ետուր իշխանութիւն գնալ ի վերայ իժի եւ քարբի
եւ կոխել զամենայն զօրութիւնս թշնամւոյն,
անեբկիւղս արասցես զմեզ յամենայն մեքենայից նորա,
եւ դիս պաՀեա՛ որպէս բիբ ական ընդ Հովանեաւ թեւոց քոց:

41 Յորժամ երթայցեմ Տէր ի ճանապարՀս, մի՛ թողուր զիս միայն.
այլ առաքեա՛ զօգնականութիւն քո զՀետ իմ՝
պաՀել զիս յամենայն փորձութեանց սատանայի ի տուէ եւ ի
գիշերի
եւ մի՛ տալ թոյլ մեղանչել մտաց իմոց,
այլ կոծել զկոծ մեծ ի վերայ մեղաց եւ անօրէնութեանց իմոց:

42 ՊաՀեա՛ զիս Տէր՝ ի բանից եւ ի գործոց,
ի տեսութեանց եւ ի գերէհ խորՀրդոց.
եւ գերկիւղ դատաստանի քոյ տպաւորեա՛ ի սրտի իմում՝
անդադար յօժարութեամբ մտօք փութալ եւ պաՀել զպատուիրանս
քո:

43 Փակեա՛ Տէր՝ զզդուն մեղաց իմոց,
եւ բա՛ց ինձ զզդուն լուսոյ եւ արդարութեան.
դի երկիւղալից սիրով եկից զՀետ կոչողիդ իմոյ արարչիդ,
որ ասացեր՝ «Եկայք առ իս
ամենայն աշխատեալք եւ ծանրաբեռնեալք,
եւ ես Հանգուցից զձեզ»:
եւ դարձեալ թէ՝
«Որ խնդրէ՝ առնու,
եւ որ Հայցէ՝ գտանէ,
եւ որ բաղխէ՝ բացցի նմա»:

40 Send, O Lord, Your angel of peace
         as a protector and guardian of my soul.
    Just as You gave power to walk upon the snake and the serpent,[35]
         and to trample down every power of the enemy,[36]
    May You make us fearless before all his devices,
    and guard me like the pupil of Your eye in the shadow of Your wings.[37]

41 O Lord, whenever I go out on my path do not leave me alone,
    Send Your assistance after me
         to guard me day and night from all the temptations of Satan,
         and to give me no occasion to sin in my thoughts,
         but to strike a great blow against my sins and my iniquities.

42 Protect me, O Lord, from those words and deeds,
         spectacles and thoughts that hold me captive.
    Imprint on my heart the fear of Your judgment
         that with firm resolve of mind I may hasten to keep Your commandments.

43 Close, O Lord, the gate of my sins,
    Open to me the gate of light and justice
         so that with loving fear I may follow You, my Creator,
         who called me when You said,
         "Come to me all who labor and are heavy laden,
              and I will give you rest."[38]
    And again [when You said],
         "The one who asks receives,
         The one who seeks finds,
         and to the one who knocks it will be opened."[39]

---

[35] Cf. Genesis 3:15, Mark 16:18.
[36] Cf. Luke 10:19.
[37] Psalm 36:7, 57:1.
[38] Matthew 11:28 (29 Arm). It is to be noted that here as elsewhere, when the author quotes from the biblical text it is nearly always, for all intents and purposes, exactly the same as found in the text of the Zohrab edition of the Armenian bible; differences, usually only minor omissions, can easily be explained by the demands of the rhetorical nature of these prayers.
[39] Matthew 7:8.

44 Նայեա՛ Տէր՝ ի մերկութիւն անձին իմոյ
      զոր կողոպտեաց թշնամին,
   եւ այժմ խայտառակ եւ ամօթալից կամ
      առաջի քո աստուածային գիտութեանդ,
   մարդասիրեա՛ եւ զգեցո՛ ինձ զՀանդերձ Հարսանեաց,
   եւ մօ՛յծ եւ ուրախացո՛ զիս ի կոչումն բազմելոց քոց:

45 Զգեցո՛ ինձ Տէր զպատմուճանն պարածին՝
      զոր մերկացայ մեղօք իմովք.
   ցո՛յց զանոխակալութիւնդ քո յիս,
   եւ լուսափայլ ողորմութեամբ քո զարդարեա՛ զմերկութիւնս իմ:

46 Լո՛ւր Տէր՝ աղաղակի անտակիս,
      որ ամօթով կամ առաջի քո.
   զգանձն Հայրենի վատնեալ՝ սովամած կորնչիմ.
   կերակրի՛ Հաւասար եղէ խոզից անասնոց անբանից,
      եւ նմանեցայ նոցա:

47 Մի՛ մերժեր զիս Տէր՝ ի Հայրական գթոյ քոյ.
   Համարձակիմ ի խնամս սիրոյ քոյ
   ի ծնողէդ վերջացայ եւ գործիւթիւն իմ ուրացայ:
   «Հա՛յր մեղայ յերկինս եւ առաջի քո,
    չեմ արժանի կոչիլ որդի քո,
    արա՛ զիս իբրեւ զմի ի վարձկանաց քոց:»

48 Զարդարեա՛ զիս Տէր՝ մեծաւ երկիւղիւ քո.
   եւ դարձո՛ յանտակութենէ յարդարութիւն,
   յաղտեղութենէ ի սրբութիւն, ի ծուլութենէ ի զգաստութիւն.
   ժուժկալութեամբ եւ Համբերութեամբ գնալ
      ի ճանապարհս քո ուղիղս:

49 Դադարեցո՛ զիս Տէր՝ ի չարաչար խորՀրդոց իմոց
      եւ յառնելոյ զկամս մտաց իմոց եւ մարմնոյ իմոյ.
   զաՀագին օր գալստեան քո նկարեա՛ առաջի աչաց իմոց՝
      դողալ եւ սարսիլ ի դատաստանաց քոց:

44 Look, O Lord, upon the nakedness of my soul
         which the enemy has stripped.[40]
    I now stand before Your divine compassion,
         covered with shame and disgrace.
    Be compassionate and clothe me in a wedding garment,
    Bring me in and give me joy by inviting me in to be seated.[41]

45 Clothe me, O Lord, in that former garment
         that I stripped off by my sins.
    Show me that You will not be vengeful toward me,
    and in Your resplendent mercy clothe my nakedness.[42]

46 Hear, O Lord, my cry for I am the prodigal son
         who stands in shame before You.
    I have consumed my patrimonial treasure and am dying of hunger.
    In order to find nourishment I have become a companion
         of stupid irrational pigs and I have become like them.[43]

47 Do not deprive me, O Lord, of Your fatherly compassion;
         I boldly presume on Your loving care.
    I did renounce Your fatherhood and I denied my sonship:
         "O Father, I have sinned against heaven and before You.
         I am not worthy to be called Your son.
         Treat me as one of Your hired servants."[44]

48 Adorn me, O Lord, with great fear of You,
    and turn me from wantonness to righteousness,
         from filthiness to purity, and from idleness to watchfulness,
         so that I may walk steadfastly and patiently
              along Your straight paths.

49 Stop me, O Lord, from my evil thoughts
         and from doing the will of my mind and my flesh.
    Paint before my eyes the terrible day of Your coming
         that I may tremble and quake before Your judgments.

---

[40] The author may have in mind here the parable of the Good Samaritan; cf. Luke 10:29–37; but this is also a common *topos* in early Christian literature.

[41] Cf. Luke 22:30.

[42] Cf. Genesis 3:21.

[43] Cf. Luke 15:11–32.

[44] Luke 15:18–19.

50 Պայծառացո՛ Տէր՝ զլապտեր հոգւոյ իմոյ
    որպէս գիմաստուն կուսանացն.
    եւ շնորհեա՛ պատրաստիլ արթնութեամբ
    ընդ առաջ ելանել երկնաւոր փեսային
    զի մի՛ մնացից արտաքս որպէս գյիմար կուսանն:

51 Մանո՛ւմ ինձ Տէր՝ գճանապարհս քո,
    եւ ուսո՛ ինձ գարդարութիւնս քո.
    Հեռացո՛ Տէր՝ զմարմինս իմ ի խորհրդոց չարեաց,
    եւ Հաստատեա՛ յերկիւղ բարեաց՝
    սուրբ եւ անարատ կալ առաջի քո յամենայն ժամ:

52 Զանօրէնութիւնս իմ ջնջեա՛ Տէր՝.
    ի յոյս բարեաց եւ յերկիւղ քո զմիտս իմ բեւեռեա՛,
    լցեալ սիրով եւ Հաստատուն Հաւատով
    սպասել եւ ակն ունել մեծի գալստեան քոյ:

53 Զօրացո՛ զիս Տէր՝ ի սէր պատուիրանաց քոց,
    անսալ երկիւղիւ Հրամանաց քոց,
    սարսիլ եւ դողալ ի դատաստանաց քոց,
    խնդրել գարդարութիւն եւ գիրաւունս երեսաց քոց,
    եւ առնուլ զպարգեւս շնորհաց քոց:

54 Արձակեա՛ զիս Տէր՝ ի կապանաց մեղաց իմոց,
    եւ գՀնացեալս մեղօք՝ վերստին նորոգեա՛.
    եւ գիսաւրեալս ի ցանկութեանց մարմնոյ՝ լուսաւորեա՛
    գնալ ի ճանապարհս խաղաղութեան,
    զի տեսցեն աչք իմ զփրկութիւն քո
    զոր պատրաստեցեր սրբոց քոց:

55 Բժշկեա՛ Տէր՝ զանբժկելի Հիւանդութիւնս իմ՝
    որ կարկամեալ դնիմ ի մահիճս մեղաց իմոց,
    եւ դեգերեալ կամ ի դուռն երկրորդ սելովմայ՝
    սպասել եւ ակն ունիլ մեծի գալստեան քոյ:

50   Light, O Lord, a lamp for my soul
         just like [those of] the wise virgins.
     Grant that I be prepared to go forth with great watchfulness
         to meet You, O heavenly bridegroom,
         and not remain outside like the foolish virgins.[45]

51   Make known to me, O Lord, Your paths
     and teach me Your just ways.[46]
     Keep, O Lord, my flesh far away from evil thoughts,
     and strengthen me in good and fearful [thoughts],
         that I may always stand before You holy and without reproach.

52   Wipe away my impious deeds, O Lord,
     and fasten my mind onto the hope of good deeds and the fear of You,
         that filled with love and, with unshakable faith,
         I may await and look to Your great coming.

53   Strengthen me, O Lord, in the love of Your commandments,
         that I might obey Your statutes in fear,
         quake and tremble at Your judgments,
         pursue justice and uprightness before Your face,
         and receive the gifts of Your grace.

54   Release me, O Lord, from the bonds of my sins.[47]
     Rejuvenate me once more for I am worn out by sin.
     Bestow Your light upon me who am darkened by the desires of my flesh,
         that I may walk upon the paths of peace
         and that my eyes may see Your salvation
         which You have prepared[48] for Your holy ones.

55   Heal, O Lord, my incurable infirmities,
         for I lie crippled[49] upon the bed of my sins,
         and I frequently stand at the gate of a second Siloam[50]
         waiting and looking for Your great coming.

---

[45] Cf. Matthew 25:1–13.
[46] Cf. Psalm 25:4, but the author here also brings in several closely related themes.
[47] Cf. Psalm 107:14, 116:16, Isaiah 58:6.
[48] Cf. Luke 2:30.
[49] This word is found only once in the Armenian bible, in the description of the infirm woman in Luke 13:11.
[50] Cf. John 9:1–12.

56 Հրամայեա՛ ինձ Տէր՝ որպէս անդամալուծին
առողջանալ, խորտակել գանկողինս ցաւոց իմոց,
շրջիլ ընդ կամարարս քո ի տան Տեառն,
եւ ի դպիթս Աստուծոյ ծաղկիլ եւ ոչ մեղանչել:

57 Խորտակեա՛ Տէր՝ զբռնութիւն սատանայի,
համտ եւ ի բաց ընկեա՛ զզօրութիւն նորա.
արգել դյարձակումն նորա ի վերայ իմ,
զի մի՛ տարապարհակ վարեալ զմարմին իմ տանիցի
յընդարձակութիւն ճանապարհի՝
որ տանի ի կորուստ եւ յապականութիւն:

58 Յիշեա՛ Տէր՝ զրադեալ եւ մոռացեալ մտաց իմոց
զահաւոր եւ զտեսկալի գալուստ քո
եւ զդատաստանն անաչառ,
զպատիւ եւ զփառս արդարոցն,
եւ զանները̕լի տանջանս մեղաւորացն,
եւ նորոք զարհուրեալ դողացդ զմարմին իմ
տեսանել զմահ հանապազ առջի աչաց իմոց:

59 Բեւեռեա՛ Տէր՝ զմարմին իմ ընդ երկիւղ քո,
եւ ընդ սէր պատուիրանաց քոց զհոգի իմ,
եւ զհրամայեալն ի նմա՝ երկիւղիւ լսել,
եւ առանց ճանձրութեան կատարել միշտ.
եւ մերկանալ ի մեղաց եւ ի ցանկութեանց կենցաղոյս,
եւ պայծառանալ վարուք առաքինութեան:

60 Փրկեա՛ զիս Տէր՝ ի գայթակղից նենգից սատանայի,
որ բազում մեքենայիւք պատեալ պաշարէ զիս.
աւար առեալ զմիտս իմ՝
վարէ ի գերութիւն ցանկութեան մեղաց,
առնելով ծաղր եւ այլն կատականաց թշնամեաց իմոց:

56 Command me, O Lord, as You did that paralytic,
    to be healed and to smash the bed of my affliction,[51]
    and, by Your good pleasure, to walk in the house of the Lord
    and to flourish in the courts of [our] God[52] and not to sin.

57 Smash, O Lord, the power of Satan,
    Cut off and cast his strength far away.
    Prohibit his assault upon me
        lest he compel my flesh and bear me
            along that wide path
        that leads to ruin and destruction.[53]

58 Bring back, O Lord, to my distracted and forgetful mind
        Your dread and terrible coming
        Your impartial judgment,
        the honor and glory for the righteous,
        and the unremitting torments for sinners.
    By these things make my flesh tremble and quake,
        to see death constantly before my eyes.

59 Fasten my body, O Lord, onto the fear of You
        and my soul onto the love of Your commandments,
        to listen with fear to whatever You order for it,
        and always to accomplish it without delay,
        to strip myself of sin and of the desires for this present life,
        and to become resplendent with virtuous habits.

60 Save me, O Lord, from the secret darts of Satan,
        who with his many devices surrounds me and hems me in.
    He takes my mind hostage
    and leads it off captive to the enjoyment of sin,
        making me an object of ridicule and derision to my enemies.[54]

---

[51] Cf. Matthew 9:2–8.
[52] Cf. Psalm 92:13.
[53] Cf. Matthew 7:13, and parallels.
[54] Cf. Psalm 109:25.

61 Ամրացո՛ զիս Տէր՝ յերկիւղ քո,
և զօրացո՛ զտկարացեալս զօրութեամբ քով.
զՀիւանդութիւն Հոգւոյ իմոյ առողջացո՛,
զցաւս մարմնոյ բժշկեա՛,
և զՉերմութիւն սիրոյ քո Հաստատեա՛ ի սրտի իմում՝
չարչարակից լինել սրբոց քոց:

62 Դարձո՛ Տէր՝ զզերեայս ի սատանայէ,
և զմեղօք վաճառեայս լեգիտոտական և ի խիստ տանջանացն.
փրկեա՛ ի բոնակալ չար սպասաւորաց դիւացն.
և յեղեզնակորխս կալոյ մեղացն Հանցես
և տարցես զիս յերկիրն աւետեաց:

63 Ընկզմեա՛ Տէր՝ զԹշնամին իմ որպէս զզօրութիւն փարաւոնի
զի սպառնացեալ ի վերայ իմ խրոխտայ,
Հետամուտ եղեալ զկնի իմ դարձուցանէ՛ զիս յառաջին յանցանսն
ընդ իշխանութեամբ իւրով՝ ծառայել մեղաց և անօրէնութեանց:

64 Խաղաղացո՛ զիս Տէր՝ ի ծփանաց ալեաց խռովութեանց խորՀրդոց,
և զբազմութեան յորձանս մեղաց իմոց ցածո՛,
և կառավարեա՛ զմիտս իմ ժամանել
յանքոյթ և ի խաղաղ նաւաՀանգիստն Հոգւոյդ սրբոյ:

65 Զերծո՛ զիս Տէր՝ ի լերինս քարանձաւի
կամ ի տեղի անապատի,
ուր և ողորմութիւն քո առաջնորդեսցէ ինձ՝
Հանդիպիլ մեծի փառաց անուան քոյ.
տո՛ւր ինձ զԹեւս աղաւնակերպ Հոգւոյդ սրբոյ՝
Թոչիլ և վերանալ խոնիլ յերամս արդարոց:

61   Fortify me, O Lord, in the fear of You
     and with Your strength give strength to me who am so weak.
     Restore to health the sickness of my soul,
     Heal the sores of my flesh,[55]
     and in my heart establish the fervor of Your love
         that I may become a companion of Your holy ones.

62   Bring me back, O Lord, for I have been taken captive by Satan;
         by my sins I have been sold into the bitter torments of the Egyptians.[56]
     Save me from those tyrannical evil servants of the demons.
     Take me away from this reed-filled quagmire of sin[57]
     and bring me into the land of the Good News.

63   Drown, O Lord, my enemy, [as You did] the army of Pharaoh,[58]
         who haughtily utters threats against me,
         and pursues me to bring me back to my former transgressions
         and, under his power, to be a servant to sin and lawlessness.

64   Grant me peace, O Lord, from the billowy waves of my turbulent thoughts,
     Abate the many whirlpools of my sins.
     Steer my mind that it may come
         To the safe and peaceful harbor of Your Holy Spirit.[59]

65   Carry me off, O Lord, to a mountain cave
         or to some desert place
         — wherever Your mercy may guide me —
         to encounter the great glory of Your name.
     Give to me the dove-like wings of Your Holy Spirit,[60]
         to fly up on high and be united with the assembly of the just.

---

[55] A phrase taken from the parable of the rich man and Lazarus; cf. Luke 16:20.

[56] The images employed here are all taken from the story of Joseph being sold by his brothers into the slavery of Egypt, cf. Genesis 38.

[57] This phrase, of course, refers to what scholars now prefer to call the Reed Sea, rather than the traditional Red Sea, where the Egyptian army drowned during the exodus from Egypt; see the climax of the story in Exodus 14:26–31. Whatever its proper name, it has traditionally been the symbol for the cleansing of sin.

[58] Cf. Exodus 14:28.

[59] The author seems to be drawing his images here from Psalm 107:25–30.

[60] The author here combines the image of Psalm 55:6, with the traditional image of the Holy Spirit as a dove; cf. Matthew 3:16, and parallels.

66 Ժամանեցո՛ զիս Տէր՝ յօթեանս արդարոց քոց,
և գՀանգիստ աշխատութեան սուրբ Հարցն պարգևեսա՛ ինձ.
անտես արա՛ զյանցանս իմ,
և դասաւորեալ պայծառացո՛ ընդ սուրբս
    և ընդ սիրելիս անուան քոյ:

67 Հաստատեա՛ Տէր՝ զխաղաղութիւն և զպայծառութիւն
    լուսոյ կենաց անճին իմոյ,
    զի մի՛ խտորիցիմ յաջ կամ յաՀեակ,
    և դատապարտիմ յալուր գալստեան քոյ
    պաՀանջելով զյետին նաքարակիտն մինչ խապառ:

68 Մի՛ մերժեր զիս ի բազմազուժ ողորմութեանց քոց.
    զապաւինեալս ի քեզ՝ ամրացո՛
    և աներկիւղ պաՀեա՛ յամենայն որոգայթից սատանայի,
    զի մի՛ գերի վարեալ տանիցէ զմիտս իմ
    ի զբաղումն և ի չար ծառայութիւն:

69 Ուսո՛ զիս Տէր՝ առնել զարդարութիւն, խօսիլ զճշմարտութիւն,
    սիրել զսրբութիւն և ատել զաղտեղութիւն,
    խտտորիլ ի չարեաց և գնալ ի ճանապարՀս բարեաց:

70 Ապրեցո՛ զիս Տէր՝ յորսողացն այնոցիկ որք գան ի վերայ իմ
    ըմբռնել զիս ի մեղս և ի ծուլութիւն անժուժկալութեան,
    մոռացումն առնել յանցանաց իմոց,
    և ոչ տալ վիշկլ գօր Հատուցման
        և գարսափելի պատասխանին՝ որ ասէ.
    «երթայք յինէն անիծեալք ի Հուրն յաւիտենից»:

71 Կանգնեա՛ զիս Տէր՝ ի գլորմանէս,
    և ի բազմամեղ անդնդային խորութենէս վերացո՛
    և բարձրացո՛ թևօք Հոգւոյդ սրբոյ
        ի պարապումն աղօթից և ի խնդրուածս Հաճոյից,
    ի ցանձումն մեղաց,
    ի նորոգումն կենաց,
    և ի լուսաւորութիւն մտաց,
    և ի կատարումն սուրբ պատուիրանաց քոց:

66 Bring me, O Lord, into the dwellings of Your just ones,
and grant me, with the holy fathers, that rest from labor.
Overlook my transgressions,
Set me to shine among the holy ones[61]
   and among those who love Your name.[62]

67 Restore, O Lord, the peace and splendor
   of the light of life to my soul,
      lest I turn aside to the right or to the left,[63]
      receive condemnation on the day of Your coming,
      and You exact from me my last penny.[64]

68 Do not drive me away, O Lord, from the bounty of Your mercy.
Give courage to me who trust in You.
Keep me without fear from every snare of Satan
   lest he take my mind captive
   and bear it off into distraction and slavery to evil.

69 Teach me, O Lord, to do what is right, to speak the truth,[65]
   to love holiness and to hate impiety,
      to turn away from evil and to walk upon the paths of goodness.

70 Deliver me, O Lord, from those hunters who have come out against me
   to entrap me in sin and intemperate slothfulness,
   to make me forgetful of my transgressions,
      and to prevent me from remembering the day of retribution
         and that dreaded verdict:
"Depart from me, you cursed ones, into the eternal fire."[66]

71 Lift me back up, O Lord, for I have fallen down,
Raise me up from the deep abyss of my many sins.
Carry me up on the wings of Your Holy Spirit
   that I may occupy myself in prayer and in joyful entreaties,
in being cleansed from sin,
in the renewal of life,
in the enlightenment of mind,
and in the accomplishment of Your holy commandments.

---

[61] Cf. Daniel 12:3.
[62] Cf. Psalms 5:11 (5:12, Arm).
[63] Cf. Deuteronomy 2:27, et al.
[64] Cf. Matthew 5:26.
[65] Cf. Psalm 52:3.
[66] Matthew 25:41.

72 Խնդրեմ՛ Տէր՝ գեղծեալ եւ գկորուսեալ քո պատկերս,
որ ի մէջ ազբի եւ տղմի մեղաց թաւալեալ կամ,
գիտ՛ աձեալ աւելաւ շնորՀի քո, եւ դիր
ի գանձանակն անմեղութեան՝ յորմէ անկաւ։

73 Եկ Տէր՝ ի տեսութիւն Հիանդացեալ Հոգւոյ իմոյ,
դիր գձեռն քո ի վերայ իմ, եւ բժշկեաց ասելով՝
«գօրացիր առ գմաՀիձա քո, եւ երթ»
ի ճանապարՀն կենաց արդարութեան։

74 Եկ Տէր՝ ի խնդիր մոլորելոյս,
որ յաձեալ շրջիմ արտաքոյ Հօտի պատուիրանաց քոց.
եւ գագանաբեկ եղեալ քարավէժ մեղօք
կառափնատիմ ի դիւաց.
ըմբոնեմ եւ աձ ի փարախն Հայրենի,
եւ խառնեմ ի գալիձս Հօտի քոյ։

75 Հետեւեմ Տէր՝ գՀետ ձողոպրելոյս ի քէն.
արագապէս փութացիր, Հաս եւ ըմբոնեմ
գապաստամբեալս ի ճայնէ կոչման քոյ,
եւ դիր ի բանտ կապանաց անխզելի սիրոյ քոյ։

76 Մի՛ թողուր դիս Տէր՝ Հեռանալ
ի սիրոյ պատուիրանաց քոց եւ ի վարուց առաքինութեանց.
այլ յօրդորեմ առաւելուլ յամենայն գործս արդարութեան՝
առանց մեղաց եւ առանց իրիք խափանուածոց
պաշտել գքեզ սրբութեամբ եւ արդարութեամբ
առաջի քո գամենայն աւուրս կենաց իմոց։

77 Մի՛ մատներ դիս Տէր՝ ի ցանկութիւն մեղաց
եւ ի Հեշտութիւն կամաց,
ի քուն աչաց եւ ի ցանկութիւն մտաց,
այլ պարապեմ երկիւղի քո.
եւ ապրեցօ յամենաՀնար չար դիւացն
եւ յաշխարՀական գրօսանաց։

72 Seek, O Lord, for Your disfigured and corrupted image
          which is wallowing in the dung and slime of sin.
    With the rake of Your grace, find it and put it back
          into the treasure box of sinlessness from which it fell out.[67]

73 Come, O Lord, look upon my sickened soul.
    Set Your hand upon me and heal me, saying,
          "Rise up, take your pallet and walk"[68]
          upon the path of the life of righteousness.[69]

74 Come, O Lord, in search of me who am lost,
          for I have wandered about outside the fold of Your commandments.
          I have been torn by wild beasts, stoned for my sins,
               and struck down by demons.
    Take hold of me, put me in the sheep-pen of Your Father,
    and put me in together with the lambs of Your fold.[70]

75 Come after me, O Lord, who have escaped from You.
    Make great haste, catch and seize me,
          who have rebelled against the sound of Your voice,[71]
    and put me in the prison house of Your inescapable love.

76 Do not leave me, O Lord, to distance myself
          from the love of Your commandments or from a life of virtue,
    But make me grow and increase in every work of righteousness,
          so that, without sin and with no other hindrance,
               I might serve before You "in holiness and righteousness
                    all the days of my life".[72]

77 Do not hand me over, O Lord, to the pleasures of sin,
          to the desires of the will,
               to sleep for the eyes, or to the pleasures of the mind.
    But shelter me in the fear of You,
    Deliver me from every cunning and evil demon
          and from all worldly amusements.

---

[67] Referring to the image of man, lost by the fall of Adam.
[68] Matthew 9:6, Mark 2:9, Luke 5:24, John 5:8.
[69] Cf. Proverbs 12:28.
[70] Cf. John 10:1–18.
[71] Cf. Genesis 2:8; but note overtones to Jesus as the Good Shepherd, John 10:3–5, 16.
[72] Luke 1:75.

78 Մի՛ յապաղեր Տէր՝ տալ ինձ գիրկութիւն հոգւոյ
    եւ գջերմութիւն սրտի,
    զպարկեշտութիւն կերակրոյ եւ գժուժկալութիւն մարմնոյ,
    գրղխումն արտասուաց, գանդագար աղօթս,
    գհնագանդութիւն, գխոնարհութիւն եւ գհամբերութիւն յուսոյ:

79 Յաղթեա՛ Տէր՝ հակառակամարտին իմոյ, եւ գորածի՛ զիս
    ընդդիմակաց լինել պատերազմողին ի վերայ իմ.
    եւ ցցեցի՛ ինձ գզրահն հաւատոյ՝
    պաշօք եւ աղօթիւք
    սրբել գախտս ցանկական եւ գխորհուրդս մարմնական,
    եւ առնուլ գշնորհս փրկական:

80 Տո՛ւր ինձ Տէր՝ տեղի ապաշխարութեան,
    աշխատութեան հանգիստ,
    խաղաղութեան հոգի
    եւ արդարութեան ճանապարհ,
    ամրութեան զէն եւ պահապան փրկութեան,
    հաստատութեան յոյս եւ պնդութեան երկիւղ:

81 Անցո՛ զիս Տէր՝ ընդ հուն անցից մեղաց
    խորաշուխ ծովահեղձ ցանկական կենցաղոյս՝
    ի լոյս աչաց
    եւ ի տեսութիւն մտաց.
    ի հանգիստ կենաց
    եւ ի հանդիպումն շնորհաց,
    եւ ի չափիդա ճանապարհացն արդարութեան:

82 Շնորհեա՛ ինձ Տէր՝ լալ աչաց,
    արտասուաց հոսումն,
    մեղաց սուգ,
    մտաց սրտի երկիւղ,
    ոսկերաց իմոց սարսափումն
    եւ դողումն վասն տանջանաց,
    կենաց ճանապարհ,
    եւ անեղծար պաղատանս:

78 Delay no longer, O Lord, to grant salvation to my soul,
    and a burning ardor to my heart,
    moderation in nourishment and chastity of the flesh,
    a stream of tears and incessant prayer,
    humility, obedience and patient hope.

79 Subdue, O Lord, my adversary and give me the strength
    to resist that one who wages war against me.
Clothe me with the breast-plate of faith,[73]
    with fasting and prayer,[74]
    to purify the passions of desire and fleshly thoughts,
    and to receive Your saving grace.

80 Grant me, O Lord, an opportunity for repentance,
    rest from my labor,[75]
    a spirit of peace,
    the way of righteousness,
    strong armament[76] and a guardian of salvation,
    firm hope and unwavering fear.[77]

81 Bring me, O Lord, through the ford of the river of sins,
    of my plummeting, drowning, covetous course of life
    into light for my eyes,
    into vision for my mind,
    into rest in that life,
    to the attainment of Your graces,
    and to the path of the ways of righteousness.

82 Grant to me, O Lord, weeping of the eyes,
    pouring out of tears,
    mourning for my sins,
    fear of the thoughts in my heart,
    quaking of my bones,
    trembling at my punishments,
    the path of life,
    and unceasing supplication.

---

[73] Cf. Ephesians 6:14–16; the author here 'coalesces' the "breast-plate of righteousness" and the "shield of faith".
[74] Cf. Matthew 17:21.
[75] Cf. Revelation 14:13.
[76] Cf. Ephesians 6:11–16.
[77] Cf. 4 Maccabees 17:4.

83 Արիացմ զիս Տէր՝ ի պատուիրանաց պահպանութիւն,
ի յորովայնի ժուժկալութիւն.
ի մարտ պատերազմի բանսարկուն յաղթութիւն,
ի մարմնի մեռանիլ,
եւ պայծառանալ ի Հանդիսի։

84 Լցմ զիս Տէր՝ երկիւղի քո եւ դղձմամբ,
արտասուօք եւ Հառաչանօք,
սիրով եւ սրբութեամբ,
խոնրհօք եւ ճշմարտութեամբ,
գիտութեամբ եւ ամենայն առաքինութեամբ։

85 Ձնջեա՛ Տէր՝ զբազմութիւն մեղաց իմոց,
եւ թօթափեա՛ զմրուր դառնութեան յանցանացս.
եւ պարարեա՛ զսիրտ իմ արբմամբ սուրբ Հոգւոյդ.
եւ գփշաբեր մարմին իմ լցմ խնորհօք,
զարգացմ եւ ի պտղաբերութիւն փոխարկեա՛։

86 Երեւեցմ Տէր՝ գշնորհս քո ի ծառայս քո,
զգուշ եւ գողորմութիւն քո ի պաշտօնեայս քո.
եւ տածարացմ զիս բնակարան լինիլ ամենասուրբ Հոգւոյդ՝
մի՛ եւս ծառայել մեղաց եւ ապականութեանց։

87 Բժշկեա՛ զիս Տէր՝ ի Հպարտութենէ, եւ յամբարտաւանութենէ,
ի սնափառութենէ եւ ի փառասիրութենէ,
ի մարդահաճութենէ եւ ի կեղծաւորութենէ եւ յօրակալութենէ,
ի բարկութենէ եւ ի սրտմտութենէ,
ի նախանձուէ եւ ի յատելութենէ
եւ ի դատելոյ զոք եւ ի չարութենէ եւ յամենայն մեղաց։

88 Փրկեա՛ զիս Տէր՝ ի մարդկային գովեստից ի փառաց եւ ի մեծարանաց.
զխաւարս լոյս կարծելով՝
Համբաւեն ի վերայ իմ բարի,
գեղկելիս երանելի,
գողորմելիս առաքինի,
եւ ես եմ արտասուելի եւ անմխիթար մեղօք լի։

83 Give me the strength, O Lord, to keep Your commandments,
    to exercise control over my belly,
    to gain victory in battle against the adversary,
    to die to the flesh,
    and to be resplendent at the "Rest."[78]

84 Fill me, O Lord, with fear of You and with contrition,
    with tears and groans,
    with love and holiness,
    with grace and truth,
    with knowledge and with every virtue.

85 Wipe away, O Lord, the multitude of my sins,
Drain away the bitter dregs of my transgressions,
Saturate my heart with the watering of Your Holy Spirit,
and fill my thorn-bearing flesh with Your grace,
Adorn it and transform it so that it may bear fruit.[79]

86 Manifest, O Lord, Your grace to me, Your servant,
    Your compassion and Your mercy to me who worships You.
Make me a temple to be a dwelling for Your All-Holy Spirit[80]
    so that I no longer serve sin and unrighteousness.

87 Heal me, O Lord, from pride and haughtiness,
    from vanity and love of glory,
    from flattery, hypocrisy, and vengefulness,
    from anger and indignation,
    from envy and hatred,
    from judging anyone, from evil and from all sin.

88 Preserve me, O Lord, from human praise, glory and honor
    from those who reckon any good to me,
    and who consider light me who am dark,
    blessed me who am deplorable,
    virtuous me who am pitiable,
    — and I am lamentable and filled with so many sins!

---

[78] I.e., the 'rest' promised by God to those who remain faithful; cf. Psalm 95:11, Hebrews 3:11, 18; 4:1–11.

[79] The images here are clearly taken from the parable of the sower; cf. Matthew 13:3–23, and parallels.

[80] Cf. 1 Corinthians 6:19.

89 Մածկեա՛ զիս Տէր՝ ի լուսոյ սուտ գովութեանց եւ յերանութեանց,
  զի ոչ գիտեն զմեղս իմ
 եւ կոչեն զիս սուրբ, զի երեւիմ սրբութեամբ,
  եւ լի եմ աղտեղութեամբ.
 կերպարանիմ առաքինութեամբ, եւ կեամ անառակութեամբ,
 փայլիմ երկիւղածութեամբ, եւ վարիմ մարդահաճութեամբ,
 ճանաչեմ գձմարտութիւն, եւ խօսիմ դատութիւն.
 գիտեմ գարդարութիւն, եւ գործեմ գանօրէնութիւն։

90 Քաւեա՛ զիս Տէր՝ ի մեղաց եւ ի բամբասանաց,
  ի մոռացեալ յանցանաց եւ յամենայն սխալանաց.
 եւ թող ինձ զանժուժկալութիւն եւ զծուլութիւն
 գործկորստութիւն եւ գդատարկաբանութիւն,
 գցանկութիւն եւ գաղտեղութիւն,
 գհայհոյութիւն եւ զամենայն բիծս չարեաց։

91 Կացո՛ զիս Տէր՝ հաստատուն
  եւ անշարժ ի տեղի փորձանաց պատերախմի՝
 առանց երկիւղի քաջ եւ պինտ Հաւատով
  եւ յորդորական սրտով
 գօրավիգն լինել ընդդէմ եկեղոց դիաց ի վերայ իմ.
 զինեա՛ զիս ամրակուռ զինու քո՝
  տալ պատերազմ եւ յաղթել
 թշնամւոյն Հակառակամարտի, որ կամի խապատ զիս որսալ։

92 Զրնկդմեալս Տէր՝ ի խորս մեղաց՝ հանցես
 եւ բերցես ի լոյս պատուիրանաց քոց.
 եւ առ քեզ կոչեցես գհեռացեալս ի քէն,
 եւ թողցես գգործս իմ անառակութեան.
 դապաւինեալս ի քեզ ամրացուցես,
 եւ գգառանեալս ի քեզ մխիթարեսցես.
 գարձակեալս ի կապոյ պատուիրանաց քոց՝ ընդունեսցես,
 եւ ընդ լուծ սիրոյ քոյ բեւեռեսցես։

89   Hide me, O Lord, from hearing false praises and blessings,
        for they do not know my sins.
   They call me holy for I have the appearance of holiness
        but I am filled with impurity.
   I have the semblance of virtue but I live in wantonness[81].
   I have the aura of piety but I act for the sake of flattery.
   I recognize the truth but I speak falsehood.
   I know what is upright but I do what is unjust.

90   Grant me, O Lord, pardon from my sins and from my slander,
        from being unmindful of all my transgressions and failings.
   Forgive me my sins of sloth and intemperance,
        of gluttony and idle speech,
        of envy and impurity,
        of blasphemy and of every stain of evil.

91   Set me firm, O Lord,
        Make me immoveable in the battle of temptations,
        so that without fear, with strong and steadfast faith
            and with willing heart,
       I may bravely defend myself against the demons that come out against me.
   Arm me with Your strong armor[82]
        that I may wage battle and be victorious
        over that antagonistic enemy who wishes to hunt me to the death.

92   May You raise me up, O Lord, for I am drowning in the depths of my sin,
   May You bear me up into the light of Your commandments.
   May You call me to You for I am far from You,
   May You forgive my deeds of wantonness[83].
   May You give strength to me who trust in You,
   and give comfort to me who turn to You.
   May You catch me for I have slipped the bond of Your commandments,
   May You fasten me onto the yoke of Your love.

---

[81] The word used here is taken from the description of the prodigal son; cf. Luke 15:13.

[82] Cf. Ephesians 6:11ff.

[83] Again, the word used here is taken from the description of the prodigal son; cf. Luke 15:13.

93 Զգութ սիրոյ քո Տէր՝ միաւորեա՛ լիս,
և զարգելեալս ի բանտի կապանաց՝ արձակեա՛
և խղճեա՛ զկապանս մեղաց իմոց.
առաջնորդեա՛ ինձ ի ճանապարհ արդարութեան,
և տեղի յարկից պատրաստեա՛, և պսակեա՛ ընդ սուրբս քո։

94 Հաղորդս արա՛ զիս Տէր՝ աստուածային սիրոյ քոյ,
    սիրել զպատուիրանս քո
    և գնալ ի ճանապարհս քո,
    չարչարիլ մինչև ցմահ վասն անուանդ քո,
    մտանել ի փառս
    և դասիլ ընդ սուրբս քո,
    և ուրախանալ միշտ ընդ կամարարս քո։

95 Գթա՛ Տէր ի մեղուցեալ և յեղկելի անձն իմ.
խափանեա՛ դանատակ ցանկութիւնս իմ.
սրբեա՛ զաղտեղութիւն մեղաց իմոց,
և քաւեա՛ զանօրէնութիւնս իմ.
բժշկեա՛ գվիրաւորեալ Հոգիս,
և առողջացո՛ զՀիւանդացեալ մարմին իմ.
ցրուեա՛ զչարն լիսէն և ժողովեա՛ լիս զբարիս,
և լից զպակասութիւնս իմ գործութեամբ քո Տէր։

96 Առաջի քո անկանիմ և խնդրեմ գթողութիւն մեղաց իմոց.
դպաղատանս իմ ընկա՛լ, և քաւիչ լեր յանցանաց իմոց.
պայծառացո՛ և լուսաւորեա՛ գխորՀուրդս և գմիտս իմ.
կարողացո՛ զմարմին իմ
        անդադար կալ ի փառաբանութիւն անուանդ քում սրբոյ։

97 Զանկեալս մեղօք կանգնեա՛, Տէր,
և գխոցեալս ի թշնամոյն դեղապատեա՛.
բա՛րձ զցաւս մեղաց,
և վերացո՛ զկսկիծ յանցանաց.
յափշտակեա՛ ի դառն դաՀճաց,
և ազատեա՛ յանողորմ տանջանացն,
և ի մարմնական լլփանաց Հեռացո՛,
և ի դասս ճգնաւորացն դասեցո՛։

93 Unite me to Your tender love, O Lord,
Release me for I am confined in the jail of my transgressions,
Cut off the bond of [my] sins.
Lead me onto the path of righteousness.
Prepare a place of shelter and crown me among Your saints.[84]

94 Give me a share, O Lord, in Your divine love
    that I may love Your commandments,
    that I may walk on Your paths,
    that I may suffer unto death for the sake of Your name,
    that I may enter into Your glory,[85]
    that I may be enrolled among Your saints,[86]
    and that I may rejoice always with those who have done Your will.

95 Have pity, O Lord, upon my sinful and miserable soul.
Bring an end to my licentious desires.
Cleanse the impurity of my sins
and pardon me for my iniquities.
Heal my wounded spirit
and cure my sickened flesh.
Drive out from me [all] evils and gather up in me [all] good things;
Fill up my deficiencies, O Lord, with Your power.

96 Before You I prostrate myself and beg forgiveness for my sins.
Receive my entreaties and grant me pardon for my transgressions.
Enlighten and illumine my mind and my thoughts,
give strength to my flesh
    that I might always stand and give praise to Your Holy Name.

97 Raise me up, O Lord, for I have fallen into sin,
and cure me for I have been wounded by the enemy.
Remove the pains of [my] sins
and take away the afflictions of [my] transgressions.
Snatch [me] away from brutal torturers,
and free [me] from merciless torments.
Keep me far from carnal gluttony
and enroll me among the ranks of ascetics.

---

[84] Cf. Revelation 2:10.
[85] Cf. Luke 24:26.
[86] Cf. Psalm 69:28.

98 Լե՛ր վերակացու եւ պահապան անձին իմոյ, Տէր իմ Յիսուս.
պահեա՛ զիս ի դիւաց, եւ փրկեա՛ զիս ի մարդկային փորձանաց:
Հակառակողաց յաղթեա՛,
եւ կացո՛ զիս ի մէջ պատերազմողաց՝ քաջ եւ ընտիր լինիլ.
գործակցեա՛ ինձ լինիլ քաւարան մեղաց,
    եւ համբերել վշտաց առաքինական գործովք
    եւ հանդիպիլ քում աստուածային շնորհաց:

99 Վա՜յ ինձ Տէ՛ր՝ վա՜յ ինձ, զի մեղօք կործանեցայ,
    եւ մտօք իմովք ապտեղացայ.
ի բարեաց ունայնացայ, եւ ի սիրոյ ցամաքեցայ.
ի լալոյ խաւարեցայ, եւ ի գնալոյ դադարեցայ:
Ոչ ունիմ աչս լալոյ եւ արտասուաց,
ծփիմ տարակուսեալ,
    զի յոյս եւ ակն բարւոյ ոչ ունիմ:

100 Կանգնեա՛ Տէ՛ր՝ գտարաբերեալ անձն իմ,
որ լի եմ մեղօք եւ անժիւ յանցանօք.
    եւ խարշեալ եւ տրոհեալ եմ ամենայն անդամօքս
յոտից մինչեւ ցգլուխս ապականեալ,
    եւ չի՛ք հնար բժշկութեան՝ եթէ ոչ ի քէն Տէր իմ Յիսուս.
խոնարհեա՛ առ վիրաւորեալս դեղատուութեամբ,
եւ մի՛ գարշիր ի շարահուտ ախտացելոյս մեղօք:

101 Հեռացո՛ Տէ՛ր՝ զբերան իմ ի բամբասելոյ,
    եւ զլեզու իմ ի չար խօսելոյ,
դաչս իմ յարատ հայելոյ,
    եւ զականջս իմ ի չար լուր լսելոյ,
զձեռս իմ ի յափշտակելոյ,
    եւ զոտս իմ ի յանառակ գնացս երթալոյ,
եւ զամենայն անդամս իմ պարապեալ զզաստացո՛՛
    միշտ զհաճոյս քո կատարել:

98 Be the overseer and guardian of my soul, my Lord Jesus,
    Protect me from demons and save me from human temptations.
    Overcome those who oppose me,
    Help me to stand courageous and distinguished in battle.
    Let me be a co-worker in the pardoning of sins
        that, with virtuous deeds, I may persevere in affliction
        and obtain Your divine grace.

99 Woe to me, O Lord, woe to me, for I have come to ruin in my sins,
        and in my thoughts I have defiled myself.
    I am bereft of [all] good, and am drained of all love.
    I have been so blinded by weeping[87] that I can no longer walk;
    I do not have eyes for weeping or for lamentation.
    I am so tossed and shaken about,
        that I no longer have hope or expectation of [any] good.

100 Re-establish, O Lord, my floundering soul.
    I am full of sins and innumerable transgressions,
        in all my limbs there is burning[88] and racking pain.
    From my feet to the very top of my head I am disfigured,
        and there is no means for healing except from You, my Lord Jesus.
    Deign to heal me for I am wounded,
    and do not be repulsed by my foul and morbid sins.

101 Keep, O Lord, my mouth far away from slander,
        and my tongue from evil speech,[89]
        my eyes from too much staring,
        my ears from listening to evil rumors,
        my hands from robbery,
        my feet from going on lewd paths.
    Rouse and protect all my limbs,
        that they may always accomplish Your pleasure.

---

[87] Cf. Lamentations 2:11.
[88] Cf. Job 30:17.
[89] Cf. Psalm 34:13, 1 Peter 3:10.

102 *Մեղա՛յ քեզ Տէր՝ մեղայ.*
    զի յանցեայ զպատուիրանաւ քով.
    ի լուսոյ կենաց եկայ
        եւ մտի ի խաւար մեղաց.
    ցանկանալով ադտեղութեան՝ ի սիրոյ քոյ Հեռացայ,
    ըմբոնեցայ ի չարէն՝ եւ եղէ որդի կորստեան,
    ողորմեաս ինձ բազմամեղիս բարերար,
        զի դու միայն ես մարդասէր:

103 *Ի քեզ Տէր ապաւինիմ՝*
    որ քաւարան ես մեղաւորաց,
    բարւոք շտեմարան,
    եւ փախուցելոյս դարան,
    զԹշնամին իմ արամ փախստական:
    Օգնական դայլ ոք ոչ ունիմ,
        բայց զքեզ միայն ունիմ պաՀապան անճին իմոյ.
    ի վտանգից փրկեա՛,
    ի յորոգայթից ապրեցո՛,
    եւ արժանի արա՛ դիս լինել որդի լուսոյ քո յաւիտենին:

104 *Ողորմեա՛ ինձ Տէր կենաց*
    եւ քաւիչ մեղաց,
    կատարիչ խնդրուածաց
    եւ արձակիչ կապանաց,
    բաշխող պարգեւաց
    եւ տուիչ ամենայն շնորՀաց:

105 *Լո՛ւր Տէր գաղաչանս իմ, եւ ընկալ դպագատանս իմ.*
    քաւեա՛ զյանցանս իմ, եւ կատարեա՛ զխնդրուածս իմ.
    արձակեա՛ զկապանս իմ եւ բժշկեա՛ զՀոգի իմ.
    առողջացո՛ զմարմինս իմ, եւ ուղղեա՛ զզնացս իմ.
    փութացո՛ զիս ժամանել յոթեւանս սրբոց քոց:

106 *Հայածեա՛ Տէր՝ զբազում ախտաժետութիւնս իմ,*
    զցաւս ի մարմնոյս եւ զադտ ի Հոգւոյս,
    զբուն ի գլխոյս եւ դյազումն յորկորոյ:
    ՊաՀեա՛ զխորՀուրդս իմ անդբաղ, զսիրտ իմ սուրբ,
    եւ զմիտս իմ լուսաւոր եւ զգաստ,
    զգանկութիւնս իմ առ քեզ,
    եւ դյօժարութիւն յաղօթս ի տուէ եւ ի գիշերի:

102 I have sinned against You, O Lord, I have sinned,[90]
    for I have transgressed Your commandments.
I have gone out from the light of life,
    and I have entered into the darkness of sin.
In my desire for impurity I have gone far from Your love.
I am overtaken by evil and I have become a child of perdition.
Have mercy on me, a great sinner, O Beneficent One,
    for You alone are the Lover of mankind.

103 In You, O Lord, I take my refuge,
    for You are a place of atonement to sinners,
    a treasure house of good,
    and a safe-house for those who are fleeing.
Make my enemy a fugitive.
I have no other helper,
    except You alone, Protector of my soul.
Deliver me from danger,
Rescue me from the traps,
and make me worthy to become a child of Your light forever.

104 Have mercy on me, O Lord of life
    Who forgives our sins,
    Who fulfills our petitions,
    Who breaks our bonds,
    Who distributes gifts,
    and Who gives out all graces.

105 Hear, O Lord, my prayer and receive my supplications,
Pardon my transgressions and bring to fulfillment all my petitions.
Break my bonds and heal my spirit,
Restore my flesh and make straight my paths.[91]
Make me arrive quickly at the dwelling place of your saints.[92]

106 Cast out, O Lord, my many sicknesses,
    afflictions of my body and stains on my soul,
    slumber from my head and satiety from my throat.
Keep my thoughts undisturbed and my heart pure,
    my mind illumined and alert,
    my desires for You,
    and my inclination for prayer day and night.

---

[90] Cf. Psalm 51:4.
[91] Cf. Psalm 5:8.
[92] Cf. Matthew 3:3, Mark 1:3, Luke 3:4, John 1:23.

107 Բղխեա՛ Տէր՝ ի գլուխ իմ աղբիւր վտակաց,
     արոգեա՛ եւ զանդա մտաց իմոց.
     զազտ յանցանաց իմոց լուա՛,
     եւ սրբեա՛ զԹարախ վիրաց իմոց.
     գփուշ մեղաց իմոց խլեա՛
     եւ տնկեա՛ զբոյս կենաց։
     Աճեցո՛ Տէր զարդարութիւն,
     եւ նուաստացո՛ զանօրէնութիւն.
     մերո՛ զմարմնոյս ցանկութիւն,
     եւ նորոգեա՛ զՀոգւոյս կենդանութիւն։

108 Կոչեա՛ Տէր՝ զմեղուցեալ անձն իմ ի քեզ,
     զի մերձենալ առ քեզ ոչ իշխեմ.
     պատկառիմ յամօթոյ եւ զարհուրիմ ի գործոց իմոց.
     ոչ ունիմ առ քեզ Համարձակութիւն,
     զի ես ինձէն եմ կորուսեալ.
     ի սուրբ պատուիրանաց քոց Հեռացայ
     եւ մերկացայ ի փառաց քոց,
     այլ դու Տէր՝ զիմս վիս եւ ողորմեա՛,
     զի ստեղծուած եմ անարատ ձեռաց քոց։

109 Ոչ իշխեմ Տէր՝ անյույս լինիլ,
     զի ողորմած ես եւ գԹած,
     եւ փառս անձառս խոստացար դարձելոց մեղաւորաց.
     այլ ես զարհուրիմ եւ դողամ, եւ երկնչիմ
     ի բազում եւ յանժիւ մեղաց իմոց,
     զի պատրեալ խաբեցայ յորսողէն.
     եւ արդ զիՆչ լինիմ եղկելիս՝
     որ տարակուսեալ եմ ի կենաց եւ տարագրեալ։

107 Pour, O Lord, onto my head a fountain of running water,
Irrigate the fields of my mind,
Wash away the stains of my transgressions,
Cleanse the pus from my wounds,
Pluck out the thorns of my sins
and plant the herb of life.
Increase, O Lord, my righteousness
Suppress my lawlessness,
Kill the desires of my flesh
and renew the vitality of my spirit.

108 Summon, O Lord, my sinful soul to Yourself
     for I am incapable of drawing near to You.
I am covered with shame and am in dread over my deeds.
I have no freedom before you,
     for I am dragging myself into ruin.
From Your holy commandments I have distanced myself,
     and I have stripped myself of Your glory,[93]
but You, O Lord, have pity on me and have mercy,
     for I am a creation of Your immaculate hands.[94]

109 I am not able to fall into despair,
     for You are merciful and compassionate,
     and You promised ineffable glory to sinners who repent.[95]
But I am terrified, trembling, and in great fear
     due to my many and innumerable sins,
for I have been deceived and seduced by the hunter.
And now, how miserable have I become
     who am banished and excluded from salvation.

---

[93] The phrasing is from Job 19:9, although there Job claims that it is God who stripped him.

[94] The notion that God created using His hands stems from Job 10:8 and Psalm 118:73; cf. Agatʻangeghos, *Patmutʻiwn*, 152: *ստեղծեալ զմարդն ձեռամբ իւրովք*. Some later authors identified these hands as the Son and the Holy Spirit.

[95] Cf. 1 Corinthians 2:9.

110 Արա՛ զիս Տէր՝ ի սուգ եւ յարտասուս վասն մեղաց իմոց,
զի ծանրաբեռնեալ եմ անօրէնութեամբ
եւ յագեալ ադտեղի խորհրդով.
շատ ներեցեր ինձ, զի ոչ խրատեցեր զիս ի մարմնի.
արդ սարսեալ դողամ, զի ոչ մնան ինձ այսպիսի չարիք։
Աղաչեմ բարերար Տէր՝
մի՛ կոչեր զիս յատենի,
եւ տանջանաց մի՛ մատներ զիս.
այլ փրկեա՛ ի Հրոյ գեհենին
եւ ի վտանգից ապրեցո՛ եւ ողորմեա՛ ինձ,
զի դու միայն ես մարդասէր։

111 Վա՜յ ինձ Տէր՝ զի ճիանք տարակուսանաց պատեն զիս,
եւ գիխտ իմ խռովեն.
զոր աղօթեմ՝ ոչ գիտեմ,
սաղմոսեմ՝ եւ ոչ իմանամ.
շրթունք իմ բարբառի,
եւ միտք իմ ճողոպրեալ յածի այսր եւ անդր՝
եւ զկայումն ոչ ունի, եւ ի պէտս իմ ոչ գտանի,
եւ ուր կամիմ զի իջէ, անդ ոչ դադարի.
ոչ տեսանի արդեօք եւ ոչ ըմբռնի.
զուր աշխատիմ եւ ոչ ինչ օգտիմ.
որպէս ճայն Հնչեալ պղնձի կամ ծնծղայի՝
թափուր եւ ունայն գտանիմ,
եւ անպտուղ լինիմ յամենայն բարեաց։

110 Lead me, O Lord, into mourning and lamentation over my sins,
>   for I am overburdened with my unrighteousness
>   and am sated with my filthy thoughts.
> Be very forgiving to me whom You never chastised in the flesh.
> Now I am shuddering and trembling lest such evils remain in me.
> I pray to You, O beneficent Lord:
>   Do not summon me to Your throne,
>   or hand me over to torment,
> Rather, save me from the fires of Gehenna.[96]
> Deliver me from punishments and have mercy on me,
>   for You alone are the Lover of mankind.

111 Woe to me, O Lord, for waves of anxiety beset me
>   and they agitate my heart.
> I do not understand what I am praying;
> I recite a psalm but I do not understand.
> My lips utter the words,
>   but my mind roams and wanders here and there;
> It has no stability and it is never found at my tasks,
> wherever I wish it to be it does not remain there.
> It certainly is not seen and it is not controllable;
> At whatever I am working it gives me no help.
> Like the noise of a clanging gong or a cymbal,[97]
> I find myself empty and void,
>   and I am barren of all good deeds.

---

[96] Cf. Matthew 5:22, and parallels.
[97] Cf. 1 Corinthians 13:1.

112 Ընկալ Տէր գմղորեայս՝
    որ փախուցեալ կամ ի լերինս,
որպէս ծառայ չար ի Տեառնէ հալածեալ եմ վասն մեղաց։
Եւ ի սուրբ եղբարց հրաժարեալ եմ,
    ի սուրբ պաշտամանց հեռացեալ.
զի սիրող էի մեղաց եւ նախատինք կրօնաւորաց,
    անյագ ի զրկանաց եւ խափանիչ սուրբ պատուիրանաց։
Անգութ էի աղքատաց, եւ հակառակ սպասաւորաց.
անողորմ հիւանդաց էի եւ անմխիթար աշխատողաց.
չէի իսկ արժանի կեալ ի մէջ ճգնաւորաց։

113 Հանգո՛ Տէր՝ գշնորհս Հոգւոյդ սրբոյ ի վերայ իմ,
    որ միայն եմ ի պատերազմի առանց օգնականի.
սրբեա՛ Տէր՝ գտառար Հոգւոյ իմոյ,
եւ առ իս լեր ընդ երեկոյս։
բա՛ց պաշա Հոգւոյ իմոյ,
եւ լուսաւորեա՛ զմիտս եւ գխորհուրդս իմ։
Տո՛ւր ինձ գործութիւն Տէր իմ Յիսուս,
եւ ընկալ գորհնաբանութիւն բերանոյ իմոյ.
ի խոր քնոյ գիշերայ դարթռ՛ դիս
    գոհանալ եւ օրհնել գքեզ,
    որով գմեղս իմ քաւեցից.
շնորհեա՛ ինձ սուգ եւ արտասուս լալոյ
եւ սգալոյ եւ անդադար աղօթելոյ առաջի քո։

114 Դատեա՛ Տէր՝ գդատապարտողն իմ՝
    որ յանդգնի ի վերայ իմ,
    մարտ եղեալ ընդ իս
    ցանկութեամբ եւ անժուժկալութեամբ,
    ծուլութեամբ եւ որկորստութեամբ,
    փառասիրութեամբ եւ մարդահաճութեամբ,
    բարկութեամբ եւ սրտմտութեամբ,
    ատելութեամբ եւ չարաչար հայհոյութեամբ,
    սնափառութեամբ եւ սնապարծութեամբ,
    հպարտութեամբ եւ ամբարտաւանութեամբ,
բանիւք եւ գործովք, եւ խորհրդովք գորածողով լինի ի վերայ իմ,
եւ ընկզմէ՛ գիս ի խորս չարեաց։

112 Receive, O Lord, me who have strayed,
    and have fled into the mountains;
Like an evil servant I have been banished from the Lord
    because of my sins.
I have been renounced by the holy brothers,
    and removed from the sacred services,
For I was a lover of sin and an offence to ascetics,
    insatiable for fraud and a suppressor of the holy commandments.
I had no compassion for the poor and was hostile to servants;
I was without mercy for the sick and I offered no comfort to the weary.
I was, therefore, the most unworthy among the ascetics.[98]

113 Let, O Lord, the grace of Your Holy Spirit rest upon me
    who am alone in battle without any help.
Purify, O Lord, the temple of my spirit,
and be with me throughout the evening;
Open the eyes of my spirit,
and illumine my mind and my thoughts.
Give me strength, my Lord Jesus,
and receive the praise from my mouth;
Wake me from the deep sleep of the night
    to bless You and to praise You
    by which I might atone for my sins.
Grant that I may mourn, weep tears of lamentation,
    and pray before You continuously.

114 Condemn, O Lord, that one who condemns me,
    who boldly rises up against me,
    and wages war against me
    with desires and intemperance,
    with idleness and gluttony,
    with vainglory and love of flattery,
    with anger and indignation,
    with hate and excessive blasphemy,
    with vanity and conceit,
    with pride and haughtiness.
With words, deeds, and thoughts he levies his army against me
    and plunges me into the depths of evil.

---

[98] In lines 6 and 10, I have translated two different words as "ascetics": կրօնաւոր and ճգնաւոր. Generally, these two words both indicate, in a non-specific way, one who toils away at asceticism — often a monk, but not necessarily so; the former is the word that the author of these prayers uses when he pleads to be enrolled among them, #97, line 8, above. It is, in any case, an instance where Armenian has a slightly larger vocabulary than does English.

115 Սփռեա՛ Տէր՝ գշնորհս քո ի վերայ մասանց անդամոց իմոց.
ցո՛ Տէր՝ զմարմին իմ արիութեամբ եւ ժուժկալութեամբ,
    եւ զՀոգի իմ երկիւղիւ եւ գողութեամբ.
    զսիրտ իմ սիրով եւ արդարութեամբ քո,
    եւ զմիտս իմ լուսով եւ իմաստութեամբ քո.
    զխորՀուրդս իմ Հանճարով եւ գիտութեամբ,
    եւ զոտս իմ գնալ ի շաւիղս արդարութեան.
    զձեռս իմ շօշափելով ի գործս ապաշխարութեան,
    եւ զբերան իմ անդադար սաղմոսել քեզ գոՀութեամբ.
    զաչս իմ յորդաբուղխ արտասուօբ,
    եւ զՀոտոտելիս իմ Հոտոտել պատրաստես զՀոտ գիտութեան ի կեանսդ,
    զլսելիս իմ լսելով զձայնն աւետեաց որ ասէ.
        «Թողեալ լիցին քեզ ամենայն մեղք քո».
    եւ թէ «Այսօր եղեւ փրկութիւն տանս այսմիկ»:

116 Մինչեւ յե՞րբ Տէր՝ անսաս չարագործին՝
    որ ոչ յագի իմով կորստեամբ,
    այլ Հանապազ սկիզբն առնէ չարեաց,
    եւ ի բաց կորզեալ խափանէ զիս
        ի բարեաց եւ յառաքինութեանց.
    եւ Հեռացուցանէ զիս ի սրբութեանց,
    եւ յախտէնից կենաց արտաքս Հանէ զիս:
Խաւարեցուցանէ զլուսաւորութիւն աչաց,
    եւ ապականելով գերէ զմիտս իմ
    եւ վարէ զիս ի չար ծառայութիւն յանցանաց.
    եւ ի ձեռս անօրէն դաՀճաց մատնէ զիս,
    եւ տանի ի տեղի չարչարանաց,
    եւ արկանէ ի բանտ կապանաց մաՀու,
    կացուցանէ ի մէջ խաւարասէր սպասաւորաց,
    եւ ի տոռունս մեղաց կապէ զիս:
Եւ արդ ես եղկելիս դի՞նչ լինիցիմ,
    եթէ ոչ դու Տէր՝ օգնեսցես ինձ:

115 Spread, O Lord, Your grace over every inch of my limbs;
   Fill, O Lord, my flesh with courage and patience,
      my spirit with fear and trepidation,
      my heart with Your love and fidelity,
      my mind with Your light and wisdom,
      my thoughts with intelligence and knowledge,
      my feet to go on the paths of uprightness,
      my hands to put to the works of repentance,
      my mouth to sing psalms to You with continual praise,
      and my eyes with copious tears.
   Prepare my nostrils to smell the scent of knowledge in You, O Life,
      my ears to hear the voice of the Good News that says:
         "May all your sins be forgiven you!"[99]
         and "Today, salvation has come to this house."[100]

116 How long, O Lord, will You give ear to this evildoer,
      who is not content with my destruction,
      but who makes me begin over and over in evil [deeds],
      and snatches me away prohibiting me
         from good [deeds] and virtue,
      and distances me from holiness
      and draws me away from eternal life.
   He darkens the light of my eyes,
      corrupts and seduces my mind,
      and drives me into evil servitude to transgressions.
   Through my iniquity he brings me to the executioners,
      hands me over to the place of torture,
      casts me into the prison house of death,
      sets me among those servants who love darkness,
      and binds me with the cords of sin.
   So now what shall I, who am so deplorable, become
      if You, O Lord, will not help me?

---

[99] Matthew 9:5, and parallels.
[100] Luke 19:9.

117 Տես, Տէր, զլալիս եւ զողբալիս,
զպաղատելիս եւ զեղկելիս,
ինձ ողորմեաւ անօրինելոյս,
եւ շնորհեաւ յորդ արտասուս ի գիշերի,
եւ ծագեաւ գթութեամբ զնշոյլ շնորհաց առաւօտու։
Բա՛ց զխաւարեալ աչս սրտի իմոյ,
եւ բժշկեաւ զՀիւանդացեալ Հոգի իմ.
ընկա՛լ զդարձ մեղաւորիս,
եւ մի՛ բարկանար բազմամեղիս՝ Տէր իմ Յիսուս.
եւ քանզի անմիւ ունիմ զշարիս,
ջնջեաւ լինէն եւ տուր ինձ զշնորՀս բարեաց։

118 Համարձակիմ Տէր, աղօթել առ քեզ,
բայց ոչ գիտեմ զՀածոյսն քո
խնդրեմ եւ ոչ իմանամ զօգտականն Հոգւոյս.
յայտնեաւ ինձ ողորմած Տէր, զկամս քո,
եւ ուսո՛ ինձ զպատուիրանս քո։
Զբարիս՝ զոր ոչ խնդրեմ եւ իմանամ, տուր ինձ Տէր.
եւ եթէ ոչ գործեմ զբարիս բարի արա ինձ Տէր.
եւ եթէ ոչ խնդրեմ զողորմութիւն, ողորմութիւն շնորհեաւ ինձ,
եւ զՀեռացեալս առ քեզ կոչեաւ.
եւ եթէ ոչ կամիմ, բռնաւորեաւ եւ ի քեզ կորզեաւ.
եւ եթէ կամիմ եւ եթէ ոչ կամիմ, դարձո՛ դիս.
եւ եթէ ըմբռնիմ յումեքէ, գերծո՛ դիս.
եթէ յերկրաւորս զբաղեցայց, ի խորՀուրդս Հոգեւորս զբաղեցո՛ դիս.
եթէ այսր եւ անդր գնալ ցանդիմ, մի՛ թողուր դիս՝
մինչեւ ըմբռնեալ տարցես
ի տեղի յարկի փառաց քոց։

119 Տէր իմ եւ Աստուած իմ Յիսուս Քրիստոս,
դու ես իմ օգնական, ի ձեռս քո եմ.
դու գիտես զօգուտն իմ, օգնեա՛ ինձ.
մի՛ թողուր դիս մեղանչել քեզ,
դի մոլորական եմ ի չար դիւաց.
մի՛ թողուր դիս Հետեւիլ կամաց իմոց,
մի՛ թողուր դիս կործնչիլ ի մեղս իմ,
այլ գծմա՛ լիս ի ստեղծուածս ձեռաց քոց.
մի՛ ընկենուր դիս յերեսաց քոց,
եւ զՀոգիդ Սուրբ մի՛ Հաներ յինէն։

117 See, O Lord, my weeping and my groaning,
>   my supplications and my deplorable self.
> Have mercy upon me who am such a sinner,
> Grant me the grace of abundant tears in the night,
> and, in Your mercy, let the light of Your grace shine in the morning.
> Open the darkened eyes of my heart,
> and heal my diseased spirit;
> Accept the conversion of this sinner,
> and do not be angry, my Lord Jesus, at me who am so sinful.
> Because I possess such innumerable evil deeds,
> Purge them from me and give me the grace of good deeds.

118 I am emboldened, O Lord, to pray to You,
>   but I do not know what pleases You.
> I seek but I do not know what is beneficial to my spirit.
> Reveal to me, O merciful Lord, what You wish,
> and teach me Your commandments.
> The good deeds that I neither seek nor understand, give to me, O Lord.
> Although I do no good deeds, do good to me, O Lord,
> and although I do not seek mercy, grant me mercy,
>   and call to me who am so far from You.
> Although I am unwilling, take hold of me and snatch me for Yourself,
> and whether I am willing or unwilling, bring me back,
> and if anything else lays hold of me, snatch me away.
> If I become occupied in earthly things, occupy me with spiritual thoughts,
> or if I heedlessly go here and there, do not forsake me
>   until You have snatched me and brought me
>   into that dwelling-place of Your glory.

119 My Lord and my God,[101] Jesus Christ,
> You are my help, I am in Your hands.
> You know what is beneficial to me, help me,
> Do not let me sin against You,
>   though I wander among evil demons.
> Do not let me follow my own will,
> Do not let me perish in my sins,
> But have compassion on me, a creation of Your hands.[102]
> "Do not cast me away from Your presence
>   and take not Your Holy Spirit from me."[103]

---

[101] Cf. John 20:28.
[102] Cf. n. 94, above.
[103] Psalm 51:11 (50:13 Arm).

120 Առ քեզ ապաւինեցայ,
    բժշկեա՛ զանձն իմ զի մեղայ քեզ.
    առաջի քո են ամենայն նեղիչք իմ,
    եւ ոչ դող ինձ հանգիստ բաց ի քէն։
    Տէր, կեցո՛ զիս վասն բազում ողորմութեան քո,
        քանզի ամենեքեան յարուցեալ են ի վերայ իմ,
        որք խնդրեն զանձն իմ կորուսանել զնա.
    եւ զի դու կարող ես եւ հզօր յամենայնի, փրկեա՛ զիս։

121 Մի՛ Հայր Տէր՝ ի մեղկեալ սիրտս
        եւ ի զազրասէր մարմինս իմ,
        զի հող եմ եւ մոխիր։
    սիրեմ զերկրաւորս,
    եւ ոչ փափագիմ նայիլ յերկնայինսն.
    այլ միշտ հեշտանամ ի չարիս,
    եւ ոչ տեսանեմ զանվախճան գեառն.
    եւ ոչ յիշեմ զառաջին սուրբ Հարսն գերանելին,
        այլ ընդ տիղմն աշխարհիս թաւալիմ,
        եւ ոչ մաքրեալ վերանամ դասի ընդ առաքինսն։
    Եւ զի մոռանամ զերկիւղ դատաստանին,
    եւ ոչ դողամ յահագին դառն տանջանացն՝
        որ կայ պահեալ մեղաւորաց.
    եւ ես ծույանամ անհող լինելով ի փրկութենէ կենաց.
    չնորհեա՛ ինձ Տէր՝ սուգ եւ կոծ
        անհանգիստ եւ առատ արտասուս ապաշաւանաց։

122 Մի՛ յանդիմաներ զիս Տէր յաւուրն մեծի աՀեղին,
    եւ մի՛ յատենի Հրապարակին կացուցաներ զիս ամօթալի,
    եւ ի տեղի ատենին մի՛ խայտառակեր զիս,
    եւ մի՛ կշտամբեր յատեան դատաստանին,
    եւ մի՛ թողուր ինձ լսել զոչ գիտեմն,
    եւ դաժաւոր բարբառն աչաբեկ՝
        որ ասէ, երթա՜յք յինէն ի Հուր գեհենին։

120 To You have I fled for refuge,
   Heal my soul for I have sinned against You;[104]
   All my afflictions are before You,
   and there is no respite for me except from You.
   O Lord, save me because of Your great mercy,
      because everyone has risen up against me,
      and they seek to destroy my soul.
   Because You are all-powerful and all-mighty, deliver me.

121 Do not look, O Lord, upon my languishing heart,
      nor upon my disfigured flesh,
      for I am dirt and ashes.
   I love earthly things,
   and I have no desire to look on heavenly things.
   Rather, I always find pleasure in evil things,
   and I do not see [Your] endless glory.
   I do not remember those ancient holy and blessed fathers,
      but I am wallowing in the mire of the earth;
      I do not rise up cleansed to stand among the virtuous,
   Because I forget the dreadful judgement,
   and do not tremble at the horrible and bitter torments
      that are reserved for sinners,
   and I live in idleness, heedless of the salvation of life.
   Grant to me, O Lord, weeping and mourning,
      with incessant and abundant tears of repentance.

122 Do not reproach me, O Lord, on that great and dreadful day,[105]
   Do not let me stand full of shame at the throne of Your tribunal;
   Do not put me to shame in the place of Your throne,
   and do not admonish me at Your judgement seat.
   Do not abandon me and let me not hear that "I do not know...,"[106]
      or that dreadful, horrible phrase:
      "Go from me into the fires of Gehenna."[107]

---

[104] Psalm 41:4 (40:5 Arm).
[105] Cf. Daniel 9:4, Joel 2:31, Malachi 4:5.
[106] Luke 13:27, but cf. also Matthew 7:23.
[107] Matthew 25:41, and cf. Mark 9:43.

եւ մի՛ ի բաց մերժեր ընդ վատ եւ ընդ չար ծառային.
եւ ի ճեռն անողորմ կապողի մի՛ մատներ զիս,
եւ մի՛ տար կերակուր որդանց թունաւորաց
    ի մէջ բորբոքեալ բոցոյ,
եւ մի՛ արկաներ զիս ի խաւար սառնամանեաց տարտարոսին.
այլ փրկեա՛ զիս ի սատիկ կայծականց Հրոյն,
    ի բոցեղէն գետոց արշաւանացն,
    ի սատիկ լալագին եւ խիստ տանջանացն
    եւ յողբոց տարակուսանաց,
    ի կափկափելոյ ատամանցն,
    ի տոչորմանէ խաւարային բոցոյն
    եւ ի դժնդակ դառն աղէտից խորովելոյն,
    ի բոցաձաւալ եւ ի շրջապատ Հրոյն
    եւ ի կողկողաձայն եւ յանդադար վայոյն։

123 Բազմացաւ Տէր՝ անօրէնութիւն ի վերայ իմ
    իբրիւ զբեռն ադի կամ կապարի.
    բազում է ախտ ի Հոգիս իմ,
        եւ անխտիր եմ ի մեղս մարմնոյ,
        եւ գանագան չարեօք լցեալ եմ։
    Բայց այլ ինչ ունիմ վատժարագոյն՝
        գանգղչութիւն մարմնոյ իմոյ,
        որ քան գամենայն չարիս է դառնագոյն.
    եւ գի յաղօթելն իմում ճանճրանամ,
    եւ ի սաղմոսելն ոչ իմանամ.
    ի խնդրել գերանութիւն պղերգանամ,
    եւ յերկիւղէ չնորհաց դատարկանամ.
    տկարանամ մարմնովս,
    եւ արճան ադի սիրտ իմ լինի.
    եւ ոչ ծագէ ի ներս լոյսն անշիջանելի,
    եւ յալուրն չարի ոչ սարսեալ դողամ։

Do not drive me out as an evil and wicked servant,[108]
nor hand me over to that one who binds without mercy;
Do not give [me] as nourishment to those poisonous worms
    that are in the flaming fires,
and do not cast me into dark, frigid Tartarus.[109]
Deliver me from those extreme flames of fire,
    from the eruptions of flaming rivers,
    from violent weeping and cruel tortures,
    from overwhelming lamentation,
    from the gnashing of teeth,[110]
    from the burning of the outer darkness,[111]
    from the bitter, cruel misery of being burned,
    from the flaming, swirling fire,
    and from that unending wailing and moaning.

123 Wickedness has increased, O Lord, against me
    like a cargo of salt or of lead;
There is much disease in my spirit,
    and I am indifferent to the sins of the flesh,
    I am filled with all sorts of evils.
But I have something even worse,
    — no repentance for my flesh,
    which is the most bitter evil of all!
I grow weary in my prayer,
and I do not know how to chant the Psalms;
I am too lazy to seek for blessing,
and I am empty of grace-bearing fear.
I am weak in my flesh,
and my heart has become a pillar of salt.[112]
That inextinguishable light does not rise in it,
and on the day of evil I neither tremble nor quiver.

---

[108] Cf. Matthew 25:26.

[109] With Classical roots going back as far as Homer (*Iliad* 8.13–16) and Hesiod (*Theogony* 713–735), Tartarus was a name for the underworld. The name enters biblical literature in 1 Enoch, where Tartarus is understood to be the place below Hades where two hundred fallen angels were imprisoned, a tradition preserved in 2 Pet 2:4, though not generally reflected in English translations; it is perhaps of interest here to note that the name Tartarus is found in the Armenian version of this verse but not in the Syriac.

[110] Cf. Matthew 8:12, 13:42, and parallels.

[111] Cf. Matthew 8:12, 22:13, and parallels.

[112] Cf. Genesis 19:26.

124 Շնորհեա՛ ինձ Տէր՝ երկիւղ սրբութեան եւ սգոյ,
եւ յորդեա՛ առ իս աղբերս արտասուաց,
եւ թեթեւացո՛ գծանրութին բեռանց իմոց,
եւ ամեցո՛ առ իս գուրբ աղօթս:
Փութացի՛ր Տէր՝ եւ եկ ի խնդիր մոլորելոյս,
որ մերձեալ եմ ի վախճան կորստեան.
վասն զի խաւարեցայ ի լուսոյ,
եւ ի սիրոյ պատուիրանաց քոց խափանեցայ,
ի չար թշնամւոյն յաղթեցայ,
եւ նուազեցայ յերկիւղէ քումմէ:
Տապալեցայ ի չար խորհրդոց չարին,
եւ ցամաքեցայ ի չնորհաց արտասուաց սիրոյ քոյ.
խաբեցայ յունայն բանից,
եւ ի լուսաւորութենէ մտաց մոլորեցայ.
աղտեղացայ ցանկութեամբ մեղօք
եւ գօր վախճանին մոռացայ:

125 Տարակուսիմ անյոյս լինելով՝
որ ոչ գոյ Հնար ապաշխարութեան.
զի մարմնով տկարացայ՝
պակասեալ ի գործութենէ,
եւ ձերացեալ նուազեցայ.
սակայն ի քեզ ապաւինիմ Տէր իմ,
Հասիր յօգնութիւն ծանրաբեռնեալ ընկղմելոյս,
եւ ազատեա՛ զիս ի չարեաց,
որ ազատիչ ես ի յանցանաց:

126 Ընկա՛լ Տէր՝ զգոյգն եւ զշաղփաղփ աղօթս իմ,
որ կամ առաջի քո դատապարտեալ.
յոյլ եւ ծոյլ ի զգաստութենէ,
մոլորեալ եմ ի մտաց լուսաւորութենէ,
եւ յերկիւղէ ունայնացեալ եմ:
Բերան իմ այլ ընդ այլոյ բարբանջէ.
աչք իմ պշնու եւ միտք իմ գրաղնու.
ոչ անրաւս աղօթեմ,
եւ ոչ սրտի մտօք խնդրեմ.
ոչ Հաւատով առ քեզ գոչեմ,
եւ ոչ երկիւղիւ կարդամ.
ոչ արտասուօք Հայցեմ,
եւ ոչ դողամ եւ սարսիմ վասն աւուրն պատասխանատուութեանց:

124 Grant me, O Lord, a holy fear, and mourning;
Make flow in me springs of tears,
Lighten the heaviness of my burdens,
and multiply holy prayers within me.
Make haste, O Lord, and come to seek me
    who have wandered astray, nearly to the death of destruction,
For I have darkened myself from the light,
    and from the love of Your commandments I have impeded myself.
By the evil of the enemy I have been overcome,
and I have grown weak in my fear of You.
I have been overcome by the wicked intentions of the evil one,
and I am dry of the grace of tears of love for You.
I have been seduced by the vanity of words,
and from the enlightenment of the mind I have wandered.
I have been soiled by my desire for sin,
and I have forgotten about the day of death.

125 I am cast into doubt, and am now without hope
    that there is any means of repentance,
        for I have become weak in the flesh,
            deprived of all strength
            and diminished by old age.
Nevertheless, I take refuge in You, my Lord,
Bring help to me who am weighed down and sinking,
and free me from evils,
    for You are the one who frees us from [our] transgressions.

126 Receive, O Lord, these meager and babbling prayers
    of me who stand before you worthy of condemnation,
        idle and too lazy to keep vigil.
I wander away from any enlightenment of mind,
    and I am completely devoid of any fear.
My mouth babbles on endlessly,
    my eyes just stare out, and my mind is distracted.
I do not pray unceasingly,[113]
    nor do I seek with the mind of the heart;
I do not call out to You in faith,
    nor do I call to You in fear;
I do not implore You with tears,
    nor do I tremble or shake over the day I must render an account.

---

[113] Cf. 1 Thessalonians 5:17.

Եւ արդ՝ Տէր իմ, մի՛ անսար պղերգութեանս իմոյ,
այլ փութապէս արկ յապաշխարութիւն
 և ի բովս մաքրութեան Հրոյ
 սրբեալ եւ ազատեալ ի մեղաց։
Մեծաւ ջերամբ եռացո՛ և յորդորեա՛ յարտասուս
 եւ ի պաղատանս եւ ի խնդրուածս,
եւ տպաւորեա՛ յիս զառաջին լուսաւորութեան կերպարանն։

127 Ողորմեա՛ Տէր՝ մեղաւորիս
 եւ յանցաւորիս անշիւ բազմութեամբ,
եւ դարձո՛ յապաշխարութիւն զգերիս վտարանդեալ,
եւ մո՛յծ զիս յարքունական փառն։
առաջնորդեա՛ ինձ գվերին ճանապարհն գալ առ քեզ.
 զի եթէ ոչ առաջնորդեսցես՝ ոչ կարացից գալ,
 զի դու իսկ Հրամայեցեր՝
 եթէ «Ոչ ոք գայ առ իս, եթէ ոչ Հայր իմ ձգեսցէ զնա։»
Եւ արդ՝ Տէր իմ գթած, մի՛ յիշեր զմեղս իմ
 յաճախս լրբութեանս,
եւ մի՛ զանց առներ ի ծառայէս քումմէ։
մի՛ թողուր զիս մնալ ի նոյն չարիս,
 եւ ի կեանս աշխարհիս սպանի՛լ.
 այլ որպէս տէր ընթացեալ զկնի ծառայի փախուցելոյ՝
այսպէս դարձուցանելով զիս թողցես գյանցանս իմ,
եւ արասցես Հաղորդս սրբոց կամարարաց քոց։

128 Դարձո՛ Տէր՝ զգասումն բարկութեան քո յինէն,
 որ բազում մեղօք իմովք տրտմեցուցի զքեզ։
ողորմեա՛ ապաստամբելոյս ի քէն,
եւ զանՀնարին դիզեալ կոյտս մեղաց իմոց գրուեա՛,
եւ ընդ քաղցր յձայն ճառայութեան քո բեւեռեա՛ զմիտս իմ։

And now, my Lord, give no heed to my laziness,
but quickly cast me into repentance,
    into the furnace of the cleansing fire
    to be purified and freed from sin.
Boil [me] with a great heat and move [me] to tears,
    to supplications and to entreaties;
and imprint on me that first state of illumination.[114]

127 Have mercy, O Lord, on me who have committed
    an incalculable multitude of sins and transgressions;
Convert to repentance me who am a captive and in exile;
Bring me into Your royal glory,
and lead me to go with You along that upper path,
    for if You will not lead me, I will be unable to go,
    for it is You who commanded,
    "No one comes to me unless my Father grants it."[115]
And now, my compassionate Lord, do not recall the sins
    of my incessant shamelessness;
Do not dismiss me from among Your servants,[116]
nor allow me to remain in the same evils,
    or to be ruined in the life of this world,
    but like a master running after a fleeing servant,
will You bring me back, forgive me my transgressions,
and make me a companion of Your benevolent holy ones.

128 Turn back, O Lord, Your furious anger from me
    who have grieved You by my many sins;
Have mercy on me who have rebelled against You,
Break up the enormous massive pile of my sins,
and affix my mind to the sweet yoke of service to You.

---

[114] Cf. Genesis 1:26–28; the fall of man is often interpreted in tradition as losing the original "garment of glory" with which God had originally clothed man.

[115] John 6:65.

[116] Cf. Matthew 24:48–51, and parallels.

129 Պարգեւեա՛ ինձ Տէր՝ զլալումն Դաւթի եւ գողբումն Երեմիայի,
    զՀառաչումն Պետրոսի
   եւ գյորդառատ վտակս արտասուաց կնոջ պոռնկին,
զի նստեալ լացից անդադար ի տունջեան եւ ի գիշերի,
զի թերեւս արժանի եղէց սրբիլ
    ի յաղտոյ եւ ի թառախոյ,
եւ յորդնալից վիրաց մեղաց գերձանիլ,
եւ ի բազմաբեռն չարեաց թեթեւանալ
եւ դասիլ ընդ սուրբս քո ի փառս քո։

130 Ողորմեա՛ ինձ Տէր՝ մի՛ յամենար,
    զի առանց վաստակելոյ քո յիս՝ ոչ երբէք գործի առ իս բարի,
    եւ ոչ սերմանեայն յանդա Հոգւոյ իմոյ բուսանի.
    զի սերմն քո բարի՝ որ յիս սերմանեցաւ,
    ի չար թշնամւոյն քաղեցաւ.
    եւ բուսեայն՝ ումն ի տապոյ ջերմութենէ չորացաւ,
    եւ ումն ի մէջ փշոցն անկեալ Հեղձեալ ցամաքեցաւ։
մշակելով քո յիս Տէր՝ յծեմ գերկուս աչս եգանց՝ որ յիս,
    արտասուագոչ ճայնիւ պաղատիլ առ քեզ յարաժամ,
    զի արժանի գտայց ողորմութեան քում։

131 Շնորհեա՛ Տէր՝ զխաղաղութիւն եկեղեցւոյ քում սրբոյ,
    եւ ամենայն Հաւատացելոց՝
    թագաւորաց եւ իշխանաց,
    զօրաց եւ զօրավարաց,
    ի ճակատու պատերազմաց յաղթել անօրէն բռնաւորաց։

129 Grant me, O Lord, the weeping of David,[117] the lamentation of Jeremiah,[118]
    the groaning of Peter,[119]
    and those copiously streaming tears of that prostitute,[120]
So that I may sit and weep incessantly both day and night,
That perhaps I might become worthy to be cleansed
    from impurity and corruption,
To be delivered from the multitude of wounds from my sins,
To be relieved of the great burden of my evil deeds,
and to be enrolled with Your holy ones in Your glory.

130 Have mercy on me, O Lord, do not delay,
    for without Your toiling for me, there is never any good done for me,
    nor will anything sown bud forth in my soul,
    for Your good seed that was sown in me
    was plucked away by the evil enemy,
    and of what sprouted some was dried up by the extreme heat,
    and some that fell among thorns was choked and withered.[121]
Yoke to me, O Lord, two pair of oxen when You plow me,
    that, with a voice that cries and weeps imploring You continuously,
    I might be found worthy of Your mercy.

131 Grant, O Lord, peace to Your holy Church,
    and to all the faithful,
    to kings and princes,
    to armies and generals,
    who are in the front of combat to overcome the lawless tyrant.

---

[117] Cf. 2 Samuel 12:21.

[118] There are a number of laments in the book of Jeremiah, as well as the Book of Lamentations, traditionally ascribed to Jeremiah.

[119] Cf. Matthew 26:75, and parallels.

[120] Cf. Luke 7:38, 44.

[121] Cf. Matthew 13:18–23, and parallels.

132 Ողորմեա՛ Տէր՝ առաջնորդաց եկեղեցւոյ,
    Հայրապետաց եւ վարդապետաց,
    երիցանց՝ սարկաւագաց՝ դպրաց
    եւ ամենայն ուխտի մանկանց եկեղեցւոյ,
  առնել գիրաւունս եւ գարդարութիւն յամենայն ժամ,
    Հովուել գժողովուրդս քո,
    եւ տքնիլ վասն Հոգւոց նոցա՝ ասելով.
    «Ահաւասիկ ես եւ մանկունք իմ գոր ետուր ցիս»:

133 Ողորմեա՛ Տէր՝ կարօտելոց եւ տարակուսելոց,
    որբոց եւ այրեաց եւ նեղելոց,
    վտանգելոց եւ տանց Հաւատացելոց,
    կենդանեաց եւ նրնջեցելոց,
    եւ որք ընծայաբերք են եկեղեցւոյ.
    աղքատաց, կերակրելոց, ողորմածաց, երկիւղածաց,
    տնանկաց եւ Հիւանդաց,
    նաւորդաց եւ ճանապարհորդաց,
    խոստովանողաց եւ ապաշխարողաց,
    եւ անդարձ մեղաւորաց,
  ողորմեա՛ Տէր եւ դարձո՛ գնոսա յապաշխարութիւն:

134 Ողորմեա՛ Տէր՝ եղբարց մերոց, ծնողաց
    եւ ամենայն արեան մերձաւորաց,
    կրօնաւորաց եւ միանձանց ճգնաւորաց,
    եւ որք գողորմութիւն պարգեւեցին մեզ,
    եւ որք յանձն արարին գինքեանս յաղօթս մեր յիշել:
  Ողորմեա՛ Տէր՝ բարերար,
    եւ ըստ իւրաքանչիւրոց պիտոյից բաշխեա՛ առատապէս
    գշնորՀս Հոգւոյդ սրբոյ ի վերայ ամենեցուն սոցա.
  գարդարեա՛ եւ միացո՛ ի սէր աստուածութեան քոյ:

132 Have mercy, O Lord, on the leaders of the Church,
>   the hierarchs and the Vardapets,[122]
>   priests, deacons, acolytes,
>   and all the 'children of the covenant'[123] of the Church,
> That they may bring about justice and righteousness at all times,
>   to shepherd Your people,
>   and to be watchful over their souls, saying
>   "Behold my children and I whom You gave to me."[124]

133 Have mercy, O Lord, on those who are weak and in need:
>   on orphans, widows, and the afflicted,
>   the tormented and on the houses of the faithful,
>   on the living and on those who have fallen asleep,
>   and on those who have made gifts to the Church,
>   on the poor, the hungry, the pitiable and the frightened,
>   on the impoverished and the infirm,
>   on sailors, travelers,
>   confessors and penitents,
>   and on stubborn sinners,
> Have mercy, O Lord, and lead them all to repentance.

134 Have mercy, O Lord, on our brothers, our parents,
>   and on all our blood relatives,
>   on the monks, the solitary ascetics,
>   and on those who freely show compassion to us,
>   and on those who dedicate their prayers to remember us.
> Have mercy, O Beneficent Lord,
>   and according to each one's needs distribute liberally
>   the graces of Your Holy Spirit on them all;
> adorn them and unite them in the love of Your Divinity.

---

[122] This last term is often translated as "doctor" or "teacher", but as these prayers seem to be a medieval Armenian composition and the role of Vardapet was a very important one in the Armenian Church, I have retained the title rather than to translate it. For the importance of the institution, see R.W. Thomson, "Vardapet in the Early Armenian Church".

[123] The "sons and daughters of the covenant" were a prominent and important class of ascetics in the early Syrian church, see G. Nedungatt, "The Covenanters of the Syriac speaking Church"; but they were also known in Armenia, see M.E. Shirinian, "Reflections on the 'Sons and Daughters of the Covenant' in the Armenian Sources".

[124] Hebrews 2:13.

135 Աղաչեմ Տէր՝ եւ անկանիմ առաջի սրբոյ խաչի քոյ,
    բարեխօսութեամբ սորա գաղաչանս իմ ընկալ
        եւ գխնդրուածս իմ կատարեա՛,
    եւ գործութեամբ սորա գորացդ դիս ի կռմանս յոր կոչեցայ,
        եւ ի պատուիրանս քո յոր լուսացայ։
Տո՛ւր ինձ Տէր՝ դաս ի գործութիւն եւ ի ժուժկալութիւն,
    ի գգաստութիւն եւ յառողջութիւն՝
        լինիլ պահապան անձին իմոյ
            ի տունջեան եւ ի գիշերի եւ յամենայն ժամու,
            ի ննջել եւ ի յառնել,
            ի գնալ եւ ի դադարիլ,
            ի գործել եւ ի վաստակիլ,
            յաղօթել եւ ի պահել,
        եւ զՀամօյս կամաց քոց կատարել։
Սա՛ եղիցի ինձ բերդ ամուր,
    եւ աշտարակ Հզօր յերեսաց թշնամւոյն.
գարդարեա՛ դիս սովաւ ի գարդ Հոգեդին
    եւ ի լոյս իմանալի.
Եւ յաւուրն աՀեղի բարբառող Գաբրիէլի յերեւիկ սրբոյ խաչիդ՝
    լուսաւորեա՛ գլսաւրբեայ Հոգիս,
    վերանայ լուսով ընդ առաջ անմահ փեսայիդ՝
    խառնիլ յերամս Հայրապետաց
        եւ ի դաս մարտիրոսաց եւ ի գունդա Հրեշտակացն։

136 Բարեխօսութեամբ սրբուՀւոյ Աստուածածնիդ՝
        անարատ եւ միշտ կուսիդ
    եւ Յովհաննու կարապետին
    եւ սրբոյն Ստեփաննոսի առաջին մարտիրոսին,
    եւ սրբոյն Գրիգորի Լուսաւորչին եւ ամենայն սրբոց վկայից քոց՝
        որք միացեալ ի սէր աստուածութեանդ քոյ։
լո՛ւր ինձ եղկելուս՝ եւ մեղուցելոյս ողորմեա՛.
խնդիր արա՛ ինձ կորուսելոյս,
եւ գյորելոյս ձեռնտու լեր,
եւ մոլորելոյս առաջնորդեա՛,
եւ ի խաւարէ Հանցես դիս ի լոյս,
եւ Հոգւոյ իմոյ ազատութիւն շնորՀեա՛։
Հաստատեա՛ ի սէր քո. եւ բեւեռեա՛ յերկիւղ քո.

135 I pray, O Lord, and I prostrate myself before Your holy cross,
   Through its intercession receive my prayers
      and fulfill my requests;
   By its power, strengthen me for the calling to which I was called,
      and for Your commandments in which I have placed my trust.
   Give it to me, O Lord, for power and for endurance,
      for adornment and for health,
         that it might become the guardian of my soul,
            day and night, and at all times:
            when sleeping and when rising,[125]
            when going and when returning,
            when working and when wearied,
            when praying and when fasting,
         that I might accomplish what is pleasing to Your will.
   May it become for me an unshakeable fortress,
      and a mighty tower before the enemy.
   Adorn me with it in a spiritual garment,
      and in immaterial light.
   And on that dreadful day that Gabriel announced[126] the appearance of Your cross,
   Give light to my darkened soul,
      that it might rise up in light before You, O Immortal Bridegroom,
      and be united with the assembly of hierarchs,
         with the bands of martyrs and the ranks of angels.

136 Through the intercession of the Holy Mother of God,
         immaculate and ever-virgin,
      and of John, the Fore-runner
      and of St. Stephen, the first martyr,
      and of St. Gregory the Illuminator,[127] and of all Your
      holy martyrs,
         who are united in the love of Your Divinity,
   Hear me who am miserable, and have mercy on me a sinner,
   Search for me who am perishing,
   Give help to me who am tumbling down,
   Give direction to me who am wandering;
   Draw me out of the darkness into the light,
   and grant freedom to my soul.
   Fortify me in loving You, and affix me to the fear of You,

---

[125] Cf. Deuteronomy 6:7, 11:19; Psalm 139:2.
[126] Cf. Luke 1:30–37.
[127] It is unlikely that Ephrem had any knowledge of St. Gregory; see the introduction, above, p. 11.

գտածար Հոգւոյ իմոյ մաքրեմ, եւ առ իս օթեւանեմ:
Փակեմ դդուռն մեղաց իմոց, եւ պարապեմ շուրջանակի յոստէ իմէ,
եւ ի մարդոյ չարէ եւ յանիրաւէ փրկեմ.
եւ զարդարեմ զիս գործովք առաքինութեամբ,
եւ պարգեւեմ ինձ զանձառ երանութիւն քո:
Կենդանեաց մերոց ողորմեա՛,
            եւ զՀոգիս ննջեցելոց մերոց լուսաւորեալ
            պայծառացո՛ յարքայութեանդ երկնից:

137 Բարեխօս առ քեզ ունիմք
        զառաքեալսն եւ զմարգարէսն, եւ զամենայն սուրբ մարտիրոսսն,
        զՀայրապետսն եւ զվարդապետսն,
      եւ լո՛ւր աղաչանաց նոցա, եւ ազատեա՛ զիս ի մեղաց իմոց.
    տնկեա՛ յիս Հոգի շնորՀաց,
    եւ յօրդորեա՛ զիս բարիս գործել:
    Ի ծուլանայն իմում բռնաւորեա՛,
    եւ ողորմութեամբդ ի քեզ կոչեա՛.
    խափանեա՛ զիս ի չար գործոց,
    եւ սերմանեա՛ յիս պտուղ բարեաց.
    քաջալերեա՛ զիս ի նեղութեան իմում,
    եւ ի վշտի իմում մխիթարեա՛:
    Արժանի արա՛ զիս Տէր՝ խաչակից լինել քեզ մինչեւ ցմաՀ,
        որպէս զի ի Հեշտութեանց աշխարՀիս Հրաժարեցայց,
    եւ եղէց երանելեացն դասակից,
    եւ աստղակին եղէց Հաղորդ,
    եւ ի դրախտին վայելեցից զկեանս անմաՀս:

138 Յաւուրն իմոյ վախճանի Հրեշտակ բարի ինձ առաքեա՛
        քաղցրութեամբ առանդել զՀոգի իմ.
        ընդ ուղիղ ճանապարհ գնացից սրբոցն՝
    Հոգւոյ իմում առաջնորդեա՛,
    եւ զգազանն դարանակալ կործանեա՛.
    անցո՛ զիս անխռով ընդ օդա խաւարինս,
    եւ դերծո՛ ի չարաժանի գազանէն.
    ապրեցո՛ եւ աներկիւղ պաՀեա՛,
    եւ ի կայանս սրբոցն Հանգո՛՝
        սպասել եւ ակն ունիլ գալստեան քոյ:

Cleanse the temple of my soul, and make Your dwelling in me.
Shut up the gate of my sins, and wall me off from my adversary;
Deliver me from the evil and lawless man,[128]
Adorn me with deeds of virtue,
and bestow upon me Your ineffable blessedness.
Have mercy on us living creatures,
>   and make the souls of us who have fallen asleep
>   resplendent and illustrious in that Kingdom of Heaven.

137 We do have intercessors with You:
>   the Apostles, the Prophets, and all the Holy Martyrs,
>   the Patriarchs and the Vardapets.[129]

So hear their prayers and set me free from my sins;
Instill in me a spirit of grace,
and fill me that I may do good works.
Act forcefully against my laziness,
and in Your mercy, call me unto You;
Keep me away from evil deeds,
and sow in me the fruit of good deeds;
Give me courage in my tribulation,
and in my affliction give me comfort.
Make me worthy, O Lord, to be crucified with You unto death,
>   that I may renounce the comforts of this world,
>   and be a partner of the blessed,
>   a companion to the thief,
>   and that I may enjoy eternal life in that Garden.[130]

138 On the day of my death, send to me a good angel
>   to deliver my soul with gentleness;
>   that I may go on the straight path of the saints.

Direct my soul
and destroy that stalking beast.[131]
Bring me peacefully through dark winds,
and keep me safe from the sharp-toothed beast;
deliver me and keep me without fear,
and give me rest in the dwelling of the saints,
>   to wait and to look for Your coming.

---

[128] Cf. Psalms 17:13, 18:48, 43:1, 59:2, 82:4, and 140:1.
[129] See n. 122, above.
[130] Cf. Luke 23:39–43.
[131] Cf. 1 Peter 5:8.

139 Յորժամ գաս Տէր՝ յերկնից
    աւեղ փառօք եւ անճիւ դասուք Հրեշտակօք,
եւ զարհուրեալ դողան առ Հասարակ տարերք ամենայն՝
    երկնայինքն եւ երկրայինքս.
յայտնարկել քո գորութեանդ՝ սարսին առ Հասարակ տարերք ամենայն
    յաՀեղ փառաց դատաւորիդ
    եւ անճառ դատաստանիդ եւ աննըերելի պատուհասիդ:
Յայնմ աւուր եւ դիս ընկա՛լ Տէր՝
    ընդ արդարս եւ ընդ կատարեալս քո,
եւ կարգեա՛ ընդ աջմէ դասուն,
եւ պսակեա՛ ընդ սուրբս քո.
եւ չնորՀեա՛ ինձ գկեանս յաւիտենից,
եւ գանձառ բարիս քո պարգեւեա՛ ինձ.
    եւ քեզ փառք արարողիդ եւ պարգեւողիդ իմոյ բարեաց:

140 Յիշեա՛ Տէր՝ գՀոգիս ննջեցելոց մերոց
    յաւուր մեծի քում գալստեանդ՝
        յորժամ գաս յերկնից անճառ փառօք,
            աՀեղ եւ ստականի գօրօք,
            Հրանիւթ եւ Հոգեղէն գուարթնօք:
ԱՀաւոր Հուր առաջի քո ընթացեալ տարածանի,
կիզէ գլերինս եւ Հալէ գբլուրս,
եւ գարարածս ամենայն առ Հասարակ տապալէ.
յայնմ աւուր աՀեղին ողորմեա՛ ինձ մարդասէր,
    գի գին սուրբ արեան քո եմ:
Յորժամ գագբիւրս ցամաքեցուցանես,
    եւ գգնացս գետոց դագարեցուցանես,
    գծովու ջրոյն գանբաւութիւն սպառեցուցանես,
    գլուսաւորս խաւարեցուցանես,
    փողն աՀագին ընդ տիեզերս ամենայն Հնչի
        եւ գմեռեալսն ամենայն գարթուցանէ
        եւ գաշխարՀս ամենայն դողացուցանէ,
        եւ արարածք ամենայն յարուցեալ կան առաջի աստուածութեանդ
            քոյ:

139 When You come, O Lord, from heaven
>> in awesome glory and with innumerable hosts of angels,[132]
> All the elements, both heavenly and earthly,
>> shudder and tremble equally.[133]
> With a show of Your power, all the elements quake equally
>> at the awesome glory of You, O judge,
>> at Your ineffable judgment, and Your irrevocable punishment.
> On that day, receive me too, O Lord,
>> along with Your just ones and Your perfect ones;
> Assign me to the right of the host,
> and crown me among Your saints.
> Grant me eternal life
> and bestow upon me Your ineffable good things,
>> and glory be to You who make and bestow good things on me.

140 Remember, O Lord, the souls of us who have fallen asleep
>> on that great day of Your coming,
>>> when You come from heaven in ineffable glory,
>>>> with the awesome and dreadful hosts,
>>>> with fiery and spiritual angels.
> An awesome fire runs and spreads out before You;
> It sets the mountains on fire and melts the hills,[134]
> and it devastates all creation at once.
> On that dreadful day, have mercy on me, O Lover of mankind,
>> for I am the price of Your holy blood.[135]
> When You dry up the springs,
>> and stop up the rivers' courses,
>> and swallow up the immense waters of the sea,
>> and turn the luminaries dark,[136]
> That dread trumpet resounds through the whole world,
>> wakes all the dead
>> and causes the entire earth to tremble,
>> and every creature rises up and stands before Your Divinity.[137]

---

[132] Cf. Matthew 16:27.
[133] Cf. Romans 8:22–23.
[134] Cf. Psalm 46:6, Isaiah 41:15.
[135] Cf. 1 Peter 1:18–19.
[136] There is no exact parallel, but cf. Revelation 6:12–14.
[137] Cf. 1 Thessalonians 4:16.

Յայնժամ դնես գդատողական աթոռ քո,
    եւ ընդ քեզ բազմեցուցանես դերկոտասան առաքեալն.
անաչառ դատաստանաւ դատիս
    եւ յամենեցունց զարդարութիւն պահանջես,
զկամարարս քո պատուես եւ դապատամբեալն
ի ձայնէ կոչման քո պատժես,
եւ զարդարան փառաւորես, զմարտիրոսան եւ զսուրբ վկայն պսակես,
զիմաստուն սուրբ կուսանն զարդարես,
եւ յիմար կուսանացն զառագաստին դուռն փակես,
եւ ի փառացն եւ յերանութեանցն հալածես,
զոզիան քո ընտրես, եւ գայծիան ի քէն ի բաց մերժես
    եւ ի գեհեանն առաքես՝ ուր լայումն է աչաց,
    եւ դառնագոյն կսկիծ ահեղ տանջանաց,
    Հրեղինացն՝ չար որդանցն Թունաւորաց կատողացն գազանաց
        եւ կրճտումն ատամանց։
Արդ՝ գժմ եւ յիս յայնժամ մարդասէր Տէր
    եւ բարերար փրկիչդ իմ Յիսու Քրիստոս.
եւ ողորմութեամբ քով գժասցիս
    ի Հոգիս ննջեցելոց մերոց՝
    որք Հաւատով ի քեզ ննջեցին,
    զորս յարուցեալ կացուցանես առաջի
        աՀաւոր քո մեծի դատաստանիդ՝
    յայնմ տիեզերական ահեղ Հրապարակին։
Յորժամ յայտնին ամենայն գործք բարւոյ եւ չարի
    անթագչելի ի մէջ ատենին,
յայնմ աւուր ահեղի Թողութիւն շնորհեա յուսացելոց քոց,
    որք յանուն քո սուրբ ննջեցին յերկրի,
    զորս գնեցեր պատուական արեամբդ քով։
Ձնչեա գձեռագիր ամենայն մկրտելոցս ի քեզ,
եւ Թող գպարտիս յանցանաց ամենայն Հաւատացելոց
    զկամայից եւ դակամայից.
ընդ աջմէ քումմէ դասեա, եւ դերանական գձայնն
    ի լսելիս ամենայն Հաւատացելոց աւետաբերեա ասելով.
եկա՛յք օրՀնեալք Հօր իմոյ՝ ժառանգեցէք պյալւտենից բարութիւնն։

At that time You shall set up Your judgment seat,
    and seat the twelve Apostles at Your side;[138]
With strictly impartial justice You judge
    and exact justice from them all;
You honor Your followers while those who rebel
You chastise with the sound of Your call;
You glorify the just, the martyrs and You crown the holy confessors;
The wise and holy virgins You adorn, while to the foolish virgins
You close the door to the bridal chamber,
You expel them from glory and blessing.[139]
You select Your sheep, while the goats You separate
    and cast them into Gehenna, where there is weeping of the eyes
    and most bitter anguish from dreadful tortures[140]:
        for the angels, evil worms, venomous, ravenous wild beasts,
            and gnashing of teeth.
Now, be compassionate to me at that time, O Lord who loves mankind,
    and my beneficent Savior, Jesus Christ,
and in Your mercy may You have compassion
    on the souls of us who have fallen asleep,
    who have fallen asleep believing in You;
    whom You raise up and stand before Your
        great and awesome judgment seat,
    in that universal, dreadful last judgment.
When all the works of both the good and the evil are revealed,
    and made manifest in the midst of [Your] tribunal.
On that dreadful day grant forgiveness to those You have taught,
    who in Your holy name fell asleep in the earth,
    whom You purchased with Your precious blood.[141]
Cancel the bill of debt[142] for all those who were baptized in You,
and forgive all Your faithful the debts for their transgressions,
    both the willing and the unwilling;
set them at Your right hand and proclaim that happy phrase
    in the hearing of all Your faithful, and say:
"Come, blessed of my Father, and inherit the eternal blessings."[143]

---

[138] Cf. Revelation 21:14.

[139] Cf. Matthew 25:10–12.

[140] Cf. Matthew 25:41–46.

[141] Cf. 1 Peter 1:19.

[142] Cf. Colossians 2:14. For a full, recent treatment of the tradition of this "bill of debt" see M. Stone, *Adam's Contract with Satan*.

[143] Matthew 25:34.

141 Արդ՝ Տէր բարերար ողորմած եւ մարդասէր,
ընկա՛լ գաղօթս եւ գինդրուածս իմ,
որ պաղատիմ եւ Հայցեմ ի քէն
վասն իմ եւ վասն ամենայն Հաւատացելոց:
Մի՛ դարձուցաներ զերեսս քո ի ժողովս,
այլ խոնարհեամ յաղաչանս իմ,
եւ լո՛ւր ինձ մարդասէր Տէր,
եւ ցոյց լիս գտվորական քո մարդասիրութեանդ գողորմութիւնն,
եւ խնայեա՛ ի մեղուցեալ ծառայս քո.
եւ կարգեա՛ զիս ընդ աջմէ դասուն, եւ մի՛ կացուցես ընդ ձախմէ
ընդ ույսն՝ որք պայրացուցին զքեզ:
Եւ մի՛ պաՀանձեր յինէն դանՀամար պարտիս յանցանաց իմոց,
եւ մի՛ դատապարտեր զմեղաւորս յայնժամ.
եւ մի՛ յայտնեսցին ծածուկ գործք ամբարշտութեան իմոյ
յանցանաց յանաչառ քո ատենին՝
առաջի Հրեշտակացն եւ Հրեշտակապետացն
եւ ամենայն սրբոց քոց սիրողաց:
Այլ յաղթեալ ի քումէ մարդասիրութենէդ՝
արասցես այցելութիւն եւ ողորմութիւն մեղուցեալ ծառայիս քո.
եւ մի՛ ըստ չար գործոց իմոց Հատուցես ինձ
եւ մի՛ Հրամայեր կապեալ ոտիւք եւ կապեալ ձեռօք
Հանել ի խաւարն արտաքին,
ուր լալ աչացն է եւ կրտձել ատամանց.
այլ ըստ քում գթութեանդ եւ բարերարութեանդ
եւ անիչաչարութեանդ ողորմեա՛ ինձ բազմամեղիս:
Յայսմ աւուր գերձ՛ զիս յամօթոյն յաւիտենից,
եւ փրկեա՛ զիս յանվախճան տանջանացն,
եւ ապրեցո՛ զիս յանները̇ի պատուՀասիցն,
եւ բա՛ց ինձ զդուռն ողորմութեան քոյ,
եւ մի՛ փակեր զդուռն արքայութեան:
Տէր իմ Տէր, Աստուած իմ Աստուած՝ Յիսուս Քրիստոս,
արժանի արա՛ զիս զանարժանս յաւուրն յայնմիկ
երանութեան պարգեաց լուսոյ
եւ անսպառ յաւիտենից ուրախութեանց
եւ բարեաց Հատուցմանց սրբոցն եւ արդարոցն՝
զփառս երանելեացն վայելել միշտ,

141 Now, O Lord, beneficent, merciful and Lover of mankind,
Receive my prayer and my entreaties
   that I beseech and seek from You
   on my behalf and on behalf of all the faithful.
Do not turn Your face away from my pleading,
but condescend to my petitions,
and hear me, O Lord, Lover of mankind.
Show me Your familiar compassion and love of mankind,
and grant pardon to Your sinful servant.
Assign me to the right side, do not stand me on the left
   with the goats who have caused You anger.[144]
Do not exact from me the innumerable debts of my transgressions,
Do not condemn this sinner at that time;
and let not the hidden deeds of my impiety and transgressions
   be revealed at Your impartial tribunal,
   in the presence of the angels and archangels,
   and all those holy ones who love You.
But, overcome by Your Love of mankind,
May You visit and have mercy on Your sinful servant.
Do not repay me according to my evil deeds,
nor command that I be bound hand and foot
   to be cast into the outer darkness,
   where there is weeping of eyes and gnashing of teeth;[145]
   but, according to Your compassion, Your beneficence,
and Your forgiveness, have mercy on me, a great sinner.[146]
On that day deliver me from eternal shame,
Save me from unending torments,
Free me from those intolerable punishments,
Open to me the gates of Your mercy,
and do not close the gate to Your kingdom.
Lord, my Lord, God my God, Jesus Christ,
On that day, make me, who am unworthy, worthy
   of the blessing of the gift of light,
   of unending, infinite joy,
   and of those good gifts of the saints and of the just:
   the glory that always befits the blessed,

---

[144] Cf. Matthew 25:33.

[145] Matthew 8:12, 13:42, 50, et al.

[146] This last phrase is exactly that same one made famous in Nersēs Shnorhali, Հաատով Խոստովանիմ.

զի մտից արժանապէս յառագաստ անմահ փեսայիդ,
եւ ժառանգեցից զանսպառ բարիսն ընդ ամենայն սուրբս քո,
    մաքուր յստակ եւ սուրբ սրտիւ՝ Համարձակ երեսօք
անՀատ տեսից զքեզ ընդ Հրեշտակս,
    եւ ընդ սուրբ սիրողս քո
վայելեցից զանՀաս զանճառելիդ
    եւ զանեզր լոյս երրորդութեանդ՝ գոՀանալով.
եւ գուզաՀաւասար արասցես ընդ սուրբս քո
    յօրՀնաբանութիւնս միշտ արժանապէս,
    Հանապազ աստուածային անտուեր լուսով քով պայծառացայց,
    եւ անդադար երգով փառաւորեցից
    եւ բարեբանեցից եւ վերօրՀնեցից զամենասուրբ զերրորդութիւնդ,
այժմ եւ յաւիտեանս յաւիտենից. ամէն.

That I may worthily enter the bridal chamber of the immortal bridegroom,
and may inherit innumerable good things with all Your saints,
    that with a pure, clean and holy heart and an open face
I may see You along with Your angels,
    and that with all those holy ones who love You,
May I enjoy and praise the incomprehensible, ineffable,
    limitless light of Your Trinity.
May You make me equal to Your holy ones,
    to sing to You in worthy fashion unending praises,
    that I might always be illuminated by Your unclouded light,
    and that I may glorify with unending song,
    praise and extol the All-Holy Trinity,
Now and unto the ages of ages. Amen.

Բ

Աղօթք դարձեալ նորին սրբոյն Եփրեմի։

Տէր երկնի եւ երկրի,
  իշխան մահու եւ կենաց,
  դատաւոր կենդանեաց եւ մեռելոց,
Քրիստոս Աստուած, յոյս եւ ապաւէն Հոգւոյս իմոյ.
  քեզ խոնարհեցուցանեմ զերկրպագութիւն
  եւ մատուցանեմ փառաբանութեամբ մաղթանս։
Լո՛ւր պարգեւիչ՝ Հայցուածոց իմոց,
  որ միայնդ ես առանց մեղաց,
  որ միայնդ ես սուրբ եւ ի սուրբս Հանգուցեալ,
  որ միայնդ ես գթած եւ ողորմած։
Ողորմեա՛ ինձ Աստուած ըստ մեծի ողորմութեան քում,
  եւ ըստ բազում գթութեան քաւեա՛ զանօրէնութիւնս իմ։
Ստեղծի՛չ իմ՝ ողորմեա՛ ինձ եւ օրհնեա՛ զիս,
  երեւեցո՛ գերեսս քո առ իս եւ Հաշտեա՛ ընդ իս։
Ապրեցուցի՛չ իմ՝ դա՛րձ առ իս, երեւեցո՛ գերեսս քո
  եւ յիշեա՛ զիս յարքայութեան քում։
Դա՛րձ առ իս Աստուած փրկիչ իմ,
  եւ դարձո՛ գարտմութիւնս քո յինէն.
մի՛ յախտեան բարկանար ինձ,
  եւ մի՛ դարձուցաներ գերեսս քո յինէն.
մի՛ բարկութեամբ խրատեր զիս,
  եւ մի՛ սրտմտութեամբ քով յանդիմաներ զիս.
մի՛ յախտեան բարկանար ինձ,
  եւ մի՛ յիշեր գչարիս իմ,
  եւ մի՛ պարտաւորեր զիս ըստ իմում անօրէնութեանս.

Part II:

More Prayers from Saint Ephrem

O Lord of heaven and of earth,[147]
    Ruler over death and life,[148]
    Judge of the living and of the dead,[149]
O Christ God, hope and refuge of my spirit,
    to You I **lay down** [my] service,
    and I offer my adoration with praise.
Listen, O giver of gifts, to my solicitations,
    You who alone are without sin,
    You who alone are holy and who give rest to the holy ones,[150]
    You who alone are compassionate and merciful.[151]
Have mercy on me, O God, according to Your great mercy,
    and according to Your great clemency pardon my iniquity.[152]
O my creator, have mercy on me and bless me,
    show Your face to me and look kindly upon me.[153]
O my Life-giver, turn towards me, show me Your face,[154]
    and remember me in Your kingdom.[155]
Turn to me, O God my Savior
    and turn Your wrath away from me;
do not be angry with me forever,[156]
    and do not turn Your face away from me;[157]
do not chastise me in Your anger,
    and do not reproach me in Your wrath;[158]
do not be angry with me forever,
    and do not remember my evil [deed]s,[159]
    nor condemn me according to my iniquity;

---

[147] Matthew 11:25, Luke 10:21, Acts 17:24, Tobit 10:13, Judith 9:12.
[148] Cf. Sirach 11:14, Acts 3:15.
[149] Acts 10:42, 2 Timothy 4:1, 1 Peter 4:5.
[150] Cf. Revelation 14:13.
[151] Cf. James 5:11.
[152] Psalm 51:1.
[153] Cf. Psalm 67:1.
[154] Cf. Psalm 69:16–17.
[155] Cf. Luke 23:42.
[156] Cf. Psalm 79:5, 85:5.
[157] Cf. Psalm 132:10.
[158] Psalm 6:1.
[159] Cf. Psalm 79:8.

մի՛ յաւիտեան պահեր ոխս,
եւ մի՛ ի սպառ բարկանար ինձ:
Մի՛ ըստ մեղաց իմոց առներ,
եւ մի՛ ըստ անօրէնութեան իմում հատուցաներ ինձ:
Մի՛ ընկենուր դիս յերեսաց քոց,
եւ մի՛ խնդրեր զգիր յանցանաց իմոց.
մի՛ դատապարտեր դիս, զի ես ինձէն գիտեմ զի անուղղայ եմ
եւ յանցաւոր ի մանկութենէ իմէ,
եւ անպատասխանի յամենայնի:
Այլ դու դատաւոր Հզօր եւ անտխակալ,
որ զյանցանս մեղացն թողեր զառառակ որդւոյն,
թո՛ղ եւ ինձ զպարտիս
մեղուցեալ եւ անարժան քո ծառայիս.
քանզի քո առատ բարերարութիւնդ յորժամ յիս ցուցցես,
յայնժամ երեւեսցի բարեգթութիւն քո,
որ արժանի եմ բիւր տանջանաց.
զի զամենայն զկեանս իմ անառակութեամբ անցուցի,
եւ ոչ կացի ի հրամանի քում:
Այլ քաղցրացի՛ր ինձ քաղցրութեամբ՝ քաղցր եւ բարի թագաւոր,
եւ հաշտեմ ընդ բազմամեղիս:
Մի՛ հայիր յիմ անհնազանդութիւնս եւ ի ծուլութիւնս.
մի՛ անարգեր դիս եւ մի՛ թողուր դիս, եւ մի՛ ընդ վայր հարկաներ դիս:
Չի թէպէտ ես գտաճար Հոգւոյդ սրբոյ ապականեցի
իմով ծուլութեամբս եւ անառակ գնացիւքս,
այլ դու գթա՛մ յիս ստեղծիչ իմ ողորմած եւ անկշառար:
Մի՛ ապականեր զհոգի իմ գեհենաժառանգ այրմամբն յախտենական.
այլ գթացեալ մարդասիրապէս՝ երկայնամիտ լեր առ իս,
եւ ներեա՛ յանցանաց իմոց,
եւ շնորհեա՛ ինձ ժամանակ զղջմամբ արտասուաց եւ ապաշխարութեան:
Եւ տուր գործուին եւ իմաստութիւն խորհիլ
գործել քո ի տուէ եւ ի գիշերի,
գործել զբարի եւ առնել զարդարութիւն առաջի երեսաց քոց:

do not hold Your anger against me forever,
    and do not be angry with me at the end.
Do not deal with [me] according to my sins,
    and do not recompense me according to my iniquity.[160]
Do not cast me away from Your face,[161]
    and do not seek an account of my transgressions.
Do not condemn me for I know that I am indeed wayward
    and a transgressor from my youth,
    and I have no answer for any of it.
But You, O judge, who are mighty and without malice,
    who forgave the transgressions and sins of the prodigal son,[162]
forgive also the debts of me,
    who am a sinner and Your unworthy servant,
for when You manifest to me Your abundant beneficence,
    then Your clemency will appear,
    for I am worthy of a myriad of punishments,
    I have spent my entire life in unrighteousness,
    and I did not stand upon Your commandment.
But sweeten me with [Your] sweetness, O sweet and good King,
    and look kindly upon me who am such a great sinner.
Look not upon my rebelliousness nor upon my slothfulness;
do not reject me, do not abandon me, and do not forsake me.
Although I have corrupted the temple of Your Holy Spirit[163]
    by my slothfulness and by my dissolute lifestyle,
nevertheless, be compassionate to me, my merciful and forgiving creator.
Do not destroy my spirit in the eternal burning of hell,
but in [Your] compassion and love for mankind be patient toward me,
    grant pardon for my transgressions,
    and grant me time for repentance with tears and mortification.
Give [me] the strength and the wisdom to meditate
    upon Your laws day and night,[164]
    to do good and to act with righteousness before Your face.

---

[160] Cf. Psalm 103:10.
[161] Cf. Psalm 27:9, 88:14.
[162] Cf. Luke 15:11–32.
[163] Cf. 1 Corinthians 6:19.
[164] Cf. Psalm 119:15, 23, 48, 78.

Համբառնամ առ քեզ Տէր դայս իմ բոլորով սրտիւ իմով.
  կարդամ առ քեզ, Քրիստոս Աստուած միածին Որդի Աստուծոյ։
Որ կամաւոր խոնարհեցար յանձառ փառաց,
  առեր զկերպարանս ծառայի եւ անպարտականդ
  յաղագս դատապարտութեան մերոյ
Համբերեցեր մինչեւ դշարշարանս խաչի եւ մահու յանձն առեր
  վասն փրկութեան ստեղծուածոց քոց։
Արդ՝ որ այսպիսի սէր ունիս առ ազգս մարդկան,
  եւ կամիս զի ամենայն մարդ կեցցէ
  եւ ի գիտութիւն ճշմարտութեան եկեսցէ,
գթա՛ ի բազմամեղս՝
  գթած եւ մարդասէր Տէր,
եւ կամեա՛ց ընդ իմ փրկութիւն, եւ արա՛ ողորմութիւն ինձ
  եղկելոյս թշուառականիս,
  որ առաւել վիրաւորեալ եմ եւ ողորմելի քան զամենայն մարդիկ։
Զի ոչ մի օր սիրեցի զքեզ ի բոլոր սրտէ իմմէ,
  եւ ոչ մի ժամ յամենայն գործութենէ իմմէ պահեցի զպատուիրանս քո.
  այլ ապերգոյթեամբ եւ գրոսանօք անցուցի զամենայն ժամանակս իմ,
  եւ ազտեղի խորհրդովք անցուցի զկեանս իմ։
Աւուրք իմ պակասեցան, եւ անօրէնութիւնք իմ բարձրացան,
  եւ ոչ գող ինձ յոչ փրկութեան եւ տեղի ապաւինի.
  բայց միայն յուսացեալ եմ եւ ապաւինեալ յարատ ողորմութիւն քո՝
  Քրիստոս Աստուած։
Եւ արդ՝ տնկեալ բղխմամբ արտասուաց աղաչեմ զքեզ,
  եւ Հառաչմամբ սրտի առ քեզ պաղատիմ.
  մինչչեւ եմ կորուսեալ
  եւ մինչչեւ է ժամանակ դարձի իմոյ Հասեալ՝
շնորհեա՛ ինձ ժամանակ ապաշխարութեան,
  եւ յառաջ քան զվախճանն արձակեա՛ դիս ի կապանաց մեղաց իմոց,
  եւ անտես արա՛ դանձիւ անօրէնութիւնս իմ։
Որ ամենայն բարութեանց ես Տէր, եւ իշխանդ ես թողուլ դմեղս,
  ծածկեա՛ եւ արա՛ անտեսութիւն անօրէնութեան իմոյ
  յամենայն մեծութենէ քումմէ։
Մխիթարեա՛ դվշտացեալ եւ գտառապեալ Հոգիս իմ.
  եւ արժանի արա՛ զիս յայսմ Հետէ ըստ կամաց քոց
  քաղաքավարել զայլ ևս պանդխտութեան իմոյ ժամանակս։
Եթէ կամիմ եւ եթէ ոչ կամիմ՝ բռնադատեա՛ դիս,
  եւ մի՛ թողուր դիս ի կամս անձին իմոյ,
  մինչեւ տարեալ Հասուսցես յօթեւանս արքայութեանդ երկնից։

I raise up my eyes to You, O Lord, along with my whole heart,
>   I implore You, O Christ God, Only-Begotten[165] Son of God.
You who willingly descended from [Your] ineffable glory,
>   took on the form of a servant[166] and, without guilt,
>   [and] because of our condemnation,
You endured [even] to take on the punishment of the cross and death
>   for the salvation of Your creatures.[167]
Now You who have such love toward the race of mankind
>   and who wish that all men should live,[168]
>   and come to the knowledge of truth,
have mercy on me who am such a great sinner,
>   O merciful Lord and Lover of mankind.
Will salvation for me and have compassion upon me
>   who am so miserable and wretched,
>   who am more wounded and pitiable than any man.
Not for one day have I loved You with my whole heart,
>   nor for one hour did I keep all Your commandments with all my strength,
>   but in idleness and in self-indulgence I have spent all my time,
>   and with impure thoughts I have squandered my life.
My days have come to an end and my iniquity has mounted up;
>   for me there is no hope of salvation nor place of refuge,
except in hoping and taking refuge in Your abundant mercy,
>   O Christ God.
And now that I have fallen, I beseech You with copious tears,
>   and with groaning heart I make supplication to You:
>   before I perish
>   and before the time of my turning back [into dust] arrives,
grant me time for repentance;
>   before the end loose me from the bonds of my sins,
>   and overlook my innumerable iniquities.
You who are Lord of all goodness, You O Prince, who forgive sins,
put aside and overlook my iniquity
>   in all Your greatness.
Comfort my afflicted and oppressed spirit,
>   and make me worthy from this point, according to Your will,
>   to conduct well the remaining time of my pilgrimage.
Whether I am willing or unwilling compel me,
>   and do not abandon me to my own will,
>   until You come and bear into my dwelling Your Kingdom of Heaven.

---

[165] John 1:14, 18; 1 John 4:9.
[166] Philippians 2:7.
[167] Cf. Philippians 2:7–8.
[168] Ezekiel 18:23, 33:11.

Լո՛ւր Տէր՝ աղօթից անարժան ծառայիս քո,
եւ պաղատանաց իմոց ունկն դիր.
    որ ասացեր՝ թէ Հայցեցէ՛ք եւ գտջիք, բաղխեցէ՛ք
    եւ բացցի ձեզ,
եւ այժմ բա՛ց ինձ Տէր զդուռն ողորմութեան՝
    որ ողբալով կարդամ առ քեզ:
Եւ մի՛ անտես առներ գաղաչանս մեղուցեալ անձին իմոյ,
    որ ոչ եկիր կոչել զարդարս, այլ զմեղաւորս յապաշխարութիւն:
Արդ՝ խոնարհեալ անձամբ եւ բեկեալ սրտիւ եւ ամօթալից երեսօք
անկանիմ առաջի քո եւ աղաղակեմ առ քեզ.
Հայր, մեղա՜յ յերկինս եւ առաջի քո.
    թէպէտ եւ ոչ եմ արժանի կոչիլ որդի քո
    յաղագս ապականեալ վարուց իմոց,
    եւ ոչ անուանել զանուն քո գարշելի բերանով իմով,
    այլ Համարձակիմ ի գթութիւն քո,
        զի գիտեմ զքեզ քաղցր եւ անոխակալ
        բազմախնամ եւ երկայնամիտ առ արարածս քո:
Եւ յաղագս այնորիկ ժտելով պաղատիմ առ քեզ.
եւ յառաջ քան զդնել ատենին աղաչեմ,
եւ նախ քան զգիտակել դրանն ապաշխարութեան
    եւ հատանել անդարձ վճռին՝
զարտասուս իմ արկանեմ առաջի անոխակալ գթութեանդ քոյ,
ողորմած Տէ՛ր երկայնամիտ, քաղցր եւ անյիշաչար.
    մի՛ ընդ քանքարաթագույան դատապարտեր զիս
    եւ մի՛ ընդ լմար կուսանացն փակեր զդուռն արքայութեան քոյ.
    մի՛ ընդ չար եւ ընդ վատ ծառայիցն լծակցեր զիս,
    եւ մի՛ ընդ անհաւատսն եւ ընդ Հերձուածողսն դնել զբաժին իմ.
    մի՛ ընդ պոռնիկան եւ ընդ չարագործան կորուսաներ զիս,
    եւ մի՛ ընդ ախտաւորսն եւ ընդ չաղախեալան Հոգւով
        Հաներ զիս ի կենացն:
Այլ գերծ՛ զիս յանեզրական տանջանացն,
    եւ ապրեցո՛ յանհանգիստ ալէկոծութեանց,
    եւ փրկեա՛ յանմաՀ մաՀուանէն,
    եւ ազատեա՛ յաւիտենական ամօթոյն,
գերծ՛ ի միշտ լալոյն եւ Հանապազորդ ողբալոյն:

Hear, O Lord, the prayers of Your unworthy servant,
and give ear to my entreaties,
>   You who said, "Seek and you shall find, knock
>   and it shall be opened to you,"[169]

so now open, O Lord, the gate of mercy, to me
>   who with lamentation now calls upon You.

Do not ignore the supplications of my sinful soul,
>   for You did not come to call the just, but sinners to repentance.[170]

Now with humbled soul, broken heart and a shame-filled face
I prostrate myself before You and I cry out to You,
"Father, I have sinned against heaven and before You;
>   no longer am I worthy to be called Your son,"[171]
>   on account of my depraved life,
>   nor to pronounce Your name with my fetid mouth,
>   but I take courage in Your compassion
>> for I know that You are sweet and forgiving,
>> and have great care and patience toward Your creatures.

For this reason I earnestly beseech You,
before [Your] long-established throne I make supplication,
and before the opening of the gate of repentance
>   and the arrival of Your irrevocable judgement

I pour out my tears before Your compassion that knows no malice:
O merciful and long-suffering, sweet and forgiving Lord,
>   do not condemn me along with those who hide their talents,[172]
>   do not close the door of Your kingdom [on me] with the foolish virgins,[173]
>   do not put me in with the wicked and slothful servant,[174]
>   and do not set down my portion with unbelievers and heretics.
>   Do not put me to death with fornicators and evil-doers,
>> and do not cast me away from life.

Rather deliver me from interminable torments,
>   free [me] from incessant troubles,
>   save me from the deathless death,
>   and free [me] from eternal shame.

Deliver [me] from continual weeping and from unceasing lamentation.

---

[169] Matthew 7:7.
[170] Matthew 9:13, and parallels.
[171] Luke 15:18–19, 21.
[172] Cf. Matthew 25:24–30.
[173] Cf. Matthew 25:1–13.
[174] Cf. Matthew 25:41–46.

Մի՛ տարագիր առներ եւ մի՛ մերժեր զիս
  ի քո դասուցն եւ յերանաւէտ կենացն.
մի՛ անբաժին Հաներ զիս ի Հայրենի ժառանգութենէն,
եւ մի՛ զրկեր զիս յերկնաւոր Հարսանեացն,
եւ մի՛ կարօտ պաՀեր զիս ի քո անճառելի տեսլենէդ:
Այլ շնորհեա՛ ինձ ընդ արժանաւորսն եւ ընդ կատարեալ ոգիսն
վերանալ լուսեղէն ամպովք ընդ առաջ քո յօդս,
եւ պարզ երեսօք եւ աչալրջութեամբ կալ առաջի քո Տէ՛ր:
Եւ վասն քո փառաւորեալ Հզօր եւ աՀեղ թագաւորութեանդ
մի՛ մտաներ ի դատաստան ընդ ծառայիս քո,
եւ մի՛ Հատուցաներ ինձ րստ անօրէնութեանս,
եւ մի՛ ամաչեցուցաներ զիս առաջի անէծի եւ աՀեղ բանակաց քոց.
Այլ ողորմեա՛ ինձ, զի ոչ ոք է Հակառակ քեզ,
եւ պարզեւեա՛ ինձ զքո արքայութիւնդ:
Ընդ սուրբս քո դասեա՛,
եւ ընդ արդարսն պսակեա՛,
ընդ սիրելիսն քո օրՀնեա՛,
  եւ ընդ կամարարս կամաց քոց
  յարագուարձ ուրախութիւնսն ուրախացո՛
եւ առատապարգեւ փառօք փառաւորեա՛ զիս՝ Տէ՛ր,
  ի լուսեղէն երամս արդարոց՝
  ընդ նոսին Հանգչիլ
    ի վերինդ Երուսաղէմ յանսուեր
    եւ յաստուածակեաց ուրախութիւնդ.
զի ընդ նոսին Համաձայնեալ փառաւորեցից
զամենասուրբ գերորդութիւնդ յաւիտեանս յաւիտենից. ամէն:

Do not banish me nor expel me
> from Your ranks or from the life of happiness.

Do not take me away destitute from [my] paternal inheritance,
> do not deprive me of the heavenly wedding-feast,
> and do not keep me without Your ineffable vision.

Rather grant that with the worthy ones and with the perfect souls
> I may rise with the wind on the celestial clouds to Your presence,
> to stand before You, with luminous and attentive face, O Lord.

For the sake of Your glorious, mighty and awesome Kingdom
> do not enter into judgement with me your servant,
> do not recompense me according to my iniquity,
> do not shame me before Your innumerable and awesome spirits.

Rather have mercy on me, for no one is [able to] oppose You,
> and present me into Your Kingdom.
> Enroll me among Your saints
> and with the just ones crown [me],
> among Your loved ones bless [me]
>> and with those who have accomplished Your will
>> make [me] joyful with an ever joyful joy.

Glorify me, O Lord, with abundant glory
> in the light-bearing troops of the just
> that along with them I may take my rest
>> in the heavenly Jerusalem that has no shadow[175]
>> and in Your divine banquet,
> so that in unison with them I may give praise
> to the All-Holy Trinity forever and ever. Amen.

---

[175] Cf. Revelation 21:23–25, 22:5.

Գ

Աղօթք նորին դարձեալ:

Տէր իմ Յիսուս Քրիստոս՝
 մի՛ մտաներ ի դատաստան ընդ ծառայիս քո,
 եւ մի՛ տար այլում զդատաստանս իմ,
 այլ ի փառաւոր բեմին մերձեսցայ դիս արժանաւորեմ.
 քանզի դոր Աստուած դատի, ողորմութեան արժանի լինի:
Լսելով զայս ի Հանձարեդաց եւ յիմաստնոց
 եւ ի սրբոց առաքելոցն զայսոսիկ՝ ասեմ.
 դի ամենայն ոք որ զԹագաւոր տեսանէ,
 Թէպէտ եւ մեղուցեալ է՝ ոչ մեռանի:
Աղաչեմ զքեզ՝ ստեղծիչ իմ եւ փրկիչ իմ,
 մի՛ դիս ի նեղեյն իմում Թյուտացուցաներ,
 մի՛ խորտակելով չարչարեր դիս:
Քանզի եԹէ արժանապես ըստ գործոց այդ արասցես ինձ,
 յերկոցունց կողմանց կազմի ինձ որոգայԹ կորստեան.
 դի յորժամ յիշեմ զգործս իմ դանրմբերելի,
 դողումն ի վերայ իմ անկանելով խորտակեն դիս,
 եւ սարսուռ դձնեալ ունի դիս
յորժամ վատահանամ Հատուցումն ընդունիմ
 ի Հանգստեանն՝ որ առաջի կայ,
 եւ ոչ կարեմ Համբերել:
Եւ յառաջագոյն յայտ առնէ ատամանց իմոց կրճտումն,
 որ անդ առաջի կայ ինձ ցաւքն եւ սարսուոքն:
Տես Տէր զլոխարՀութիւնս իմ եւ զԹառ յիս:
Աղաչեմ զքեզ՝ միածին Որդի Աստուծոյ,
 արժանի արա դիս Թողութեան մեղաց,
 եւ մի՛ Հատուցաներ ինձ ըստ վարձուց վաստակոց իմոց.
քանզի եԹէ դանօրէնուԹիւնս իմ պաՀեցես, ո՞վ տեւեսցէ քեզ.
 եւ եԹէ ըստ մեծուԹեան քում Հատուցանես մեզ ողորմուԹիւն,
 արժանի՝ գտանիմք ի դատաստանի քում.
քանզի ամենայն բերան խցցի
 եւ դատապարտեսցի ամենայն աշխարՀ առաջի Աստուծոյ:
Արդ ոչ եԹէ զքո շնորՀսդ արՀամարՀելով յառաջ բերեմ զայսոսիկ,
 այլ զզբեյայն խոսիմ՝ երկայնամիտ Քրիստոս:
Չի՞նչ օգուտ իցէ քեզ ի մարմնոյ իմոյ,
 եԹէ ի բորբոքեալ Հուրն առաքեցայց.

PART III:

MORE PRAYERS FROM [EPHREM]

My Lord Jesus Christ,
> do not enter into judgement with Your servant[176]
> and do not hand over my judgement to another,
> but make me worthy to approach Your glorious seat,
> because the one whom God judges becomes worthy of mercy.

Having heard this from the intelligent, the wise,
> and from the holy Apostles, I say
> that everyone who sees a king,
> though he be a sinner will not die.

I beseech You, my Creator and my Savior,
> do not bring misery upon me in my distress;
> do not torture me nor crush me.

For if You were properly to examine me according to my works
> there would be a ruinous trap set for me on two sides:

for when I remember my insupportable deeds
> horror falls upon me and crushes me,
> violent terror seizes me;

when I consider the retribution to be received
> at the rest that is to come,
> I am unable to bear it.

Even before [this] the gnashing of my teeth makes clear
> that sorrows and horrors stand before me.

See, O Lord, my lowliness and have pity on me.
I beseech You, O Only-Begotten Son of God,[177]
> make me worthy of the forgiveness of sins
> and do not recompense me according to the wages of my labors,[178]

for if You would retain my unrighteous [deed]s who could endure You?[179]
But if You render us mercy according to Your greatness
> we will be found worthy in Your judgement.

Because every mouth shall be silenced
> and every land shall be judged before God.

Now it is not that I bring them before You to despise Your grace
> but I speak what is written, O long-suffering Christ.

What help will there be to You from my flesh
> if You cast it into a flaming fire?

---

[176] Psalm 143:2.
[177] John 1:14, 18; 1 John 4:9.
[178] Cf. Jeremiah 25:14.
[179] Cf. Psalm 130:3.

արա՛ ընդ իս ըստ ողորմութեան քում զգուցութիւն քո,
    եւ ծանիցի ամենեցուն շնորհք քո եւ երկայնմտութիւն քո:
Եթէ զգատաստան ամենայն երկրի առնես,
    որպէս պատուիրանք քո յայտնեցին,
ոչ ապրեսցի մի ի Հաղարաց,
եւ ի բիւրոց ոչ փրկեսցին:
Այլ գի՞նչ Հոգալով խօսիմ զայս ես տառապեալս.
աղաչեմ Փրկիչ՝ ոչ գի զուգեսցես զմեղաւորս ընդ արդարսն՝
քեզ մաղթեմ, բարերարութեան որդի,
    այլ գի արժանի արասցես զգթութիւն քո սփռել ի մեզ,
յիս եւ ի մերձաւորս իմ:
Դարձեալ աղաչեմ եւ ոչ դադարեցից երբէք յայսցանէ.
    գի թէ ոչ զգուշութիւն քո ճգեսցես ի մեզ,
    ոչ ոք կարող է տեսանել զկեանս:
Աստուած՝ գթութեամբդ քո աղաչեմ զքեզ,
    մի՛ կացուցաներ գիս ընդ ուլսն ի ճախմէ քումմէ՝
        որք գայրացուցին զքեզ,
    եւ մի՛ ասիցես թէ ոչ գիտեմ զքեզ,
    այլ տո՛ւր ինձ յաղագս գթութեան քոյ
        մշտնջենաւոր ողրումն եւ գղջումն.
նուաստացո՛ գսիրտ իմ եւ սրբեա՛ զսա,
    գի լիցի տաճար շնորՀաց քոց:
Չի թէպէտ մեղաւոր եմ եւ ամբարիշտ,
    սակայն Հանապազ զգրունս քո բաղխեմ,
գի թէ դանդաղկոտ եմ եւ պղերգ,
    սակայն գճանապարհա քո կամիմ գնալ:
Տէր իմ եւ փրկիչ, ընդէ՞ր գիս լքանես.
գթա՛ յիս, վասն գի դու միայն ես առանց մեղաց.
Հա՛ն գիս ի տղմոյ անօրէնութեան իմոյ,
    գի մի՛ ընկլայց յաւիտեան:
Փրկեա՛ գիս ի բերանոյ թշնամույն իմոյ,
    գի աՀա իբրեւ գառիծ մռնչէ՝ կամելով կլանել գիս.
գարթո՛ զգօրութիւն քո, եւ եկեսցէ կեցուցանել գիս.
փայլատակեա՛ գփայլատակունս քո, եւ քայքայեա՛ զգօրութիւն նորա.

Deal with me according to Your mercy, Your clemency,
> and all Your graces and Your patience will be made manifest.

If You judge the entire world
> as Your commandments make clear,

not one in a thousand will live
and not one in ten thousand will be saved.
But what am I saying by bringing forward those who are tormented?
I beseech [You], O Savior, not to weigh sinners against the just.
I implore [You], O Son of Beneficence,
> to consider it worthy to seed Your clemency in us,
> in me and in those close to me.

I beseech You again and I will never cease from it
> for unless You spread Your clemency upon us
> no one will be able to see life.

O God, I beseech Your clemency,
> do not set me among the goats on Your left[180],
>> those who angered You,
>
> and do not say "I do not know you,"[181]
>> but in Your clemency give me
>>> incessant tears and repentance;
>>
>> humble my heart and cleanse it
>>> that it may become a temple of Your grace.

Although I am a sinner and impious,
> nevertheless I constantly knock at Your gates;

although I am slow and idle
> nevertheless I wish to walk on Your paths.[182]

My Lord and Savior why do You forsake me?
Have mercy on me because You alone are without sin;
remove me from the mire of my iniquity
> lest I sink in forever.

Deliver me from the mouth of my enemy,
> for he roars like a lion wishing to devour me;[183]

rouse up Your might that it may come and give me life;[184]
flash forth Your lightnings[185] and destroy his power;

---

[180] Cf. Matthew 25:33.
[181] Matthew 25:12.
[182] Cf. Micah 4:2.
[183] Cf. 1 Peter 5:8.
[184] Cf. Psalm 80:2.
[185] Cf. Psalm 18:14.

երկիցէ եւ գարհուրեսցի լերեսաց քոց,
  քանզի տկար է եւ ոչ ունի զօրութիւն կալ առաջի քո։
Եւ արժանաւորեա զիս ընդ փրկեալսն խաչիւ եւ արեամբ քով՝
  գոհանալ եւ փառաւորել զքեզ
  ընդ Հօր եւ ընդ Սուրբ Հոգւոյն,
  այժմ եւ միշտ եւ յաւիտեանս յաւիտենից. ամէն։

may he be frightened and terrified before Your face,
> because he is powerless and has no strength to stand before You.

Make me worthy that with those saved by Your cross and blood
> I may give thanks and praise to You
> along with the Father and the Holy Spirit
> now and always and unto the ages of ages. Amen.

Դ

Նորին դարձեալ աղօթք զղջման։

Տէր Աստուած գօրութեանց՝ աղաչեմ զքեզ,
    որ մեծդ ես եւ ահաւոր,
    աՀեղ եւ սքանչելի,
    անեղ եւ անանցանելի,
    անբաւ եւ անրովանդակելի
    եւ ամենեւին անքննելի եւ անիմանալի եւ անՀաս,
    ի վեր քան զամենայն
        եւ յամենեցունց օրՀնեալ գովեալ եւ փառաւորեալ,
        անյիշաչար գթած եւ մարդասէր։
Քանզի դու միայն ես Հայր ամենակալ
    եւ արարիչ ամենայն լինելութեանց,
    գործ ի չգոյէ գոյացուցեր,
    եւ ունիս ի Հաստատութեան.
Եւ դու Տէր՝ որ Տէր ես ամենայնի,
    եւ ամենայն արարածք քոյով Հրամանաւղ կառավարին։
Դու ես ամենեցուն օգնական եւ պաՀապան,
    դու բժշկես զվիրաւորեայսն ի բանսարկուէն,
    եւ առողջացուցանես զՀիւանդացեայս մեղօք.
    ընդունիս զխոստովանողս եւ զապաշխարողս,
    եւ քաւես եւ սրբես դյանցանսն մեղուցելոց։
Վասն որոյ ես որ կարի լի եմ մեղօք,
    առ քեզ անկանիմ յարաձամ.
    աղաչեմ եւ մաղթեմ եւ խնդրեմ ի քէն գթողութիւն.
դու նայեա յիս Փրկիչ՝ մարդասիրութեամբ քով,
    եւ ընկալ գթութեամբ քով զգերեայս ի չար թշնամւոյն։
ԽոնարՀեմ Տէր՝ ի մաղթանս իմ,
    եւ բժշկեա զՀոգւոյ իմոյ զխոցոտումն յաներեւոյթ նետից սատանայի։
Տես Տէր՝ զտառապանս քոյ ծառային,
    եւ շնորՀեա գթողութիւն անշիթի յանցանաց իմոց գոր մեղայ։
Լուր Տէր՝ ձայնի ողբալոյս եւ ցաւագին պաղատանացս,
    զի կարօտ եմ շնորՀի քոյ եւ ողորմութեանդ։
Թող Տէր՝ դյանցանս իմ բազմամեներ եւ դմեղս իմ դանՀամարս
    մինչեւ Հասեալ իցէ օր դատաստանի քոյ.
փարատեա յինէն զանգղշութեան խաւարն՝
    որ տարածեալ կայ ի սրտիս եւ դեղշ Հաստատեմ։
յորդորեմ դիս յարտասուս
    եւ ի դեղշ ապաշխարութեան Հանապազ։

Part IV:

More Prayers from [Ephrem] on Repentance

O Lord, God of might, I beseech You,
    You who are great and awesome,
    terrible and marvelous,
    uncreated and eternal,
    infinite and unfathomable,
    altogether unsearchable, incomprehensible and inconceivable,
    above all and in all
        blessed, praiseworthy and glorious,
        forgiving, merciful, and Lover of mankind.
Because You alone are Father, all-powerful,
    and creator of all that has come to be,
    which You brought into being from non-being,
    and which You hold in constancy.
Indeed You are the Lord, who are Lord of everything,
    and all creatures are governed by Your command.
You are the helper and the keeper of everyone,
You heal those who have been wounded by the adversary,
You restore those who have fallen sick in their sins,
You receive those who make confession and repent,
and You pardon and cleanse the transgressions of sinners.
Therefore, I who am exceedingly filled with sin,
    prostrate myself before You continuously,
    I beseech, entreat and beg from You forgiveness.
Look upon me, O Savior, in Your love for mankind,
    and in Your clemency, receive me who am captive to the evil enemy.
Incline, O Lord, to my entreaties
    and heal my soul wounded by the invisible arrows of Satan.
Behold, O Lord, the tribulations of Your servant,
    grant forgiveness for the innumerable transgressions that I
    have committed.
Hear, O Lord, the voice of my laments and of my mournful supplications,
    for I am in need of Your grace and Your mercy.
Forgive, O Lord, my many transgressions and my innumerable sins
    even unto the day Your judgement arrives.
Remove from me the darkness of my lack of contrition
    which is widespread in my heart, and set [in its place] compunction.
Urge me on to tears
    and to continual compunction and repentance.

Շնորհեա՛ ինձ Փրկիչ՝ զղջումն արտասուաց մարգարէին,
    որով զմահիճս թանայր,
    զի եւ ես զվէր հոգւոյս իմոյ լուացից
        հեծեծանօք եւ պաղատանօք եւ ողբագին արտասուօք:
Գիտեմ Տէր՝ զի յանցանք իմ անթիւ են առաջի քո՝
        մարդասէր,
    այլ եւ անբաւ են ողորմութիւնք քո ի վերայ ապաշխարողաց.
ընդ որս եւ ինձ ողորմեա՛,
    ինձ որ առաւելս եմ անօրինեալ քան զամենայն մարդ:
Եւ չեմ արժանի ատ քեզ ի վեր հայել բարերար՝
    ի բազմութենէ պատահեալ յանցանացն զոր գործեցի.
Այլ դու Տէր՝ հայեաց ի վարանումն տարակուսանաց իմոց
    յերկիւղէ գեհենին,
եւ մի՛ անցեղջ եւ անապաշաւ հանէր զիս յաշխարհէս լի յանցանօք.
    այլ ի վայրս տարժանելի վաստակոց
    եւ ի ջան կատարեալ ապաշխարութեան
ատ զհոգի իմ յինէն,
եւ խառնեա՛ ի թիւ ճշմարիտ ապաշխարողացն արդարացելոցն՝
    որ ի փառս քո վայելեն:
Ոչ վասն իմ ինչ վարուց եմ արժանի ողորմութեան քոյ՝ մարդասէր,
այլ վասն գթութեան քոյ Տէր շնորհեա՛ ինձ թողութիւն յանցանաց իմոց,
եւ օգնեա՛ ի մարդի թշնամւոյն ծուլացելոյ ծառայիս քոյ՝ բարերար.
քանզի բազում անգամ խոստացայ զյանցանս իմ
    խոստովանել եւ ապաշխարել,
եւ անօրէն թշնամին ժամէ ի ժամ ձգելով կորոյս
    զկարողութեան ժամանակն ապաշխարելոյ:
Եւ արդ եթէ ոչ դու Տէր՝ օգնեսցես եւ շնորհիւ քո զօրացուսցես,
    չիք ինձ ի գործոց իմոց փրկութիւն.
զի թեպետ եւ բանամ զբերան իմ յաղօթել,
    եւ զձեռս իմ ատ քեզ ի վեր համբառնամ յաղաչանս,
անդրէն գսիրտ իմ սատանայ պատրուակէ,
    եւ զմիտս մերժէ յաստուածային յերկիւղէ,
    զանազան եւ զազիր խորհրդովք զբաղեցուցանէ
    եւ ընդունայն հանէ յաղօթիցն:
Վասն որոյ զՓրկիչդ իմ աղաչեմ,

Grant to me, O Savior, the tearful compunction of the prophet
> with which he used to soak his bed,[186]
>> that I too may bathe the wound of my spirit
>>> with groanings, supplications and tears of lamentation.

I know, O Lord, that my transgressions are innumerable before You,
> O Lover of mankind,
>> but Your mercy toward penitents is infinite.

Have mercy upon them and upon me,
> me who am far more impious than any man.

I am not worthy to look up to You, O Beneficent One,
> because of the multitude of transgressions that I have committed.

But You, O Lord, look upon my great agitation
> due to my fear of Gehenna;

do not take me from the world impenitent, obdurate, and full of transgressions.
> But in place of [my] unworthy deeds
> and for the care of perfect repentance

take my spirit from me
and join [it] to the number of true and justified penitents
> who revel in Your glory.

Not for any part of my life am I worthy of Your mercy, O Lover of mankind,
but because of Your clemency, O Lord, grant to me forgiveness of my transgressions;
give aid to Your idle servant in the battle against the enemy, O Beneficent One,
for many times have I promised
> to confess and repent of my transgressions,

but the wicked enemy continuously casts [his arrows]
> and undoes the time and the capacity for repentance.

And now if You, O Lord, do not help and strengthen me with Your grace,
> there is no salvation for me from my works,

for even though I open my mouth to pray
> and lift my hands up to You in supplication,[187]

then Satan veils my heart
> and drives my mind away from divine fear,
> with various obscene thoughts he distracts it
> and draws it away from prayer.

For this reason I beseech You, My Savior,

---

[186] Cf. Psalm 6:6.
[187] Cf. Psalm 63:4.

վրկեմ զիս ի պատերազմէս յայսմանէ.
    քանզի կարի նեղեալ եմ ի նեևդութենէ թշնամւոյն՝
    որ երբեմն ի Հաւատս յորդորէ յօժարամիտ սրտիւ խնդութեամբ,
    եւ երբեմն ի մեղս ընկենու ոչ լիշելով զբոց գեհենոյն՝
    զոր ոչ զգացի,
    եւ ոչ լալով լուացի զվիրաց յանցանաց իմոց փտութիւնս։
Որ շարախօցս եմ վիրաւորեալ յանՁիւ մեղացս բազմութենէ,
    եւ ոչ բաւեմ ապրել ծուլացելով անձամբս.
այլ յողորմութիւն քո յուսալով Համարձակիմ առ քեզ աղօթել
    բարերարիդ եւ մարդասիրիդ Աստուծոյ։
Ընկալ զաղաչանս իմ ցաւագնս եւ զաղաղատանս իմ աղերսաբերս,
եւ շնորհեա՛ ինձ զդջումն արտասուաց ապաշխարութեան,
    որով զմեղս իմ քաւեցից,
    եւ զարարիչդ իմ Հաշտեցուցից մաղթանօք։
ԱՀա Տէր՝ սիրտ իմ գելու յանՁիւ մեղացս վարանաց,
    եւ որովայն իմ Հեծէ առ քեզ ողբալով.
    եւ անձն իմ Հեծէ եւ աչք իմ բաղձայ արտասուաց
        լիշելով զմեղաց իմոց զբազմութիւն։
Չի լի եմ անՁիւ յանցանօք
    եւ անՀամար գործովք անօրէնութեամբ,
եւ առ քաւիչդ իմ խոստովանիմ ողբալով.
    քանզի Աստուած ես զթութեանց եւ Տէր ողորմութեանց,
    զՁամ յամենամեղս որ ի քեզ եմ ապաւինեալ, բազմագութ։
Չի կարեվէր եմ մեղօք,
    եւ տագնապիմ ախտիւ յանցանօք,
եւ խնդրեմ ի քէն բժշկիլ՝ որ բժիշկ ես Հոգւոց եւ քաւիչ յանցանաց։
Եւ արդ բժշկեա՛ Տէր,
    զի լեզու իմ վիրաւորի դատարկաբանութեամբ
    եւ ի գրախոս բամբասանաց։
Լուսաւորեա՛ Տէր՝ զաչս իմ
    յածողս ի շարաչար նայելոյ եւ յանդէպ տեսանելոյ։
Սրբեա՛ Տէր՝ զմիտս իմ
    ի խաւարային խորՀրդոց սատանայի
    եւ յամենայն չար գործոց թշնամւոյն,
եւ լցո՛ շնորՀօք եւ ողորմութեամբ քո։

save me from this battle
> because I am in great straits from the guile of the enemy
> who sometimes exhorts to faith with eager and joyful heart
> and sometimes casts into sin by not remembering the pit of Gehenna.
> I did not learn this
> nor did I by weeping wash the putrid sores of my transgressions.

For I am wounded and injured by the numberless multitude of my sins,
> and I am unable to live, my soul being so idle.

But hoping in Your mercy I dare to pray to You,
> O beneficent God and Lover of mankind.

Receive my dismal supplications, petitions and entreaties,
and grant me contrition with tears of repentance
> by which I might win pardon for my sins,
> and that I might pacify my Creator by my entreaties.

Behold, O Lord, my heart is distressed by the embarrassment of my innumerable sins,
> my innards groan as they make lamentation to You,
> and my soul groans and my eyes become soft with tears
>> as I call to mind the multitude of my sins.

For I am filled with innumerable transgressions
> and with uncountable deeds of impiety,

and to You who pardon me, I confess with lamentation
> because You are a God of clemency and a Lord of Mercy.

Have clemency on all my sins for in You I take refuge, You who are most clement.
Because I am mortally wounded by my sins
> and am tormented with disease from [my] transgressions,

I seek to be healed by You who heal souls and who pardon transgressions.
So now heal [me], O Lord,
> for my tongue is wounded by idle discourse
> and by the useless utterances of slander.

Enlighten, O Lord, my eyes
> that roam and gaze on wicked things and look upon indecent sights.

Purify, O Lord, my mind
> from the dark thoughts of Satan
> and from every evil deed of the enemy,

and fill it with Your grace and with Your mercy.

Լուա՛ Տէր՝ զախտ Հոգւոյ իմոյ
    զոր ժանդահոտ մեղաց նեխութեամբ զազրացուցի,
եւ շնորհեա՛ ինձ խորհիլ միշտ գսիրոյդ քո՝
    բաղձալ յարաժամ:
Հորդ մարդասիրի եւ բարերարի
    կարօտիմ Հանապազ,
ընկա՛լ զիս զթութեամբ որպէս զորդին անառակ.
լցո՛ զքաղց իմ եւ զծարաւ յաւատարաչխ շնորհէդ՝
    բարերա՛ր:
Եւ խնդրեմ առ քեզ մերձենալ,
    եւ միշտ շնորհաց քոց փափագիմ յարաժամ,
եւ զողորմութիւնս քո բերկրանօք ժտեմ Հայցել մաղթանօք:
Եւ դու Տէր՝ ընկա՛լ զվշտագնելոյս տառապանս,
եւ ներեա՛ քոյով մեծաւ ներողութեամբ յանցաւոր ծառայիս՝
    բարերա՛ր:
Չի թէ առանց ներելոյ գլանցանս իմ դատես,
ապա երանեմ չելելոցն յորովայնէ,
    զի Հուր գեհենին է ժառանգութիւն Հանապազ.
քանզի ոչ մնացին ճանապարՀք մեղաց՝ ընդ որս ոչ գնացի,
    եւ ի շնորհաց Սուրբ Հոգւոյդ մերկացայ:
Արդ անկեալ առ քեզ պաղատիմ,
    զթամ ի ժտութիւն թախանձանաց մաղթողիս,
եւ մի՛ մերժեր զիս յողորմութենէ քումմէ՝ ողորմած Տէր:
Չի զքեզ խնդրեցի եւ զքեզ աղաչեմ,
    լ՛ց զփափագ իմ որում միշտ Հոգի իմ կարօտի՝
        մեղաց թողութեան:
Չի ոչ թէ իբրեւ գրաբեզործ ոք Հայցեմ ի քէն Համարձակ,
այլ իբրեւ գմեծամեղ յանցաւոր ոք՝
    աղերսիւ ժտեմ յարաժամ:
Ոչ զոգի իմ մաքուր ունելով ինչ մերձենամ առ քեզ՝ մարդասէր,
այլ ի մաքրութենէդ քումմէ զժահահոտութիւն վիրաց մեղաց իմոց
    մաքրել աղաչեմ.
զի դու միայն ես Հայր իմ եւ Տէր բարերար,
    արարիչ իմ եւ փրկիչ իմ եւ կեցուցիչ իմ:
Առ ո՞ երթայց՝ մարդասէր,
կամ յումմէ՞ խնդրեցից օգնութիւն եւ վիրաց իմոց բժշկութիւն.
այլ քեզ մաղթեմ ողորմածիդ Աստուծոյ
    եւ բազմագութ իմոյ արարչիդ:

Cleanse, O Lord, the stain of my spirit
> which the stench of [my] sins has disfigured and corrupted,
and grant that I may always meditate upon Your love
> and continually desire it.
From You, O Father, Lover of mankind and Beneficent One,
> I am in constant need;
receive me with clemency as [You did] the prodigal son;[188]
fill my hunger and my thirst with Your bountiful grace,
> O Beneficent One.
And I seek to draw near to You
> and I am always desirous of Your grace
and I continuously and joyfully persist in imploring [You] with [my] petitions.
And You, O Lord, receive the entreaties of me who am deeply afflicted,
and grant pardon in Your great favor to your transgressing servant,
> O Beneficent One.
For if You were to judge my transgressions without granting any pardon
then I would be happy for those who had never come forth from the womb
> for the fire of Gehenna is their common inheritance.
Because the paths of sin did not remain, I did not walk on them,
> and I have been stripped of the graces of Your Holy Spirit.
So I fall down before You and beg of You,
> be compassionate to the earnest entreaties of me who am making supplication
> and do not exclude me from Your mercy, O merciful Lord.
For You have I sought and to You I pray,
> fulfill my desire for that which my spirit is ever in need,
>> the forgiveness of sins.
For not like someone who does good deeds do I boldly make request of You,
but like a great sinner and transgressor
> I continually entreat You with supplication.
Although I did not keep my soul clean I draw near to You, O Lover of mankind,
and I pray to You to purify the stench from the wounds of my sins
> with Your own purity,
for You alone are my father and beneficent Lord,
> my creator, my savior, and my life-giver.
To whom shall I go, O Lover of mankind?
Or from whom shall I seek help and healing for my wounds?
> But I make supplication to You, O most-merciful God
> and my most compassionate Maker?

---

[188] Cf. Luke 15:20.

Մի՛ բարկութեամբ խրատեր
եւ մի՛ սրտմտութեամբ քո յանդիմաներ՝ բարերար.
մի՛ ընդ պատժեալսն պատժեր զիս,
եւ մի՛ ընդ դատապարտեալսն դատապարտեր զիս՝ գթած.
մի՛ անողորմ պահանջանօք պահանջեր,
եւ մի՛ տոկալի գեհենիդ դողացուցաներ՝ մարդասէր:
Մի՛ յաւիտենական ամօթովն ամաչեցուցաներ զիս,
    եւ մի՛ ի մեծի աւուրն սրբոցն պատկելոյ՝
զիս պատուհասեր անողորմ եւ աններելի:
Այլ ապրեցո՛ զիս Տէր՝ ի Հրահոսան հալոցսն
    եւ ի Հրաբորբոք գեհենոյն,
յանլոյծ կապանացն
    եւ յաննչող խաւարէն,
յանաչառ դատաստանացն
    եւ յանների տանջանացն ցաւոց:
Այո՛ Տէր՝ յայտնեա՛ առ իս զգթութիւնս քո,
    դի սովոր ես ցուցանել գողորմութիւն քո առ կարօտեալս,
    նեղեալս եւ վշտագնեալս մեղօք.
եւ այժմ առ իս ցոյց զբարերարութիւնդ քո,
    որ չարաչարս եմ վիրաւորեալ առաւել քան զՍողոման.
եւ միշտ երկիւղիւ դողամ Հանապազ՝
եթէ կենդանույն Հրակիզեսցես
    իբրեւ գնոսա Հրատեղացն բարկութեամբ:
Վասն որոյ աղաչեմ զգթութիւնս քո՝ մարդասէր,
շնորհեա՛ ինձ նման նինուէացւոցն՝
    զարտմութիւն քո յողորմութիւն դարձուցանել,
    եւ կանգնիլ ի յանցանաց կործանմանէ.
դի աՀա ծով մեղաց յանդունդս ընկղմէ զիս
    վասն անօրէնութեան իմոյ առաւել քան զՋրՀեղեղն:
Այլ Հրամայեա՛ ինձ Տէր՝
    գողորմութիւնս քո տապան ամրութեան իբրեւ զՆոյի
    ապրիլ ապաշխարութեամբ ի Հրեղէն ծովէն անդնդոց:

Do not admonish [me] in Your anger
and do not reproach me in Your wrath, O Beneficent One;
do not punish me with those who are being punished,
and do not condemn me with those who are being condemned, O Compassionate One.
Do not examine me with a merciless examination,
and do not give me over to trembling in Your hideous Gehenna, O Lover of mankind.
Do not put me to shame in eternal disgrace
    and, on that great day of the crowning of the saints,
do not punish me without mercy and without forgiveness.
Rather, deliver me, O Lord, from the torrid flames of that furnace
    and from the blazing fires of Gehenna,
    from those unbreakable bonds,
    from that lightless darkness,
    from impartial judgment
    and from those intolerable pains of torture.
Yes, Lord, reveal to me Your compassion
    for You are wont to show Your mercy to those in need,
    to those afflicted and tormented by their sins.
And now show Your beneficence to me
    who am wounded far worse than Sodom.[189]
I continually quake in constant fear
    that You will burn me up alive
    just like those who were burnt up in Your anger.
For this reason, I appeal to Your compassion, O Lover of mankind,
give me the same grace as [You did] the Ninevites,[190]
    by turning Your indignation into mercy
    and raising me up from the destruction of transgressions,
for behold a sea of sins is drowning my haughty self
    because of my iniquities even more than that flood.[191]
But command for me, O Lord,
    that Your mercy be an ark of durability, just as it was for Noah,[192]
    to deliver me by repentance from this unending sea of fire.

---

[189] Cf. Genesis 19:24–28.
[190] Cf. Jonah 3:10.
[191] Cf. Genesis 7:21–23.
[192] Cf. Genesis 7:17–24; cf. also 1 Peter 3:20, 2 Peter 2:5.

Քանզի դու այն բարերար Տէրն ես,
    որ վասն մարդասիրութեան քոյ
    ի ծառայական կերպ իջեր՝
թագաւորդ, ազատեմ եւ զիս ի չար ծառայութենէ
    մեղաց իմոց եւ յանօրէնութեանց։
Որ վասն իմ թուք ի դէմս
    եւ ապտակ ի ծնօտս եւ փուշ ի գլուխս ընկալար՝ մարդասէր,
հան զփուշ յանցանաց իմոց՝
    որ չարաչար վիրաւորիմ հանապազ։
Որ վասն իմ փայտի խաչի եւ խոցման գեղարդեանն
    եւ ձեռաց կապանաց եւ բեւեռացն համբերեցեր՝ բարերար,
լո՛յծ եւ զիս ի դառն կապանաց սատանայի,
    եւ բժշկեա՛ զխոցումն անբեւոյթ գեղարդեան թշնամւոյն։
Եւ արդ՝ որ այսմ ամենայնի համբերեցեր ողորմած Տէր՝ վասն իմ,
    եւ այժմ ադաշեմ վասն մեղացս թողութիւն։
Թէպէտ վասն անբաւ ծուլութեանս իմոյ
    չեմ արժանի ողորմութեան քոյ,
սակայն վասն ժտութեան իմոյ լո՛ւր Տէր՝
    իբրեւ այլոյն թախանձանաց առ անիրաւ դատաւորին։
Եւ առ իս կատարեա՛ զբան քո Տէր իմ՝
    թէ ոչ եկի կոչել զարդարս, այլ զմեղաւորս։
Եւ գիտեմ՝ եթէ արդարքն իբրեւ զպարտս ընդունին
    ի քէն զարդարութեան պարգեւն.
բայց ինձ ողորմութիւն շնորհեա՛ իբրեւ մեծամեղի
    եւ բիւրապատիկ մահապարտի։
Որ առ ամենեսեան ես գթած,
    լո՛ւր եւ իմ ողբալոյս առ քեզ՝ բարերար,
    եւ ունկն դիր գթութեամբ պաղատանաց ճայնիս՝
        ողորմած.
դարձի՛ր զիս յուղիղ ճանապարհն իբրեւ զհայհոյիչն եւ զհալածիչն,
    եւ արդարացո՛ որպէս զմաքսաւորն։
ողորմեա՛ ինձ որպէս Քանանացւոյն.
ընկա՛լ զիս որպէս զառատակ որդին,
    եւ միսանդամ դարձի՛ր իս զշնորհն աւազանին սրբութեան

Because You are that beneficent Lord
    who, in Your love for mankind,
        descended into that form of a servant,[193]
O King, now save even me from the wicked servitude
    to my sins and to my iniquities.
You who, on my behalf, received spit on Your face,
    a slap on Your cheek and thorns on Your head,[194]
O Lover of mankind, remove the thorn of my transgressions
    with which I am constantly and cruelly wounded.
You who, on my behalf, endured the wood of the cross, the piercing by the lance
    and the bonds and the nails in the hands,[195] O Beneficent One,
release even me from the bitter bonds of Satan
and heal [me from] the wound of the invisible lance of the enemy.
And now, to You who bore all these things, O merciful Lord, on my behalf,
I now also pray for the forgiveness of my sins.
Although, because of my unbounded slothfulness
    I am not worthy of Your mercy,
nevertheless because of my persistence, hear me, O Lord,
    as [You heard] the entreaties of that widow before the unjust judge.[196]
And fulfill in me Your word, my Lord, that
    "I have not come to call the righteous, but sinners."[197]
And I know that the righteous receive gifts of righteousness
    from you like payments,
but grant to me mercy as if to a great sinner
    and one who is worthy of death many times over.
You, who are compassionate to all,
    hear also my laments to You, O Beneficent One,
    and in Your compassion give ear to the voice of my supplications,
        O Merciful One;
    turn me back to the right path like that blasphemer and persecutor,[198]
    and absolve me like the tax-collector,[199]
    have mercy on me like [You did] the Canaanite;[200]
    receive me like the prodigal son,[201]
    and once again restore to me the grace of the holy baptismal font

---

[193] Cf. Philippians 2:7.
[194] Cf. Mark 14:65, 15:17.
[195] Cf. John 19:34.
[196] Cf. Luke 18:1–6.
[197] Matthew 9:13, Mark 2:17, Luke 5:32.
[198] That is, Paul; cf. Acts of the Apostles 9:3–7, et al.
[199] Cf. Luke 18:13–14.
[200] Cf. Matthew 15:21–28.
[201] Cf. Luke 15:20–24.

գոր գանագան մեղօք Հայածեցի։
Եւ մի՛ ընդունայն առներ գագաշանս ծառայիս քո՝ բարերար.
այլ բա՛ց գգուռն ողօթից իմոց առ քեզ՝ մարդասէր.
եւ մի՛ թագուցաներ գգուռն ողորմութեան քոյ
        յամենամեղ ծառայէս՝ ողորմած։
Չի դու Տէր՝ ասացեր,
    Թէ չի՛ք ինչ գոր խնդրիցէք յԱստուծոյ՝
        եւ ոչ առնուցուք։
Վասն որոյ ամենամեղս ժտեմ Հայցելով ի քէն թողութիւն,
    գոր անսուտ խոստացար ինձ Փրկիչ։
Ոչ թէ վասն Հաճութեան ինչ գործոյ
    կամ արդարութեան իմոյ ազաչեմ զքեզ՝ մարդասէր,
այլ վասն ողորմութեան քոյ,
    գի քաղցր ես եւ բարերար եւ մարդասէր։
Աճա ես իբրեւ գպարտական եւ գմեծամեղ
    կամ առաջի քո ամօթով,
եւ դու իբրեւ գՀայր գԹած
մի՛ արգելուր գՀայցուածս իմ
    գոր խնդրեմ ի քէն գթողութիւն։
Աճա ձեռք իմ Համբարձեալ են առ քեզ,
եւ սիրտ իմ գարթուցեալ է ի խնդրել՝ Տէր՝ բարերար.
բաց գականջս իմ լսել երկիւղիւ գձայն պատգամաց քոց.
եւ բացցին աչք սրտի իմոյ գողութեամբ
Հայել առ քեզ ի բարձունս առ գԹածդ
    եւ բազումողորմդ եւ ներողդ առ մեղուցեալս.
գի դու Տէր քաղցր ես եւ երկայնամիտ,
վասն մեղաւորաց կոչեցար ողորմած,
ի դառնալ անօրինին ոչ յիշես
    գամենայն անօրէնութիւնն գոր արար։
Արդ՝ խնդրեմ ի քէն ողորմեա՛ ինձ,
    քանգի դու միայն ես քաւիչ՝
    որ գանմթիւ յանցանս յանցելոցն քաւեցեր՝
        բարերար.
գմեռեալսն մեղօք կենդանացուցեր.
գմոլորեալսն ի չար թշնամւոյն դարձուցեր.
գխաւարեալսն ի ճշմարտութենէ լուսաւորեցեր,
եւ բազմամեղիս դարձին ներեցեր մինչեւ ցայժմ։

from which I have expelled myself by my manifold sins.
Do not make void the prayers of Your servant, O Beneficent One,
> but open the gate to my prayers before You, O Lover of mankind,
> and do not close the gate of Your mercy
>> to Your servant who is full of sin, O Merciful One.
For You, O Lord, have said,
> "There is nothing that you seek from God
>> that you will not receive."[202]
For this reason, I am so bold to ask from You forgiveness for all my sins,
> for You indeed promised it to me, O Savior.
Not on account of any satisfactory deeds
> or righteousness on my part do I beseech you, O Lover of mankind,
but on account of Your mercy,
> for You are kind, and beneficent and a Lover of mankind.
Behold, like one in debt and a great sinner,
> I stand before You in shame
and You, like a compassionate Father,
do not prohibit my entreaties for Your forgiveness
> that I am addressing to you.
Behold, my hands are raised up to You,
and my heart is moved to make entreaty, O beneficent Lord;
open my ears to hear with fear the sound of Your words,
and may the eyes of my heart be opened to look,
> with trepidation, upon You on high to Your compassion,
to Your great mercy and to You who are forgiving to me who am a sinner,
for You, O Lord, are kind and long-suffering;
on account of sinners You are called Merciful,
by turning from iniquity You do not remember
> any of the lawless deeds that I have committed.
Now, I beseech You, Have mercy on me,
> because You alone are the One who gives pardon,
> You who have pardoned the uncountable transgressions of transgressors,
>> O Beneficent One;
> You have restored to life those who were dead in their sins,
> You have turned back those who have strayed over to the evil enemy,
> You have enlightened those who were blinded from the truth,
> and upon their conversion You have forgiven great sinners up to now.

---

[202] This seems to be an alternative rendering of Matthew 7:7 (=Luke 11:9): "Ask and it will be given to you."

Չի քո եմ եւ ի քո պատկեր Հաստատեցեր դիս.
ձեռօք ստեղծեր եւ շնչով կենդանացուցեր
եւ ամենայն իշխանութեամբ փառաւորեցեր դիս.
եւ եօթւր ինձ պատուիրան, եւ ոչ պահելովն անկայ ի փառացն:
Եւ դարձեալ ի գալստեան քոյ նորոգեցեր դիս՝ ողորմած.
լուացեր եւ սրբեցեր դիս աւազանին սրբութեամբ,
        եւ դարձեալ վերստին վիրաւորեցայ եւ բժշկեցեր ապաշխարութեամբ:
Եւ արդ՝ որ պայս ամենայն բարութիւնս շնորհեցեր ինձ
        ողորմութեամբ քով,
քաւեա՛ այժմ ի մեղաց եւ պահեա՛ յայսմ հետէ սրբութեամբ Տէր.
փրկեա՛ ի թշնամւոյն եւ ի ձեռաց դժոխոց,
    ի մէշտ լալոյն եւ յանդադար ողբալոյն՝
    յորում ոչ ոք լսէ եւ ներէ ի դառն ադետից տանջանացն:
Բայց դու միայն ես մարդասէր,
    քաղցր եւ երկայնամիտ, բարերար եւ բազումողորմ,
ընկա՛լ գաղաչանս իմ:
Քեզ մեղայ եւ քեզ խոստովանիմ
    եւ առ քեզ պաղատիմ.
դվերս Հոգւոյ իմոյ ցաւագին Հառաչմամբ ողբամ,
    եւ դանօրէնութիւնս իմ առաջի քո:
Աղաչեմ Հայոտեաց Տէր՝ ընդ աղայանս իմ ողորմութեամբ քով.
    ներեա եւ մարդասիրեա ի վերայ մեղուցելոյս
    եւ ընկա՛լ գթութեամբ քո գաղաչանս իմ:
Ընկա՛լ Տէր՝ զղջումն խոստովանութեան իմոյ,
    զՀառաչումն ապաշխարութեան,
եւ ջնջեա՛ զանիթւ անօրէնութիւնս մանկութեան իմոյ.
    դի տկարացայ յանցեալ իբրեւ դմարդ,
    մեղայ եւ անկայ ի խորս չարեաց:
Գիթա՛, քաւեա՛ եւ յարո՛ իբրեւ զԱստուած եւ թեթեացո՛.
կանգնեմ յաներեւոյթ գլորմանէս,
եւ ընկա՛լ գտուղ ապաշխարութիւն ապաշխարութեան իմոյ՝
    մարդասէր.
եւ թեթեացո՛ գծանրութիւն մեղաց իմոց դոր մեղայ քեզ՝
    բարերար:
Քո եմ գործ ձեռաց, մի՛ անտես առներ դիս ողորմած,
    որ առ քեզ դաչս ի վեր եմ Համբարձեալ ի մաղթել,
    դձեռս մտացս տարածեալ յաղաչանս,
    եւ ծունր իշեալ պաղատանօք զմեղս իմ

For I am Yours and You established me in Your image,[203]
with Your hands You created me and with Your breath You gave me life,[204]
and with every power of authority You glorified me.
You gave me a command, but by not keeping it I fell from that glory.[205]
When You returned at Your coming, You renewed me, O Merciful One;
You washed me and cleansed me in the basin of holiness,
    yet once again I was wounded but You healed me by my repentance.
So, You who bestowed on me all these good things
    in Your mercy,
now pardon me from my sins and keep me from now on in holiness, O Lord.
Save me from the enemy and from the power of hell,
    from eternal weeping and from unending wailing,
    where no one hears or is pardoned in the bitter misery of their torments.
But You alone are the Lover of mankind,
    kind and long-suffering, beneficent and all-Merciful,
receive my prayer.
Against You have I sinned, to You do I confess
    and to You do I make supplication.
Before You, I wail with mournful sighs for the wounds of my soul
    and for my iniquities.
In my prayers I pray: Reconcile me, O Lord; in Your mercy,
    forgive me and be charitable toward me who have sinned
    and, in Your compassion, receive my prayers.
Receive, O Lord, the contrition of my confession,
    the sorrow of my repentance,
and wipe away the innumerable lawless deeds of my youth;
    for I was weak and transgressed like a man,
    I sinned and I fell into pits of evil.
Like a God, have compassion, pardon me, raise me up and give me relief;
bring me back up from my invisible downfall,
and accept some little portion from my repentance,
    O Lover of mankind,
and give me relief from the burden of my sins that I have committed against You,
    O Beneficent One.
I am the work of Your hands, do not abandon me, O Merciful One,
    to whom I raise up my eyes to implore You
    and stretch out the hands of my mind in prayer,
    and dropping to my knee in supplication

---

[203] Cf. Genesis 1:26.
[204] Cf. Genesis 2:7; on the "hands", see n. 94, above.
[205] Cf. Genesis 2:17, 3:1–19.

խոստովանիմ առ քեզ եւ աղաչեմ ողբալով.
    Հայր' մեղայ՚յ յերկինս եւ առաջի քո,
    քաւեա՛ զանօրէնութիւնս իմ՝ ողորմած։
Եւ մի՛ այլ եւս թողուր զիս ի պատուիրանս քո մեղանչել՝
    բարերա՛ր.
այլ շնորհեա՛ ինձ առ քեզ պաղատիլ ապաշխարութեամբ՝
    պաղատանօք եւ ջանիւ աղօթից, անդադար հառաչմամբ
    եւ գորովագութ ողորմ ողբալով առ քեզ,
    Հանապազ արտասուել, աղաչել եւ խնդրել մեղաց թողութիւն,
    զի կարող ես յամենայնի մարդասիրութեամբ քո։
Պահեա՛ զիս գթութեամբ քով. գօրացո՛ զիս շնորհօք քո.
օգնեա՛ փրկեա՛ եւ բժշկեա՛ զվէրս մեղաց.
նորոգեա՛ զիս եւ Հաստատեա՛ եւ ապրեցո՛ ի չար թշնամւոյն.
ներեա՛ քաւեա՛ եւ արդարացո՛
եւ լցո՛ Հոգւով քով Սրբով։
Եւ շնորհեա՛ ինձ պաշել Հանապազ զվարս ուղիղս եւ Հաւատս
    ճշմարիտս,
    խոնարհութիւն եւ Հեզութիւն,
    Հնազանդութիւն, պատուիրանապահութիւն եւ սէր կատարեալ.
    սրբութիւն սրտի, ճշմարտութիւն լեզուի, ցնծութիւն աչաց,
    պարկեշտութիւն մարմնոյ, պնդութիւն պահոց, յօժարութիւն աղօթից,
    յորդորումն ողորմութեան, զղջումն եւ արտասուս ապաշխարութեան,
    Համբերութիւն ժուժկալութիւն,
        եւ առաւել գոհութիւն ամենայն նեղութեանց։
Զի այսու ամենայնիւ քաւեալ զիս եւ սրբեալ՝
    արժանի արա՛ զիս մարմնոյ եւ արեան քոյ սրբոյ
        եւ արքայութեանդ երկնից՝ մարդասէր։
Յամենայնի գոհացայց զքէն Հանապազ,
երկիրպագից միանգամայն երրորդութեանդ յարաժամ.
օրհնեցից գովեցից եւ փառաւորեցից գոհութեամբ անդադար
    զՀայրդ ողորմած
    եւ զՈրդիդ բարերար
    եւ զՀոգի Սուրբ կենդանարար,
այժմ եւ միշտ եւ յաւիտեանս յաւիտենից. ամէն։

I confess my sins to You and wailing I pray,
> "Father, I have sinned against heaven and before You."[206]
> Pardon my iniquities, O Merciful One.

And do not permit me any longer to sin against Your commandments,
> O Beneficent One,

but grant that I may implore You in repentance,
> with supplications and with diligent prayers,
> with incessant entreaty and tender and humble wailing before You,
> constantly weeping, praying and seeking forgiveness for my sins,
> for in Your love for mankind You are all-powerful.

Preserve me by Your compassion, strengthen me by Your grace;
help me, save me and heal the wounds of my sins;
renew me, sustain me and deliver me from the evil enemy;
forgive me, pardon me, justify me
and fill me with Your Holy Spirit.

And grant that I may always maintain an upright life and true faith,
> humility, gentleness,
>> obedience, keeping the commandments,
>>> perfect love, purity of heart, truth of tongue, joyfulness of the eyes,
>>> chastity of the body, steadfastness in fasting, a disposition to prayer,
>>> an abundance of mercy and compunction, and tears of repentance,
>>> patience, continence,
>>>> and ever more praise for every forgiveness.

Then, having pardoned and cleansed me by all these things,
make me worthy of Your holy body and blood
> and of Your heavenly kingdom, O Lover of mankind.

In everything, may I give You constant praise,
may I worship Your Trinity united at every moment.
May I bless, honor and glorify with incessant thanksgiving
> You, O Merciful Father,
> and You, O Beneficent Son,
> and You, O Holy Life-giving Spirit,

now and always, and unto the ages of ages. Amen.

---

[206] Luke 15:18, 21.

Ե

Աղօթք նորին դարձեալ:

Փառք քեզ Աստուած,
 փառք քեզ արարիչ յաւիտենից Աստուած,
 փառք քեզ.
որ շնորհեցեր Հանգիստ տկարութեանս մերում.
 որ դարթուցեր դարարամս գքեզ փառաւորել:
 Որ ի յերկնից խոնարհեցար մարմնանալ վասն մեր,
 եւ ի սուրբ Աստուածածնէն՝ Աստուած յայտնեցար:
Որ ի մէջ գիշերի վասն մեր յանցանացն ծնար ի Կուսէն
 եւ ի սուրբ այրին բազմեցար,
դանարժան ծառայս քո որ յաղքատաց եմ ծնեալ՝ սրբեցես ի մեղաց:
Որ ի մէջ գիշերի գայլով ի տաճարն արձակեցեր գծերունին,
 դանարժան գքո ծառայս արձակեմ ի մեղաց կապանաց եւ ի բանտից:
Որ ի մէջ գիշերի ճանապարհ Հորդեցեր յեգիպտոս ելանել,
 դանարժան քո ծառայս յելանելն յաշխարհէս առաջնորդեցես ի կեանս:
Որ ի մէջ գիշերի գնայիր ի վերայ ծովուն իբր ի վերայ ցամաքի,
 անարժան քո ծառայիս ձեռնտու լեր Տէր իմ՝ որպէս Պետրոսի:
Որ ի մէջ գիշերի լուացեր դոտս աշակերտացն՝
 զպատուական մարմին եւ գարիւնդ քո բաշխելով ի նոսա,
դանարժան գքո ծառայիս լուասցես գմեղա,
եւ ընկալցիս Հաղորդս մարդասիրապէս
    ընդ մետասանս բագմեալ ի սեղան խորհրդոյ:
Որ ի մէջ գիշերի վասն մեր յաղօթմ կայիր առ Հայր
 յառաջ քան զչարչարանս,
դանարժան քո ծառայիս ընկալցիս գաղօթմ
 ի ժամ գիշերիս:
Որ ի մէջ գիշերի բժկել կամեցար ի Պետրոսէ Հատեալ դունկն Մաղքոսի,
 դանարժան գքո ծառայս բժկես գվիրաւորեալս յանօրէն թշնամւոյն:

PART V:

MORE PRAYERS FROM [EPHREM]

Glory to You O God,
    Glory to You creator God from all eternity,
    Glory to You.
For You have granted us rest for our weakness,
    You roused Your creatures to give You praise,
    You lowered Yourself from heaven to take on flesh for our sake,
    and from the Holy Mother of God[207] You manifested
    Yourself as God.
You who in the midst of night for the sake of our transgressions
    were born from the Virgin and dwelt in that holy cave,[208]
May You cleanse from sin me Your unworthy servant, who was born among the poor.
You who came in the midst of night to the Temple and released the old [Simeon],[209]
    release me Your unworthy servant from the bondage and imprisonment of sin.
You who in the middle of the night set out on the path to go down to Egypt,[210]
    guide me Your unworthy servant to go out from this world to Life.
You who in the middle of the night walked upon the sea as if upon dry land,[211]
    lend a hand to me Your unworthy servant, My Lord, as You did to Peter.[212]
You who in the middle of the night washed the feet of Your disciples
    with whom You shared Your precious body and blood,[213]
    wash away the sins of me Your unworthy servant
    and may I, with love for mankind, receive communion with those eleven
        who sat at the table of Your mysteries.[214]
You who in the middle of the night prayed to the Father
    on our behalf before Your passion,[215]
    may You receive the prayers of me Your unworthy servant
    at this hour of the night.
You who in the middle of the night willed to heal the ear of Malchus cut off by Peter,[216]
    heal me Your unworthy servant who am wounded by the lawless enemy.

---

[207] Arm., *Astouadzadzin*, which translates Greek *Theotokos*.
[208] Cf. Luke 2:7, but the idea that Jesus was born in a cave is an apocryphal one; see A. Terian, *The Armenian Gospel of the Infancy*, 41–43.
[209] Cf. Luke 2:25–35.
[210] Cf. Matthew 2:13–15; cf. also Exodus 12:40–42.
[211] Cf. Matthew 14:22–27, Mark 6:45–51, John 6:16–21.
[212] Cf. Matthew 14:31.
[213] Cf. John 13:1–11.
[214] The author here seems to presume that Judas had already left.
[215] Cf. Matthew 26:36–46, Mark 14:32–42, Luke 22:40–46.
[216] Cf. John 18:10.

Որ ի մէջ գիշերի կալով առաջի Կայիափայ՝
  դատապարտեցար եւ ապտակեցար,
  զանարժան զքո ծառայս յահագին քո դատաստանին մի՛
  դատապարտեր։
Որ ի մէջ գիշերի վասն մեր Հայեցար ի Պետրոս՝
  յիշեցուցանելով նմա դյանցանս իւր,
  անարժան քո ծառայիս շնորհեա՛ զղջումն
  եւ արտասուս ի լուացումն մեղաց իմոց։
Որ ի մէջ գիշերի կամաւոր խաչի եւ մահու ընդ մեռեալս Համարեալ
  եւ ի գինուորաց պաշեցար,
  անարժան քո ծառայիս զրանակս Հրեշտակաց շնորՀեսցես պաՀապան։
Որ ի մէջ գիշերի յարեար ի մեռելոց
  կամաւ Հօր եւ սուրբ Հոգւոյն,
  զանարժան զքո ծառայս որ մեղօքս եմ մեռեալ՝ կենդանացուսցես,
  Տէր իմ։
Որ ի մէջ գիշերի վասն մեր գալոց ես միւսանգամ
  նորոգել զարարածս,
  զանարժան զքո ծառայս յանուանէ կոչեսցես
  անապական նորոգմամբ եւ նորաՀրաշ փառօք։
Որ ի մէջ գիշերի վասն քո մարդասիրութեանդ
  գիմաստուն կուսանն ընկալցին զառագաստն,
  անարժան քում ծառայիս բաց զդուռն դրախտին՝
  զառագաստն լուսոյ։
զի դու սուրբ, սուրբ, սուրբ ես, Տէր զօրութեանց։

You who in the middle of the night stood before Caiaphas
>> and were condemned and struck,[217]
> do not condemn me Your unworthy servant to Your dreadful judgement.

You who in the middle of the night for our sake looked upon Peter
>> calling back to his mind his transgressions,[218]
> grant to me Your unworthy servant repentance
>> and tears for the washing away of my sins.

You who in the middle of the night were reckoned with those to die on a cross
>> and were guarded by the soldiers,[219]
> grant to me Your unworthy servant a host of angels as guardians.

You who in the middle of the night rose up from the dead
>> by the will of the Father and the Holy Spirit,[220]
> restore to life, My Lord, me Your unworthy servant who am dead from my sins.

You who in the middle of the night will come one more time for our sake
>> to restore [Your] creatures,[221]
> may You call me Your unworthy servant by name,
>> and by Your incorruptible, regenerative and marvelous glory.

You who in the middle of the night on account of Your love for mankind
>> will receive the wise virgins into [Your] bridal chamber,[222]
> open for me Your unworthy servant the gate of the Garden,
>> that bridal chamber of light,

for You are holy, holy, holy, O Lord of hosts.[223]

---

[217] Cf. John 19:1–3.
[218] Cf. Matthew 26:74–75, Mark 14:71–72, Luke 22:61–62.
[219] Cf. Matthew 27:62–66.
[220] Cf. Matthew 28:1, Luke 24:1–3, John 20:1.
[221] Cf. 1 Thessalonians 5:2.
[222] Cf. Matthew 25:10.
[223] Isaiah 6:3.

Ձ

Աղօթք նորին դարձեալ։

Փրկեա՛ զիս Յիսուս Քրիստոս որդի Աստուծոյ՝ ի բարկութենէն որ գալոցն է.
    Որպէս փրկեցեր զԱդամ ի դժոխոցն.
    որպէս փրկեցեր զՆոյ ի Ջրհեղեղէն.
    որպէս փրկեցեր զԱբրահամ ի Հայածչացն.
    որպէս փրկեցեր զՂովտ ի Սոդոմայեցւոցն.
    որպէս փրկեցեր զԻսահակ յանհաւատիցն.
    որպէս փրկեցեր զՅակովբ ի ձեռացն Եսաւայ.
    որպէս փրկեցեր զՅովսէփ ի գբին.
    որպէս փրկեցեր զՄովսէս եւ զժողովուրդն ի Փարաւոնէ.
    որպէս փրկեցեր զԴաւիթ ի Գողիաթու.
    որպէս փրկեցեր զեղիա յեզաբելայ.
    որպէս փրկեցեր զեղիսէէ ի նախատանացն.
    որպէս փրկեցեր զՅովնան ի փորոյ կիտին.
    որպէս փրկեցեր զեզեկիա ի Հիւանդութենէն.
    որպէս փրկեցեր զերեմիա ի գբոյ տղմին.
    որպէս փրկեցեր զՇուշան ի ծերոցն.
    որպէս փրկեցեր զԴանիէլ ի բերանոյ առիւծուցն.
    որպէս փրկեցեր զերիս մանկունսն ի Հնոցին.
    որպէս փրկեցեր սուրբ զառաքեալն Պօղոս ի բազում վշտացն.

Part VI:

More Prayers from [Ephrem]

Save me, O Jesus Christ Son of God, from the wrath that is to come,[224]
    just as You saved Adam from his harsh [punishments],[225]
    just as You saved Noah from the flood,[226]
    just as You saved Abraham from his pursuers,[227]
    just as You saved Lot from the Sodomites,[228]
    just as You saved Isaac from the unbelievers,[229]
    just as You saved Jacob from the hand of Esau,[230]
    just as You saved Joseph from the pit,[231]
    just as You saved Moses and the people from Pharaoh,[232]
    just as You saved David from Goliath,[233]
    just as You saved Elijah from Jezebel,[234]
    just as You saved Elisha from those who maligned him,[235]
    just as You saved Jonah from the belly of the whale,[236]
    just as You saved Hezekiah from illness,[237]
    just as You saved Jeremiah from the pit of slime,[238]
    just as You saved Susanna from the old men,[239]
    just as You saved Daniel from the mouths of lions,[240]
    just as You saved the three youths from the furnace,[241]
    just as You saved the holy Apostle Paul from many tribulations,[242]

---

[224] Cf. Matthew 3:7, Luke 3:7.
[225] Cf. Genesis 3:24.
[226] Cf. Genesis 7:23, 8:15–18.
[227] Cf. Genesis 14:13–24.
[228] Cf. Genesis 19:1–29.
[229] Cf. Genesis 21:8–14; this could also refer to his not being killed by the Philistines in Genesis 26:1–11.
[230] Cf. Genesis 32:6–33:17.
[231] Cf. Genesis 37:17–36, 39:1–6.
[232] Cf. Exodus 12:50–15:21.
[233] Cf. 1 Samuel 17:21–54.
[234] Cf. 1 Kings 21:17–24, 2 Kings 9:4–37.
[235] Cf. 2 Kings 6:30–8:15.
[236] Cf. Jonah 1:17–2:10.
[237] Cf. 2 Kings 20:1–11.
[238] Cf. Jeremiah 38:5–13.
[239] Cf. Daniel 13:7–62.
[240] Cf. Daniel 6:16–23.
[241] Cf. Daniel 3:13–30.
[242] Cf. Acts of the Apostles, cc. 9–28, *passim*.

որպէս ւիրկեցեր զԹեկդի ի Հրոյն եւ ի գազանացն։
Որպէս ւիրկեցեր զնոսա՝ ւիրկեա՛ եւ զիս Տէր.
ողորմեա՛ ինձ Աստուած խաղաղութեան
   եւ լոյս աշխարհի՝ Փրկիչ արարածոց։
Գթա՛ Տէր՝ եւ ողորմեա՛ ինձ.
կանխեա՛ առ իս եւ ողորմեա՛.
լո՛ւր ձայնի աղօթից իմոց յամենայն ժամ։
Ծագեա՛ զլոյս գիտութեան քոյ
   ի լիմարեալ միտս իմ եւ ի մահկանացու մարմինս իմ։
Բա՛րձ յինէն գամօթ նախատանաց թշնամւոյն։
Տո՛ւր գովականութիւն խաչի քոյ,
եւ կանգնեա՛ լիս դնշան յաղթութեան բարկի քոյ,
   զի գոհացին դք էն սուրբք քո,
   եւ փառաւորեսցի անուն մեծութեան քոյ։
Ծագեա՛ լիս գողորմութիւն քո ի յաղդ սուրբ շնորհաց քոց.
եւ բա՛րձ յինէն գղատապարտութիւն անիծից պարտեաց իմոց
   ի ձեռն քաղցրութեան փրկութեան քոյ։
Խոնարհեցո՛ Տէր՝ գունկն քո եւ լո՛ւր աղօթից իմոց։
Ողորմեա՛ ինձ Տէր՝ զի նեղեալ եմ ես.
մխիթարեա՛ գիս ի գորութիւն անուանդ քոյ.
բժշկեա՛ գիս ողորմութեամբ քով,
   զի դողաց սիրտ իմ եւ ոսկերք իմ
   ի բագմութենէ յանցանաց իմոց,
Զի ո՞վ է իմ Փրկիչ, եթէ ոչ դու Տէր՝
   որ ամենեցուն գաղտնիք յայտնի են քեզ.
   չիք ինչ առաջի գորութեանդ քոյ ի ծածուկ։

      just as You saved Thekla from the fire and from the wild beasts.[243]
Just as You saved them, save me also, O Lord,
have mercy on me, O God of peace,
    Light of the World[244] and Savior of all creatures.
Be compassionate, O Lord, and have mercy on me,
hasten to me and have mercy;
hear the sound of my prayer at all times.
Shine the light of Your knowledge
    on my deranged mind and on my mortal body.
Remove from me the shameful reproaches of the enemy.
Give to me the help of Your cross,
and raise up for me the sign of Your victorious arm,[245]
    so that Your saints might praise You
    and that Your great name might be glorified.
Cultivate in me Your mercy from the salt of Your holy graces,
and remove from me the condemnation for my cursed debts
    through the sweetness of Your salvation.
Incline Your ear, O Lord, and hear my prayer.[246]
Have mercy on me, O Lord, for I am in straits,
comfort me by the power of Your name,
heal me by Your mercy
    for my heart and my bones are in throes
    from the multitude of my transgressions.
For Who is my Savior if not You, O Lord
    for all hidden things are manifest to You;
    there is nothing hidden before Your power.[247]

---

[243] *Life of Thekla.* Saint Thecla was a saint of the early Christian Church, and a reported follower of Paul of Tarsus in the 1st century A.D. She is not mentioned in the New Testament; the earliest record of her comes from the apocryphal *Acts of Paul and Thecla*, probably composed in the early second century. According to these *Acts*, Thecla was a young noble virgin who listened to Paul's "discourse on virginity" and became Paul's follower. Thecla's mother, and her fiancé Thamyris, became concerned that Thecla would follow Paul's demand "that one must fear only one God and live in chastity", and punished both Paul and Thecla. She was miraculously saved from being burned at the stake by the onset of a storm, and traveled with Paul to Pisidian Antioch. There a nobleman named Alexander desired Thecla and attempted to take her by force. Thecla fought him off, assaulting him in the process, and was put on trial for assaulting a nobleman. She was sentenced to be eaten by wild beasts, but was again saved by a series of miracles when the female beasts protected her against her male aggressors.

    [244] Cf. John 8:12.
    [245] Cf. Isaiah 41:10.
    [246] Cf. Psalm 17:6, 88:2, et al.
    [247] Cf. Ezekiel 28:3, Hebrews 4:13.

Տէր ամենակալ՝ ունկն դիր խնդրուածաց իմոց, եւ լե՛ր իմ այցելու.
    դի պակասեցաւ ի վշտաց կեանք իմ,
    եւ տկարացաւ զօրութիւն իմ,
    եւ նուաղեաց լոյս աչաց իմոց.
Չեռաւ փոր իմ, եւ ոսկերք իմ ցամաքեցաւ
    ի բազում Հոգոց մեղաց իմոց։
Մի՛ տար դիս Տէր՝ նախատինս դրացեաց իմոց,
    եւ ատելիք իմ մի՛ այպանեսցեն դիս։
Մի՛ թողուր դիս Տէր՝ վասն ողորմութեան քոյ,
եւ մի՛ մոռանար դիս, դի քեզ սպասէ անձն իմ.
    դի դու ես լոյս ժառանգութեան իմոյ։
Յետս դարձրին Հալածիչք իմ ընդունայն,
    եւ ատելիք իմ ի տարապարտուց.
Լուսաւորեա՛ դիս Տէր՝ եւ դարձո՛ գերեաս քո յիս։
Մերկացո՛ յինէն զխաւարն մոլորութեան,
    եւ Հաստատեա՛ դիս ի կենդանութիւն բանի քոյ։
Բեկ զՀպարտութիւն թշնամւոյն՝ Տէր ամենակալ.
խորտակեա՛ զյամառութիւն նորա
    դի մի՛ կարասցէ փակել զդուռն լուսոյ քոյ՝
    եկանել ինձ ի ճանապարհս արդարութեան։
Բազում են քաղցրութիւնք քո Տէր՝
    ցոդեա՛ յիս զկանուխն եւ զանագանն։
Հալեա՛ զատոն անՀնազանդութեան մտաց իմոց,
    եւ բա՛րձ զմէգ թերաՀաւատութեան ի խորՀրդոց իմոց։
Ցածո՛ յինէն զուղխս մոլեկանս Հարուածոց ցանկութեան,
    եւ ցամաքեցո՛ յինէն զաղբիւրն ստութեան։
Հերի արա՛ յինէն զձեռն ատելութեան,
    որ անրոյս առնէ զսերմն արդարութեան։
ՇնորՀեա՛ զարբ քաղցրութեան Հոգւոյդ սրբոյ՝
    զբալիչդ իմ եւ զարարիչդ,
եւ ցողով շնորՀաց քոց լուա՛ յինէն զամենայն թոյնս վնասակարս։
Մշակեա՛ յիս՝ Տէր, մշակ բարերար՝ զսերմ արդարութեան քոյ,
եւ պաՀեա՛ ի նենգութենէն թշնամւոյն,
    դի մի՛ սերմանեսցէ յիս զսերմն չար։
Ընդ յարկաւ արա՛ դիս ապաւէն իմ եւ փրկիչ իմ,
    ի Հակառակութենէ թշնամւոյն։
Մազեա՛ զնշոյլ ճառագայթից ճշմարտութեան քոյ յիս,
եւ առաջնորդեա՛ ինձ մինչեւ ի քաղաքն սրբոց։

O Lord Almighty, give ear to my supplications and come to visit me[248]
    for my life has wasted away in my afflictions,
    my strength has weakened,
    the light of my eyes has grown dim,
    my belly has grown hot and my bones have dried out
        from the great anguish over my sins.
Do not, O Lord, give me to the reproaches of my neighbors,
    and let not those who hate me scoff at me.
Do not abandon me, O Lord, on account of Your mercy,
and do not forget me for my soul waits for You,
    for You are the hope of my inheritance.
My pursuers pursue me in vain
    and those who hate me without need.
Enlighten me, O Lord, and turn Your face to me.
Strip me of the darkness of error
    and set me firm in the life of Your word.
Break down the arrogance of the enemy, O Lord Almighty,
crush his obstinacy
    lest he manage to shut the gate so that Your light
    not come to me on the path of righteousness.
Plentiful are Your sweet [rains], O Lord,
sprinkle on me the early and the late ones.[249]
Melt the ice of disobedience from my mind,
and remove the fog of mistrust from my thoughts.
Take away from me the raging torrents of desires for pleasures
and dry up in me the spring of falsehood.
Put far away from me the power of hatred,
    which renders the seed of righteousness unfruitful.
Grant to me the sweet sunlight of Your Holy Spirit,
    whom You [appointed] to pardon me and to [re]create me,
and with the dew of Your grace wash off of me every harmful poison.
Cultivate in me, O Lord and Beneficent Husbandman, the seed of Your righteousness
and keep me from the deception of the enemy
    lest he sow in me his bad seed.
Keep me safe, my Refuge and my Savior,
    from the hostility of the enemy.
Shine the light from the rays of Your truth upon me
and lead me into the city of Your saints.

---

[248] Cf. Isaiah 55:3.
[249] Cf. James 5:7.

Արժանաւորեա՛ զիս Աստուած իմ՝ հաւասարիկ ընդ սուրբս քո,
  փառաւորել զանուն քո, որ ազդիւրդ ես կենաց եւ փրկութեան։
Բան քո կենդանի լի է ամենայն երանութեամբ.
  տո՛ւր ինձ եւ լցո՛ զիս, զի կատարեալ եմ.
  օգնեա՛ ինձ, զի տկարացեալ եմ։
Արա՛ զմեզ արժանի սրբութեամբ ճաշակել ի հոգեւոր օրինացդ,
  զի եղիցի մեզ պարիսպ յամենայն նեղութենէ թշնամւոյն։
Մի՛ տար գերել զոտկար միտս մեր
  պղտոր խարդախութեամբք իւրովք։
Արբո՛ մեզ Տէր՝ յոյս մեր՝ ի քաղցրութենէ գործեան ճշմարտութեան քոյ,
  զի ապրեցուք ի սատակագոյն ալեաց փոթութեանց աշխարհիս։
Տնկեա՛ զմեզ Տէր Տէր՝ ի վերայ անսխալ հաստող քոց
  ի մէջ ջուրց գնացից պատուիրանաց քոց։
Յածողեա՛ մեզ Տէր՝ ի բարի խորհուրդս ի տուէ եւ ի գիշերի,
  զի առանց զրադման կացցուք ի գուարթութիւն լուսոյ քոյ՝
  բարերա՛ր։
Եւ բացցես մեզ զգուն կենդանութեան լուսոյ քոյ
  արժանի լինել մեզ սիրոյդ քում։
Աղաչեմք Տէր՝ զքաղցր եւ զգթած տէրութիւնդ քո,
  տո՛ւր մեզ ի սիրոյդ քումմէ, եւ յաւել ի մեզ շնորհաց քոց,
  զի արժանի եղիցուք լինել պաշտօնեայք կամաց քոց։
Բուրեսցեն շրթունք մեր որպէս խունկ գաղօսս մեր
  յամենայն ժամ առաջի մեծութեանդ քոյ։
Հաշտեա՛ ընդ մեզ Տէր՝ զի բարի ես.
  եւ թագաւորեցո՛ ի մեզ գլադջութիւնս քո,
  եւ տո՛ւր մեզ զնահատակութիւն քաջութեան խաչիդ քով։
Յորդորեա՛ զմեզ Տէր՝ ի սէր քաղցրութեան բանի քոյ,
  եւ հորդեա՛ զճանապարհս առաջի ոտից մերոց.
  կարողս արա՛ զմեզ Տէր՝ ատ կոչումնդ երկնաւոր կատարել ոտիւք։
Բա՛ց մեզ Տէր՝ զգուն հարսանեաց քոց,
  եւ զարդարեա՛ ի զարդ սրբութեան հոգեւոր պատմուճանիդ՝
    եւ վայելուչ պայծառութեան կենդանի գեղով պատուիրանաց քոց։
Չքեզ ադաչեմք Տէր Աստուած մեր՝ յոյս փրկութեան մերոյ,
զքէն գոհանամք բերանովք մերովք՝
  տալ փառս եւ խոստովանութիւն եւ երկրպագութիւն
  աստուածութեանդ քում։

Make me worthy, O my God, to be united with Your saints,
> and to glorify Your name for You are the source of life and of salvation.

Your living word is full of every blessing,
> give it to me and fill me for I am worn out,
> help me for I am weak.

Make us worthy to be nourished in holiness by Your spiritual law,
> that it may be for us a fortified wall against every affliction of the enemy.

Do not allow our weak minds
> to become prisoners to his perverse deceptions.

Give us to drink, O Lord our Hope, from the sweetness of Your powerful truth
> so that we may be saved from the violent waves of temptation of the world.

Plant us, Lord, O Lord, in Your infallible faith
> amidst the water courses of Your commandments.

Help us to prosper, O Lord, in good thoughts both day and night
> that we may stand without distraction in the enjoyment of Your light,
> O Beneficent One.

And may you open for us the gate of Your living light
> that we may be worthy of Your love.

We beseech, O Lord, Your sweet and compassionate Lordship,
to give us from Your love and even more to us from Your grace,
> that we might become worthy to be ministers of Your will.

May our lips put forth our prayers like incense[250]
> at all times before Your greatness.

Treat us favorably, O Lord, for You are Good,
and make Your triumphs reign over us
and give us bravery and courage by Your cross.

Exhort us, O Lord, to the love of Your sweet word
and prepare the paths before our feet.

Make us capable, O Lord, of Your heavenly call with perfect feet.

Open to us, O Lord, the gate of Your wedding feast
and adorn us in the holy clothing of Your spiritual garment
> and in splendor suitable to the living beauty of Your commandments.

We beseech You, O Lord Our God, the Hope of Our Salvation,
we praise You with our mouths
> to give glory, thanksgiving[251] and worship
> to Your Divinity.

---

[250] Cf. Psalm 141:2.

[251] The Armenian word used here, խոստովանութիւն, is usually translated confession, as to confess one's sins, but the sense here is of confess as "proclaim, acknowledge"; I have thus opted for thanksgiving, as a putative underlying Syriac word could convey both senses of confess and thanksgiving.

Առաւօտ մեծ ամենայն առաւօտուց
 եւ լուսատու ամենայն լուսաւորաց՝
ծագեա՛ ի մեզ զլոյս ճշմարտութեան քոյ.
ի բաց արա՛ ի մէնջ զմէգն եւ զխաւարն ստուերական գիշերոյ,
 զի մի՛ կուրացուսցէ զտեսիլս խորհրդոց մերոց,
կանխեա՛ առ մեզ զլոյս քոյ գիտութեան,
 զի գնասցուք ի ճանապարհս քո ուղիղս։
Յոյս մեր եւ Փրկիչ՝ բա՛ց մեզ զդուռն լուսոյ քոյ,
 եւ արժանի արա՛ փառաւորել զքեզ ի հայն ցնծութեան։
Մտցեն աղօթք իմ առաջի քո՝ Տէր,
 մի՛ դարձուցանէր ի մէնջ զերեսս քո վասն մեղաց մերոց,
 վրկիչ Հոգւոց մերոց եւ դարձուցիչ մոլորութեանց մերոց։
Ընկա՛լ զմեզ Տէր բարերար,
 եւ խլեա՛ զխոչ չարին առաջի ոտից մերոց,
 եւ բա՛րձ զգայթակղութիւն նորա ի գնացից մերոց։
Թագաւոր մեր եւ Աստուած՝ թո՛ղ մեզ զմեղս մեր եւ դյանցանս,
 զի դու ես քաւիչ մեր։
Լից զմեզ Փրկիչ՝ սրբութեամբ Հոգւոյդ սրբոյ բարերարի,
 զի դա է Հաշտեցուցիչ մեր ընդ կամս քո,
 եւ փառաւորեցցի անուն քո սուրբ։
Տո՛ւր մեզ Տէր՝ սիրտ նոր եւ Հոգի նորոգ,
 եւ լից սիրով քով սրբով։
Բա՛ց Տէր՝ զՀոանս քաղցր անձրեւաց քոց,
 եւ յորդեսցես ընդ ակօս ականջաց մերոց,
 զի զուարթասցին բոյսք սերման քոյ սրբոյ ի մեզ,
 որ արժանի արարեր զանարժանութիւնս մեր
     կարդալ զանուն քո սուրբ։
Ցանգեա՛ Տէր՝ եւ ամրացո՛ զամենայն խրամատութիւնս թշնամւոյն,
 զի մի՛ ճռաքաղ արասցէ զպտուղ կենդանութեան մտաց մերոց,
 եւ գրկիցիմք յօրհնութեանդ քումմէ։
Չի չիք ոք նման քեզ Տէր՝ ի սուրբս,
 եւ բարերար եւ պարգեւատու կարօտելոց եւ իրաւարար գրկելոց։
Արձարձեա՛ ի նուաղեալ յանձինս մեր զլոյս աստուածութեանդ քոյ,
 եւ օդն չարութեան մի՛ շնչեսցէ ի լոյս Հաւատոց մերոց,
 այլ ամաչեցեալ դարձցի յետս։
Մի՛ կարօտ առներ զմեզ ի քո շնորհացդ՝ Աստուած մեր,
 զի չիք ոք որ մխիթարէ զմեզ, եւ ոչ ոք է որ օգնէ,

O Morning greater than all mornings
>	that gives light to all luminaries,
shine on us the light of Your truth
and remove from us the fog and the darkness of the shadowy night,
>	lest it blind the vision of our thoughts;
hasten to us the light of Your knowledge
>	that we may go upon Your straight paths.
Our Hope and Savior, open to us the gate of Your light
and make us worthy to glorify You with voice of exultation.
Let my prayer come before you, O Lord,[252]
do not turn Your face away from us because of our sins,
>	O Savior of our souls who brings us back from our wanderings.
Receive us, O Beneficent Lord,
and sweep away every stumbling block of the evil one before our feet,
and remove his every obstacle from our paths.
Our King and God, forgive us our sins and transgressions,
>	for You are the one who pardons us.
Fill us, O Savior, with the holiness of Your Beneficent Holy Spirit,
>	for He is the one who reconciles us to Your will,
>	and may Your holy name be glorified.
Give to us, O Lord, a new heart,
>	fill it with Your holy love and a renewed spirit.[253]
Open, O Lord, the sweet streams of Your rains,
may You make them flow abundantly through the furrows of our ears
>	so that the plants of Your holy seed might rise up in us
>	whose unworthiness You have made worthy
>>		to invoke Your holy name.
Shore up, O Lord, and reinforce all the breaches of the enemy
>	lest that grape-gleaner glean the fruit of life from our minds
>	and we be deprived of Your blessing.
There is no one like You, O Lord, among the saints,
>	nor anyone so beneficent and generous to the needy and the truly indigent.
Kindle in our languishing souls the light of Your divinity,
>	and let not the air of evil blow out the light of our faith
>	but let it turn back ashamed.
Do not leave us deprived of Your grace, Our God,
>	for there is no one else to comfort us and no one to help us.

---

[252] Psalm 88:2.
[253] Cf. Ezekiel 36:26–27.

բա՛ց զա՛չ քո սուրբ՝ որ բացիչդ ես փակելոց,
    եւ արձակիչդ ես կապելոց,
    անդորրիչ նեղելոց,
    տուիչ կարօտելոց, մխիթարիչ զաւորաց,
    բժիշկ ախտացելոց, գտիչ կորուսելոց,
    քաւիչ յանցուցելոց եւ թողիչ մեղաց։
Դու ես շտեմարան բարութեան ի յերկինս եւ ի յերկրի։
Աղաչեմ գքաղցրութիւնդ քո Տէր՝
    մի՛ արգելուր ի մէնջ գողորմութիւն քո
    վասն բազում յանցանաց մերոց.
այլ բա՛ց մեզ Տէր գի մոցուք,
    եւ տու՛ր մեզ՝ գի ատցուք.
Վասն քո սուրբ անուանդ մի՛ յամօթ առներ գմեզ,
եւ մի՛ բարկանար մեզ Տէր,
եւ մի՛ չիշեր դանօրէնութիւնս մեր եւ դչարիս դոր գործեցաք։
Կամեաց Տէր, գի կեցցուք,
    եւ ողորմեաց, գի ապրեսցուք։
Ներեա՛ մեզ Տէր՝ գի եկեսցուք ի գիտութիւն ճշմարտութեան,
եւ մի՛ պահանջեր գմեզ ըստ մերում չարութեանս.
այլ տու՛ր ձեռն օգնականութեան,
    գի մի՛ ոտնհար լիցին թշնամիք մեր
    ի վրիպել գմեզ ի վրկութենէ քումմէ։
Կանգնեա՛ Տէր՝ գգլորումն մեր
եւ մի՛ տար գմեզ ի նախատինս դրացեաց մերոց։
Չի թեպետ եւ մեղաք,
    սակայն դու բարերար վիրկիչ Աստուած՝
մի՛ անտես առներ, այլ գթա՛ ի մեզ
եւ առաջնորդեա՛ մեզ ի նաւահանգիստ խաղաղութեան քո,
եւ հաստատեա՛ ի մեզ ի վերայ չինութեան ի կարգս արդարութեան.
Խափանեա՛ Տէր՝ գթշուառացուցիչս մեր,
եւ հալածիչք մեր դարձին յետս իւրեանց,
    եւ մեք հասցուք ի քաղցրութիւն օթեվանաց պատուիրանաց քոց
    յամենայն ժամ գոհանալ գքէն, եւ փառս տալ անուանդ քում սրբոյ։
Տէր վիրկիչ եւ Աստուած բազումողորմ, ողորմեա՛ Տէր՝
եւ մի՛ թողուր գիս վասն անուանդ քոյ սրբոյ։

Open Your holy right hand, You who open all closed things
>   who untie all the bound
>   who calm all the tormented,
>   who give to the needy, who comfort the mourning,
>   who heal the sick, who find the lost,
>   who pardon transgressors and who forgive sins.

You are the storehouse of every good thing in heaven and on earth.
I beseech Your sweetness, O Lord,
do not withhold Your mercy from us
>   because of our many transgressions,

but open to us, O Lord, so that we might enter
and give to us that we might receive.
Because of Your holy name do not put us to shame
and do not be angry with us, O Lord;
remember not our iniquities nor the evils that we have committed.
Will it, O Lord, that we might be saved
>   and have mercy that we might live.

Forgive us, O Lord, that we might come to the knowledge of truth,
and do not examine us according to our wickedness,
but give us Your helping hand
>   lest our enemies kick us
>   to turn us aside from Your salvation.

Raise us back up from our fall
and do not hand us over to the reproaches of our neighbors.
For although we have sinned,
>   nevertheless, You are a beneficent savior, O God.

Do not abandon us but have compassion on us,
lead us into the haven of Your peace,
and establish us in the structural institution of justice.[254]
Keep away, O Lord, those who would make us miserable
and may those who persecute us turn away,
>   and may we come into the sweet lodgings of Your commandments
>   to praise You at all times and to give glory to Your holy name.

Lord Savior and Most-merciful God, have mercy, O Lord,
>   and for the sake of Your holy name do not abandon me.

---

[254] There appears to be something missing or misspelled here; it is difficult to make sense of the Armenian as it stands.

Տէր գիտութեան եւ Աստուած ամենայն իմաստութեան,
տուր մեզ Տէր՝ զքո գիտութիւնդ եւ զքո կատարեալ իմաստութիւնդ
  դի զգաստացուք ի ցնորից մոլորութեանց,
  այնմ՝ որ եհան զմեզ ի դրախտէն փափկութեան,
  եւ մերժեաց զմեզ ի գիտութենէ սիրոյ քո կենդանութեան։
Հայեցի՛ Տէր՝ ակն ողորմութեան քոյ ի ցաւագին վիշտս մեր
  առ ի բժշկել զմեզ յանՃնարին տրտմութենէս,
  որ խառնեալ ունի բազում խոռվութիւնս։
Հայտեա՛ Տէր՝ ընդ մեզ վասն մեծագոր անուանդ քոյ,
եւ ողորմեա՛ մերոյ տկարութեանս։
Խափանեա՛ ի մէնջ Տէր՝ զվնասակար խորՀուրդս եւ զճայնս՝
  որ Հեռի են ի քաղցրութենէդ քումմէ։
Տէր գԹած՝ մի՛ Թողուր զմեզ ի սպառ,
  դի քո եմք ստեղծուածք։
Եւ մի՛ բարկանար մեզ,
  դի դու գԹած ես եւ մարդասէր։
Յիշեա՛ Տէր՝ զուխտն որ ընդ սիրելիսն քո,
եւ բարձ ի մէնջ զյաւարն ապիշութեան
  Թանձրամած ստուերին կորստեան,
  որ ընկղմէն զմիտս զգաստութեան մերոյ,
  եւ վարատէն ի քո խնամոցդ։
Տո՛ւր մեզ Տէր՝ գլոյս քո կենդանարար գսուրբ եւ գխաղաղարար
  ի պաՀպանուԹիւն եւ ի սրբուԹիւն մտաց մերոց։
Վասն բարեխոսուԹեան ՀրեշտակաՑ քոց ընկա՛լ գաղաչանս մեր.
եւ արժանաւորեա՛ դասի՛ ընդ նոսին՝
  օրՀնել եւ փառաւորել դքեզ անդադար ձայնիւ։
Յիշեա՛ եւ գիմ նուաստուԹիւնս,
եւ նայեա՛ ի խնդրուածս իմ.
եւ լուր ձայնի պաղատանաց մերոց,
  որպէս ուսուցեր՝ եԹէ
  յաղօԹս կացէք եւ մի՛ ձանձրանայք։
Եւ դարձեալ՝ Թէ յաղօԹս կացջիք, դի մի՛ մտջիք ի փորձութիւն։
Դարձեալ Հրամայեցեր՝ եԹէ չիք ինչ դոր խնդրիցէք յԱստուծոյ,
  եԹէ ոչ տացէ ձեզ։
Արդ այժմ մեք Տէր՝ ոչ վասն Հածութեան գործոց մերոց
  կամ յարդարութիւնս մեր ապաստան լեալ աղաչեմք դքեզ,
  այլ վասն ողորմուԹեան եւ մարդասիրուԹեան քոյ,
  դի քաղցր ես եւ բարերար,
    եւ մեք իբրեւ գպարտականս եւ գմեծամեղս կամք առաջի քո։

O Lord of knowledge and God of all wisdom,
give us, O Lord, Your knowledge and Your perfect wisdom
    so that we might recall ourselves from our courses of error,
    from that one who drove us out of that garden of delight,
    and who stripped us of the knowledge of love of Your life.[255]
May the eye of Your mercy, O Lord, look upon our painful afflictions
    with a view to healing us from excessive sorrows
    in which are mingled many troubles.
Reconcile us, O Lord, because of Your all-powerful name,
and have mercy on our weaknesses.
Keep away from us, O Lord, pernicious thoughts and voices
    that are far from Your sweetness.
O compassionate Lord, do not completely abandon us
    for we are Your creatures,
and do not be angry with us
    for You are compassionate and the Lover of mankind.
Remember, O Lord, the covenant with Your beloved
and remove from us the darkness of lethargy,
    the dense shadow of destruction
    that is inundating our sober minds
    and that drives us away from Your solicitude.
Give us, O Lord, Your holy, life-giving and peace-making light
    for the protection and the purification of our minds.
Through the intercession of Your angels receive our petitions
and make us worthy to be enrolled along with them
    to bless You and to give You glory with unending voice.
Remember also my base self,
have regard for my supplications,
and hear the voice of our invocations,
    just as You taught:
    "Pray and do not grow weary";[256]
and also, "If you pray do not enter into temptation".[257]
In another place You commanded, "If you ask nothing of God,
    then He will give you nothing".[258]
Even now, O Lord, we beseech You, not because of any satisfaction in our deeds
    nor that we have any confidence in our righteousness,
    but rather because of Your mercy and of Your love for mankind,
    for You are gentle and You are beneficent
        and like great sinners in debt we stand before You.

---

[255] Cf. Genesis 3:1–15, and cf. 2 Corinthians 11:3.
[256] Luke 18:1.
[257] Luke 22:40, 46.
[258] John 16:23, though in a negative formulation here.

Դու իբրեւ զՀայր գթած, իբրեւ զՏէր քաղցր՝ լուր աղօթից մերոց,
    զի գարթիցեն զգայութիւնք մեր խնդրել Համարձակ:
Բաց զականջս մեր լսել զձայն պաղատմանց քոց,
    եւ բացցին աչք սրտից մերոց Հայիլ առ քեզ ի բարձունս:
Լուր աղօթից մերոց եւ ընկալ զխնդրուածս մեր
եւ արա՛ զկամս մեր. լուր ճայնի աղօթից իմոց.
խնայեա՛ ի ժողովուրդս քո ի ժամանակի նեղութեան,
եւ փութա՛ առնել զգթութիւն քո:
Մի՛ բարկութեամբ քով խրատեր զմեզ,
եւ մի՛ սրտմտութեամբ քով ակն յանդիման առներ զմեզ.
    զի ժողովուրդ քո եմք, եւ ձեռակերտք ձեռաց քոց,
    եւ ստեղծուած մատանց քոց:
Ի քո պատկեր Հաստատեցեր զմեզ,
    եւ Հոգի առ ի քէն փչեցեր ի մեզ.
մի՛ յալիտեան բարկանար մեզ, եւ մի՛ ի բացէ առնիր ի ծառայից քոց:
Մինչ մոյորեալք էաք՝ դարձուցեր զմեզ,
    շարշարեալք՝ եւ փրկեցեր,
    ցրուեալք՝ եւ ժողովեցեր,
    խաւարեալք՝ եւ լուսաւորեցեր,
    արգելեալք՝ եւ Հաներ յանդորր,
    կապեալք՝ եւ արձակեցեր ի կապանաց.
անյոյս էաք, եւ կոչեցեր զմեզ ի յոյս քո.
մեղաւոր էաք, եւ կամեցար զի արդարասցուք.
ոչ խնդրեցաք՝ եւ եկիր առ մեզ, եւ արեամբ քով փրկեցեր զմեզ,
    եւ ի ձեռն քո ծանեաք մեք զմեզ.
ոչ ճանճրացուցաք մեք զքեզ խնդրուածովք, եւ իջեր ի դժոխս.
մեք Հանապազ բարկացուցանեմք զքեզ, եւ դու եկիր վասն մեր
    յանարգանս.
անչափ էին անօրէնութիւնք մեր առաջի քո,
    եւ փրկեցեր զմեզ շարշարանօք քոյովք:
Եւ այժմ աղաչեմք զքեզ՝ Տէր եւ Աստուած մեր,
երկիրպագանեմք եւ գոՀանամք զքէն, եւ փառաւորեմք զողորմութիւն քո:
Ի ձեռն սիրելի որդւոյ քոյ լուր աղօթից մերոց,
եւ ընկալ զխնդրուածս մեր. տես զնախատինս մեր,
նայեա՛ ի տառապանս մեր,
եւ գթացի սիրտ քո ի ժողովուրդ քո՝
    որ մատնեցաւ յաւար եւ ի յափշտակութիւն:

You, like a compassionate father, like a gentle Lord, hear our prayers
> that our senses might be roused to boldly seek You.
Open our ears to hear the sound of Your words,
> and may the eyes of our hearts be opened to look upon You in the heights.
Hear our prayer and receive our supplications;
fulfill our desires and hear the sound of my prayer,
spare Your people in their time of tribulation
and hasten to show them Your compassion.
Do not chastise us in Your anger
nor reprove us in Your wrath,
> for we are Your people, the work of Your hands
> and the creation of Your fingers.
In Your image You fashioned us
> and You blew a spirit from You into us.[259]
Never be angry with us and do not remove Yourself from Your servants.
When we were going astray You turned us back,
> were committing evil You saved us,
> were being scattered You gathered us in;
> were in darkness You enlightened us,
> were being imprisoned You brought us to safety,
> were being bound You loosened us from our bonds;
when we were without hope You called us into Your hope,
when we were sinners You willed that we become righteous.
We did not seek it but You came to us and by Your blood You saved us,
> and through You we came to know ourselves.
We did not trouble You with our entreaties yet You descended into hell,
we constantly made You angry yet You came because of our insults,
our iniquities were beyond measure before You
> yet You saved us by Your sufferings.
And now we beseech You, Our Lord and Our God,
we worship You and we praise You and we glorify Your mercy.
Through Your beloved Son hear our prayer
receive our petitions and behold our offences,
look upon our afflictions,
and may Your heart have compassion upon Your people
> who were handed over to plunder and to pillage.

---

[259] Cf. Genesis 1:26, 2:7.

Հայեա՛ եւ ի սուրբ տաճարս քո՛ որ աւերեցաւ,
    եւ ի սեղանս քո՛ որ կործանեցաւ,
    եւ ի քահանայս քո՛ որ կոտորեցան,
    եւ յուխտս քո՛ որ ցրուեցան,
    եւ ի կուսակարանս քո՛ որ կքեցան ի ցրումն եւ ի յաւարումն։
Յաճախեաց ամօթ մեր,
ցրուեցաւ ժողովուրդ քո,
Հեղաւ իբրեւ զջուր ուխտ քո սուրբ։
Խնայեա՛ ի մեզ Տէր՛ զի մատնեցաք ի նախատինս
    եւ ի չարչարանս եւ յամօթ։
Առ ո՞վ աղաղակեսցուք,
    զի լուիցէ աղօթից մերոց.
առ ո՞վ երթիցուք,
    զի աՀա ծառայ քո եմք։
Խրատեցեր զմեզ բարկութեամբ.
    արա՛ առ մեզ գողորմութիւն քո։
Կեղեցան կեանք մեր.
    մի՛ յապաղեր՛ զի մի՛ վՀատիցիմք։
Մի՛ երկայնամիտ լինիր ի նեղութիւնս մեր եւ ի տառապանս.
    որպէս աղաչեաց զքեզ մարգարէն քո՛
    որ նեղեալն էր իբրեւ զմեզ եւ ասէր.
    մի՛ խրատեր զմեզ երկայնամտութեամբ։
Լո՛ւր աղօթից մերոց,
    որպէս լուար Մովսիսի սիրելոյ քոյ.
եւ մի՛ ատցեն վրէժմ թշնամիք մեր իբրեւ զՓարաւոն,
    որ նեղեաց զժողովուրդ քո։
Ընկա՛լ զխնդրուածս մեր,
    որպէս ընկալար զխնդրուածս Յեսուայ որդւոյ Նաւեայ,
    եւ սատակեցաւ Ամաղէկ եւ բարձաւ յիշատակ նորա։
Դու ես Աստուած առաջնորդ, եւ Տէր եւ թագաւոր վերջնոցս։
Լուար Մովսիսի, եւ ընկղմեցեր զՓարաւոն.
լուար Աչարոնի, եւ արգելաւ մաՀ բարկութեան։
Դարձուցեր զգասումն բարկութեան քոյ
    ի ճեռն նախանձախնդրին քո ՓենեՀէսի.

Look upon Your holy temple that was destroyed
> upon Your altar that was laid waste
> upon Your priests who were killed
> upon Your congregations who were scattered
> and upon Your Testaments that were sealed up in dispersion and plunder.

Our shame has increased,
Your people are scattered,
Your holy covenant has been poured out like water.
Hasten to us, O Lord, for we have been handed over to reproach
> and torments and to shame.

To whom shall we cry
> that he might listen to our prayers?

To whom shall we go
> for behold, we are Your servants.

Admonish us in Your anger,
> show us Your compassion.

Our lives have been wounded,
> do not delay lest we become discouraged.

Do not suffer patiently our torments or our afflictions,
> as Your prophet, who was tormented as we are,
> prayed to You and said,
> "Do not admonish us with long-suffering".[260]

Hear our prayer
> as You heard [the prayer] of Moses, Your beloved,[261]

and let not our enemies take vengeance on us as Pharaoh did,
> who tormented Your people.[262]

Receive our petitions
> as You received the petitions of Joshua, the son of Nun,
> when Amalek was slain and his memory was wiped away.[263]

You are the God of the first ones and Lord and King of the last ones.
You listened to Moses and You drowned Pharaoh,[264]
You heard Aaron and an angry death was avoided.[265]
You brought back Your angry wrath
> through Phinehas, Your avenger.[266]

---

[260] I am unable to find the source of this quotation.

[261] Cf., e.g., Numbers 11:2, 21:7.

[262] Cf. Exodus 8:30–32.

[263] Cf. Exodus 17:8–16, though there is no mention of Joshua speaking to God, nor was the memory of Amalek wiped away.

[264] Cf. Exodus 14:26–31.

[265] Cf. Numbers 12:9–15.

[266] Cf. Numbers 25:6–15.

օգնեցեր Յեսուայ, եւ յամօթ եղեն թշնամիք նորա։
Լուար Սամփսոնի ի ժամանակի նեղութեան,
    եւ խնդրեցեր գվրէժս յայլազգեացն՝ որք բարկացուցին զքեզ։
Առեր եւ գվրէժն Դաւթի ի Սաուղայ՝ որ Հալածէր զնա,
    եւ Հաներ նմա իրաունս յԱքիտողոմայ՝ որ խորվեցոյցն զնա։
Քաւեա՞ց գծողովուրդն քո Սամուէլ առաջի քո,
    եւ ցուցեր գմեծութիւն քո,
    փոխանակ զի անարգեցին գԹագաւորութիւն քո։
Արարեր իրաունս Եղիայի Հալածականի,
    եւ սատակեցեր չաղազս նորա զմարզարէսն Բահաղու։
Պահեցաւ Միքիէ բազում ողորմութեամբ քով,
    եւ անկաւ կործանեցաւ սատակեցաւ Հալածիչն իւր ի պատերազմի։
Յուցեր գաքանչելիս քո ի Հալածիչսան Եղիսէի
    ի ժամանակի իբրեւ մտին ի չիրմին՝ տեսին գմեծութիւն քո։
Լուար Եզեկիայի ի ժամանակի
    իբրեւ արգելեալ պաչարեալ կայր ի նեղութեան,
    եւ ցուցեր գզորութիւն քո ի Սենեքարիմ եւ ի զօրս նորա։
Լուար Եսայեայ եւ օգնեցեր Յովսափաթու,
    եւ խնդրեցեր գվրէժս նեղչաց նոցա։
Լուար Յովնանու ի խորոց անդնդոց ծովուն ի փորչ ձկանն
    եւ ալեացն որ պաչարեցին զնա։
Լուար Դանիէլի ի ժամանակի իբրեւ ընկեցին զնա ի գուբն,
    եւ ապրեցուցեր զնա ի բերանոյ առիւծուցն։
Օգնեցեր Անանիայի եւ ընկերաց նորա ի Հնոցի Հրոյն,
    եւ եկեր բոցն բորբոքեալ զչարախոսս նոցա։
Լուար Մուրթքէի եւ Եսթերայ ի նեղութեան իւրեանց,
    փրկեցեր գծողովուրդ քո, եւ յամօթ եղեւ Համան Հալածիչն։

You helped Joshua and his enemies were put to shame.[267]
You heard Samson in a time of tribulation
    and You sought vengeance on those foreigners who had angered You.[268]
You also wrought the vengeance of David on Saul who was persecuting him[269]
    and You gave him the rights from Absalom who had risen up against him.[270]
Samuel pardoned Your people in Your presence,
    and You manifested Your greatness
    insofar as they had rejected Your kingdom.[271]
You rendered justice to the persecuted Elijah
    and on his behalf You slew the prophets of Baal.[272]
Micah was preserved by Your great mercy
    and his persecutor fell, was overthrown and slain in battle.[273]
You manifested Your wondrous deeds to the persecutors of Elisha,
    when they came to the tomb, they saw Your greatness.[274]
You heard Ezekiel at the time
    when he was obstructed and blockaded in straits
and You showed Your power to Sennacherib and his armies.[275]
You heard Isaiah and You helped Jehosaphat
    and You sought vengeance on their oppressors.
You heard Jonah from the great depths of the sea from the belly of the fish[276]
    and from the waves that surrounded him.[277]
You heard Daniel at the time they threw him into the den
    and You saved him from the mouths of the lions.[278]
You helped Ananiah and his companions in the fiery furnace
    and the burning flames consumed those who were slandering them.[279]
You heard Mordechai and Esther in their affliction,
    You saved Your people, and You put Haman, their
    persecutor, to shame.[280]

---

[267] There is no clear reference for this; cf. Joshua 1–12 for his conquests.
[268] Cf. Judges 16:28–31.
[269] Cf. 1 Samuel 31:1–13.
[270] Cf. 2 Samuel 18:15.
[271] Cf. 1 Samuel 8:4–22, 2 Samuel 7:8–16.
[272] Cf. 1 Kings 18:17–40.
[273] The reference here is not clear; Judges 18?
[274] Cf. 2 Kings 13:14–23.
[275] Cf. 2 Kings 19:35–36.
[276] Curiously, the word for fish is used here, as the Armenian is the only version of Jonah that specifically reads whale, as the traditional story maintains.
[277] Cf. Jonah 2:1–10.
[278] Cf. Daniel 6:16–28.
[279] Cf. Daniel 3:13–22.
[280] Cf. Esther 4:8–18, 14:1–19, 7:1–10.

Հանէր գերեմիա ի գրոյ տղմոյն,
	եւ եռուր զնա ի շնորհս եւ յողորմութիւն
	առաջի արքային բաբելացւոց։
Խնայեա՛ Տէր ի ժողովուրդս քո՝ որ չարչարեցաւ.
խնայեա՛ Տէր եւ լուր աղօթից իմոց,
	զի տաճար սրբութեան ատեցաւ,
	եւ տեղին քաւութեան պատարագաց կործանեցաւ։
Քահանայք մեր կոտորեցան, եւ ճորճ ի գլուխ եղեն կուսանք մեր։
խնայեա՛ ի մեզ՝ Տէր մեր.
խնայեա՛ յաղքատս եւ ի տնանկս եւ ի տառապեալս,
	զի չի՛ք տեղի Հանգստեան, ուր դիցեն զգլուխս իւրեանց։
Ճանապարհք մեր թափուր են, եւ շաւիղք մեր անհետք.
աչք մեր խաւարեցան, եւ սիրտք մեր մաշեցան։
Լուր աղօթից մերոց եւ ընկալ զխնդրուածս մեր։
Եւ թէ մեք անօրինեցաք եւ դառնացուցաք զքեզ,
դու՛ Տէ՛ր ըստ մեծի անուանդ քո խնայեա՛ ի մեզ։
Չիք մեր այլ յոյս եւ ոչ տուն ապաւինի եւ Հանգստեան տեղի
	քան զքեզ արտաքոյ,
զի քո են երկինք եւ քո է երկիր,
քո է տիւ եւ քո է գիշեր,
զարեգակն եւ զլուսինն դու Հաստատեցեր։
Զքեզ փառաւորեն ծովք այեօք իւրեանց,
	եւ եղեր նոցա սահման եւ ոչ ելանեն ընդ Հրամանս քո։
Կապեալ կայ ծով աւազով եւ կատարէ զՀրամանս քո։
Քեզ Հայեցեալ սպասեն ամենայն բնութիւնք,
	եւ ձեռն քո բաւական է ամենայն արարածոց քոց.
	եւ չիք ինչ՝ որ կարէ Հակառակ կալ կամաց քոց։
Քո են լուսաւորք երկնից,
	եւ Հողմք եւ մրրիկ զանուն քո փառաւորեն։
Քեզ Հայեցեալ սպասեն գազանք անապատի,
	թռչունք երկնից եւ ձկունք ծովուն։
Արի՛ օգնել մեզ մեծագոր զօրութեամբ քով,
	զի ծանիցեն ամենայն ազգք երկրի, զի չիք իբրեւ զքեզ,
	եւ չիք այլ Աստուած բաց ի քէն։

You brought Jeremiah out from the mud pit
>and You granted him grace and mercy
>before the king of the Babylonians.[281]
Spare, O Lord, Your people who have been tormented;
spare me, O Lord, and hear my prayer
>for Your holy temple is in ruins
>and the place of expiatory sacrifices has been destroyed.
Our priests have been slaughtered and our virgins are in deep mourning.
Spare us, Our Lord,
spare the poor, those in poverty and in affliction,
>for they have no resting place where they might put their heads.
Our roads are deserted and our paths overgrown,
our eyes have grown dark and our hearts have shriveled up.
Hear our prayers and receive our petitions.
And though we have committed iniquity and have turned away from You,
You, O Lord, spare us according to Your great name.
There is no other hope for us nor any other house of refuge
>nor any place of rest apart from You,
for Yours are the heavens and Yours is the earth,[282]
Yours is the day and Yours is the night[283]
and You established the sun and the moon.[284]
The seas with their waves glorify You
>and You set down their border,
>at Your command they do not go beyond.[285]
The sea is bound by sand and fulfills Your command.[286]
All natures look to You and serve You
>and Your power is sufficient for all Your creatures,
>and there is nothing that can stand against Your will.
Yours are the luminaries of the heavens
>and the winds and storms glorify Your name.[287]
To You do the beasts of the wilderness look and serve,
>as do the birds of the skies and the fish of the sea.
Come to our aid with Your mighty power
>so that all the nations of the earth might know that there is no one like You
>and that there is no other God apart from You.

---

[281] Cf. Jeremiah 38:7–13.
[282] Psalm 89:11.
[283] Psalm 74:16.
[284] Psalm 74:16.
[285] Cf. Proverbs 8:29.
[286] Cf. Jeremiah 5:22.
[287] Cf. Daniel 3:40, 42–43, Psalm 148:8.

Ասաց Փարաւոն՝ ո՞վ է Աստուած.
    և ընկղմեցեր զնա իբրև զպատերազմող ի ծովն աշագին։
Համարեցաւ զքեզ Սենեքարիմ իբրև զղիան Հեթանոսաց,
    և արարեր զնա առակ նշաւակի, զի ցուցեր նմա զմեծութիւն քո։
Օգնեցեր Մատաթիայի որ եղև քինանախանձու օրինաց քոց։
Լուար Յուդայի և Շմաւոնի և եղբարց նորա,
    և օգնեցեր նոցա աքանչելեօք ի մարտս պատերազմաց՝
    զոր արարեր ի ձեռն նոցա։
Զարթիցեն գթութիւնք քո՝ Տէր.
Թո՛ղ զմնացուածս ժողովրդեան քոյ՝ որ մատնեցաւ յաւար.
արա՛ նորոգումն տաճարի քոյ յալուրս մեր.
բարձրացո՛ զգլուխս մեր՝ որ կորացան յալուրս մեր ի մեղս մեր.
ընկա՛լ զպատարագս ժողովրդեան քոյ,
    և քաղցրացին քեզ աղօթք մեր։
Բացցին դրունք փակեալք, և կանգնեցցին դրունք կործանեալք։
Ժողովեսցին ժողովուրդք գերեալք,
    և ուրախ եղիցուք ի նորոգութիւն տաճարի քոյ յալուրս մեր։
Գոչեսցէ առաջի քո արիւն արդարոցն,
    և եղիցի քեզ ի Հաճութիւն իբրև զբուրվառ խնկոց։
Խնայեա՛ Տէր ի ժողովուրդս քո և ի սուրբ ուխտ քո՝
    որ անկաւ ի ձեռս անօրինաց,
    և ուտն Հարին ի վերայ բեկմանս մերոյ։
Սովոր իսկ ես՝ Թագաւոր մեր, ցուցանել զգթութիւն քո ի մեզ.
    և սովոր իսկ են ծառայք խնդրել Հանապազ յողորմութեանց քոց։
Ի քաղցրութիւն մարդասիրութեանդ ապաւինեալ աղաչեմք զքեզ,
    զի և ի չարաց ոչ արգելուս զբարերարութիւն քո։
Մաղես զարեգակն ի վերայ չարեաց և բարեաց,
    և ածես անձրև ի վերայ արդարոց և մեղաւորաց։
Քանզի Հանապազ գիտեմք, եթէ սովոր իսկ ես լսել նեղելոց.
    օգնեցեր Հայածականաց,
    զօրացուցեր զտկարս,
    բարձրացուցեր զխոնարՀս,
    ապրեցուցեր զչարչարեալս,
    փրկեցեր զյափշտակեալս.
    լուսաւորեցեր զխաւարեալս,
    լցուցեր զքաղցեալս,

Pharaoh said, "Who is God?",[288]
    and You drowned him like an adversary in that dreadful sea.[289]
Sennacharib accounted You one of the demons of the pagans,
    and You made him an object of mockery, for You showed him Your greatness.[290]
You helped Mattathias who became a zealot for Your laws.[291]
You heard Judah and Simeon and his brothers
    and You helped them with mighty deeds
    in those battles that You wrought through them.[292]
Let Your compassion rise up, O Lord,
Forgive the remnant of Your people who were handed over to plunder,
Restore Your temple in our days;
Raise up our heads which are bent down in our days for our sins,
Receive the sacrifices of Your people
    and may our prayers be sweet to You.
May closed gates be opened and demolished gates rebuilt.
May Your scattered people be gathered together
    and may there be joy in the restoration of Your temple in our captivity.
May the blood of the just call out before You
    and may [that blood] be as pleasing to You as a censer of incense.
Spare, O Lord, Your people and Your holy covenant
    which has fallen into the hands of the impious
    who have trampled upon our brokenness.
You are indeed accustomed, Our King, to show Your compassion to us
    and Your servants are indeed accustomed to seek Your mercies at all times.
Trusting in Your sweet love for mankind we pray to You
    for even from evil ones You do not withhold Your beneficence.
You shine the sun upon both the evil and the good
    and You pour down rain upon both just and sinners.[293]
Because we know always that You are accustomed to listen to those in straits:
    You have helped those who are persecuted,
    You have given strength to the weak,
    You have raised up the lowly,
    You have saved those in torment,
    You have delivered those who have been plundered,
    You have enlightened those in darkness,
    You have made rich those who are poor,

---

[288] Exodus 5:2.
[289] Cf. Exodus 14:26–31.
[290] Cf. 1 Kings 18:13–19:37.
[291] Cf. 1 Maccabees 2:1–70.
[292] Cf. Judges 1:2–21.
[293] Matthew 5:45.

մեծացուցեր գաղքատս,
կանգնեցեր գտնանկս։
Զայս ամենայն արարեր յամենայն դարս ծառայից քոց՝
որք յուսացան ի քեզ։
Դու ես որ ցուցեր մեզ՝ թէ ես եմ առաջին եւ ես եմ յապայ։
Դու ես Աստուած առաջնոգն եւ թագաւոր վերջնոցս.
քո է աշխարհ, եւ քո է աշխարհն երկինք
եւ ամենայն որ ինչ եղեւն եւ որ լինելոցն է առ յապա։
Առ ո՞վ երթիցուք, գի լուիցէ մեզ
ու՞մ Հայեսցուք, գի եկեսցէ օգնականութիւն.
ու՞մ ակն կալցուք, գի փրկեսցէ գմեզ.
առ ո՞վ աղաղակեսցուք, գի ընկալցի գաղօթս մեր
Քո եմք, եւ դու ես Աստուած մեր,
եւ քեզ վայելէ փառք իշխանութիւն եւ պատիւ,
այժմ եւ միշտ եւ յաւիտեանս յաւիտենից. ամէն։

>   You have exalted the poor,
>   You have raised up the weak.
> All these things You have done in every generation for Your servants who hope in You.
> You are the one who made manifest to us that "I am the first and I am the last".[294]
> You are the God of the forefathers and the King of the last ones,
> Yours is the earth, and Yours is the earth, the heavens
>   and everything that has come to be and that will come to be in the end.
> To whom shall we go who might hear us?
> To whom shall we look that help might come to us?
> For whom shall we look that he might save us?
> Upon whom shall we call that he might receive our prayers?
> We are Yours and You are our God
>   and to You is fitting glory, authority and honor,
> now and always and unto the ages of ages. Amen.

---

[294] Revelation 1:17; see also 1:8, 21:6, 22:13.

Է

Աղօթք նորին դարձեալ:

Աղաչեմ զքեզ՝ Քրիստոս փրկիչ աշխարհի,
  նայեաց յիս եւ ողորմեաց ինձ.
  փրկեա՛ զիս ի բազմութենէ անօրէնութեանց իմոց,
  քանզի անարգեցի զամենայն զբարիս
    զոր արարեր յիս ի մանկութենէ իմէ:
Զիս զտխմար եւ զանմիտ՝
  արարեր անօթ լի գիտութեամբ եւ իմաստութեամբ.
  Յածախեաց յիս զչորհս քո.
  լցո՛ զքաղց իմ, եւ զծարաւ իմ զովացո՛,
  եւ լուսաւորեա՛ զխսաւրեալ միտս իմ,
  եւ ժողովեա՛ ի մոլորութենէ զխորհուրդս իմ:
Եւ այժմ երկիր պագանեմ եւ աղաչեմ,
  անկանիմ եւ Հայցեմ խոստովանելով քում բարերարութեանդ.
դադարեցո՛ յիս զՀոսանս չնորհի քոյ
եւ պահեա՛ ինձ զնա ի գանձի քում,
  դի դարձեալ տացես ինձ զնա յայնմիկ:
Մի՛ բարկանար ինձ մարդասէր,
  դի ոչ Հանդուրժեմ սպառնալեաց քոց:
Յաղագս այստրիկ աղաչեմ ժտելով,
առաւել քան զչափ յածախեա՛ յիս.
  վասն դի լեզու իմ տկարացաւ՝
  ոչ կարելով խոսիլ զչնորհէդ քումէ:
Հիացան եւ միտք իմ՝
  ոչ բերելով զբազմութիւն այեաց նորա:
Կերպարան եւ ճառագայթ օրհնելոյ Հօր.
դադարեցո՛ աստ ի յիս ի Հոսանաց նորա,
  դի իբրեւ զչուր բղղակիդեցց զերիկամունս եւ զսիրտ իմ.
արդ դարձեալ պարզեւեա՛ ինձ զնա, եւ կեցո՛ զիս յարքայութեան քում:
Մի՛ յիշեր զանօրէնութիւնս իմ.
յանդգնիմ Հայցեմ, տուր ինձ զլնդրուածս իմ.
ծածկեա՛ զանօրէնութիւնս իմ յամենայն գիտութեանդ քումէ.
ընկալ զարտասուս. մերձեցի՛ առ քեզ ողբումն իմ.
յիշեա՛ զարտասուս իմ զոր արտասուեցի առաջի սրբոց վկայից քոց,
  դի զթացիս յիս յալուր յայնմիկ,
  եւ ծածկեսցես ընդ Հովանաւ թեւոց չնորհի քոց:
Քանզի թէ արասցես ինձ ըստ տնօրէնութեան իմոյ,
  եղուկ ես թշուառականս՝ դի՞նչ ինձ լինիցի:

PART VII:

MORE PRAYERS FROM [EPHREM]

I pray to you, O Christ, Savior of the world.
    Look upon me and have mercy on me.
    Save me from the multitude of my iniquities,
        for I have disdained all the good things
            You have done for me since I was a child.
Foolish and stupid as I am now,
    You fashioned me as a vessel filled with knowledge and wisdom.
    Multiply in me Your graces.
    Satisfy my hunger, quench my thirst,
        enlighten my darkened mind,
        and focus my thoughts from wandering.
Now I worship You and pray to You.
I prostrate myself and beg You, confessing Your goodness.
Discontinue for me the stream of Your mercy
and keep it for me in Your treasury
    so that You might give it back to me on that day.
Do not be angry with me, O Lover of mankind,
    for I cannot endure Your threats.
For this reason I fervently beg you,
increase beyond measure Your grace in me,
    for my tongue has grown weak,
        unable to speak of it;
my mind is seized in amazement,
    unable to bear the multitude of its waves.
O Image and Radiance of the Father's blessing,
cease its flow into me here
    so that like fire it may enflame my insides and my heart.
Now again grant me Your grace, and let me live in Your kingdom.
Do not remember my depravity.
I boldly ask You, grant me my requests.
Hide my iniquities from all Your omniscience.
Accept my tears. Let my lament draw near to You.
Remember the tears I cried before Your holy martyrs
    so that You might show me compassion on that day;
    may You cover me with the protection of the wings of Your grace.
For if You respond according to my iniquities,
    miserable wretch that I am, what shall become of me?

Իսկ ես լալով եւ արտասուօք պաղատիմ քում մարդասիրութեանդ,
որկեամ զիս ի բազմութենէ անօրէնութեանց իմոց,
եւ պարգեւեաս ինձ զարքայութիւնդ քո.
վիս ի մեղաւորս ցոյց զանձառ քո մարդասիրութիւնդ.
արամ զիս Հաղորդ աւազակին,
   այնմ՝ որ միով բանիւ ժառանգորդ եղեւ դրախտին.
զոր կատարելոց է խոստացեալն, անդր զիս մուծցես:
Փառք Հօր Արարչին մերում, եւ Որդւոյ փրկչին մերում,
եւ Հոգւոյն սրբոյ նորոգողին մերում
յանսպառ եւ յանեղծանելի յաւիտեան:

So with weeping and with tears, I entreat Your love of mankind,
  save me from the multitude of my iniquities,
  and grant me Your kingdom.
  Show me, a sinner, Your ineffable love for mankind.
  Make me like the thief
      who, with one word, became an heir to paradise.[295]
  To that place promised to the perfected, will You take me?
Glory to the Father, our Creator, and to the Son, our Savior,
  and to the Holy Spirit, our Restorer,
  unto unending and indelible eternity.

---

[295] Cf. Luke 23:43.

Լ

Աղօթք նորին դարձեալ:

Տէր Աստուած զօրութեանց՝
 աղաչեմ զքո բարերարութիւնդ,
 ժտեմ եւ հայցեմ ի քէն,
տո՛ւր ինձ տապան ապրեցուցիչ որպէս Նոյին՝
 ապրել ինձ ի հրեղէն ծովէն եւ յանդնդային հրահոսանցն,
 յանչէջ արգելանէն եւ յանհնարին վտանգից:
Չի դու ես Տէր Աստուած՝ որ զրանդ աստուածային ծածկեցեր
 եւ ի ծառայական կերպս իջեր վասն մեր,
 եւ զլեղի ի քիմս առեր, եւ ապտակ ի ծնօտս ընկալար:
Եւ այժմ աղաչեմ զքեզ
 ազատեա՛ զիս ի դառն ծառայութենէ սատանայի.
 զի յորժամ գձեռս իմ ի վեր ունելով աղօթեմ,
 անօրէն սատանայ խաբէ եւ ունայն հանէ զիս յաղօթից իմոց:
Լեր ինձ Աստուած՝ բերդ ամուր եւ աշտարակ հզօր,
եւ կործեմ զիս ի բերանոյ առիւծուն՝
 որ հանապազ կամի կլանել զիս.
 զի ընդ պիտանիսն ի բարձունս
 փառաւորեցից զՀայր եւ զՈրդի եւ զՍուրբ Հոգիդ,
այժմ եւ միշտ եւ յաւիտեանս յաւիտենից. ամէն:

PART VIII:

MORE PRAYERS FROM [EPHREM]

Lord, God of hosts,
    I pray to Your beneficence,
    I beseech and entreat You,
give me an ark as a deliverer as You did to Noah[296]
    to save me from the fiery sea and from the unending torrents of fire,
    from inextinguishable imprisonment and horrible punishments.
For You are the Lord God who concealed Your divine Word
    and in the form of a servant You came down on our behalf,[297]
    You received gall on Your palate[298] and You took blows on Your cheeks.[299]
And now I pray to You,
    free me from the bitterness of servitude to Satan,
    and when I pray holding up my hands,
    raise me by my prayers from the deceit of that wicked Satan.
Be to me, O God, a strong fortress and a mighty tower,
and snatch me out of the mouth of the lion
    who constantly wishes to devour me,[300]
    so that with all the advantages on high
    I might glorify You, Father, Son and Holy Spirit,
    now and always and unto the ages of the ages. Amen.

---

[296] Cf. 2 Peter 2:5.
[297] Cf. Philippians 2:7.
[298] Cf. Matthew 27:48, and parallels.
[299] Cf. Matthew 27:30, and parallels.
[300] Cf. 1 Peter 5:8.

Select Bibliography

Collected Works

Armenian

Srboyn Ep'remi Matenagrut'iwnk' [*The Writings of St. Ephrem*; in Armenian]. 4 volumes. Venice: S. Ghazar Press, 1836.

Syriac

Assemani, Joseph S., ed. *Sancti Patris Nostri Ephraem Syri Opera Omnia quae exstant graece, syriace, latine, in sex tomos distributa*. 6 volumes. Rome: , 1732–1743.

Lamy, Thomas J., ed. *Sancti Ephraemi Syri Hymni et Sermones*. 4 volumes. Machliniae: H. Dessain, 1882–1902.

Greek

Frantzolas, Konstantinos G., ed. *Hosiou Ephraim tou Syrou Erga* [*The Works of St. Ephrem the Syrian*; in Greek]. 7 volumes. Thessaloniki: Perivoli tis Panagias, 1988–1998.

The Prayers

Girk' Aghōt'its' [*Book of Prayers*; in Armenian]. Constantinople: Patriarchal Press, 1734.

Girk' Aghōt'its' asats'eal Srboyn Ep'remi Khurin Asorwoy [*A Book of Prayers composed by St. Ephrem the Syrian Priest*; in Armenian]. Jerusalem: St. James Press, 1933. Pp. 43–233.

Anushvard [Anoushavan Srpazan Tanielian]. "Yogewor Margritner." *Hask* 50 (1981) 43, 79, 123–124, 186, 221–222, 264–265, 324–325, 361–362, 402–403.

Arabajyan, A. "Surb Ep'rem Khuri Asori (306–379) ["St. Ephrem the Syrian Priest (306–379)"; in Armenian]." *Ejmiacin* (1980) 11, 28–30.

Ohanean, Vahan. *Surb Ep'rem Asori Yordorak Apashkharut'ean Zorawor Aghōt'k'* [*St. Ephrem the Syrian, An Exhortation to Repentance, Powerful Prayers*; in Armenian]. Venice: S. Ghazar Press, 2005.

Xach'atryan, Tigran. "*Surb Ep'rem Asori* [*St. Ephrem the Syrian*; in Armenian]." *Gandzasar* 3 (1993) 151–173.

Xach'atryan, Tigran. *Surb Ep'rem Asori Hordorak Apashkharutyan Zorawor Aghōt'k'* [*St. Ephrem the Syrian, An Exhortation to Repentance, Powerful Prayers*; in Armenian]. Erevan, 2005.

OTHER EDITED WORKS AND TRANSLATIONS

Akinean, Nersēs, ed. *Srboyn Epʻremi Asorwoy Meknutʻiwn Gortsotsʻ Aṛakʻelotsʻ* [*St. Ephrem the Syrian, Commentary on the Acts of the Apostles*; in Armenian]. Vienna: Mkhitarean tparan, 1921.

Amar, Joseph P., ed. *Jacob of Serug: A Metrical Homily on Holy Mar Ephrem*. Patrologia Orientalis 47.1[209]. Turnhout: Brepols, 1995.

Avdoyan, Levon. *Pseudo-Yovhannēs Mamikonean, The History of Tarōn*. Occasional Papers and Proceedings; Suren D. Fesjian Academic Publications 6. Atlanta: Scholars Press, 1993.

Azéma, Yvan, ed. *Théodoret de Cyr, Correspondance III*. Sources Chrétiennes, 111. Paris: Cerf, 1965.

Beck, Edmund, ed. *Des Heiligen Ephraem des Syrers Carmina Nisibena*. CSCO 218–219, 240–241. Louvain: Peeters, 1961, 1963.

Beck, Edmund, ed. *Des Heiligen Ephraem des Syrers Hymnen auf Abraham Kidunaya und Julianos Saba*. CSCO 322–323. Louvain: Peeters, 1972.

Beck, Edmund, ed. *Des Heiligen Ephraem des Syrers Hymnen contra Haereses*. CSCO 169–170. Louvain: Peeters, 1957.

Beck, Edmund, ed. *Des Heiligen Ephraem des Syrers Hymnen de Ecclesia*. CSCO 198–199. Louvain: Peeters, 1960.

Beck, Edmund, ed. *Des Heiligen Ephraem des Syrers Hymnen de Fide*. CSCO 154–155. Louvain: Peeters, 1955.

Beck, Edmund, ed. *Des Heiligen Ephraem des Syrers Hymnen de Ieiunio*. CSCO 246–247. Louvain: Peeters, 1964.

Beck, Edmund, ed. *Des Heiligen Ephraem des Syrers Hymnen de Nativitate (Epiphania)*. CSCO 186–187. Louvain: Peeters, 1959.

Beck, Edmund, ed. *Des Heiligen Ephraem des Syrers Hymnen de Paradiso und Contra Julianum*. CSCO 174–175. Louvain: Peeters, 1957.

Beck, Edmund, ed. *Des Heiligen Ephraem des Syrers Hymnen de Virginitate*. CSCO 223–224. Louvain: Peeters, 1962.

Beck, Edmund, ed. *Des Heiligen Ephraem des Syrers Paschahymnen*. CSCO 247–248. Louvain: Peeters, 1964.

Beck, Edmund, ed. *Des Heiligen Ephraem des Syrers Sermo de Domino Nostro*. CSCO 270–271. Louvain: Peeters, 1966.

Beck, Edmund, ed. *Des Heiligen Ephraem des Syrers Sermones de Fide*. CSCO 212–213. Louvain: Peeters, 1961.

Beck, Edmund, ed. *Des Heiligen Ephraem des Syrers Sermones*. Vol. 1. CSCO 305–306. Louvain: Peeters, 1969.

Beck, Edmund, ed. *Des Heiligen Ephraem des Syrers Sermones*. Vol. 2. CSCO 311–312. Louvain: Peeters, 1970.

Beck, Edmund, ed. *Des Heiligen Ephraem des Syrers Sermones*. Vol. 3. CSCO 320–321. Louvain: Peeters, 1972.

Beck, Edmund, ed. *Des Heiligen Ephraem des Syrers Sermones*. Vol. 4. CSCO 334–335. Louvain: Peeters, 1973.

Beck, Edmund, ed. *Ephraem Syrus. Sermones in Hebdomadam Sanctam*. CSCO 412–413. Louvain: Peeters, 1979.

Beck, Edmund, ed. *Nachträge zu Ephraem Syrus*. CSCO 363–364. Louvain: Peeters, 1975.

Bedjan, Paulus, ed. *Acta Martyrum et Sanctorum Syriace*. 7 volumes; vol. III. Paris, 1892. Pp. 621–665.

Duncombe, John. *Select Works of the Emperor Julian and Some Pieces of the Sophist Libanius*. London: J. Nichols, 1784.

Egan, George A., ed. *Saint Ephrem, An Exposition of the Gospel*. CSCO 291–292. Louvain: Peeters, 1968.

Foerster, Richard, ed. *Libanii Opera*. Bibliotheca Scriptorum Graecorum et Romanorum Teubneriana. Leipzig: Teubner, 1908. Vol. 4. Pp. 322–341.

Garitte, Gérard. "La version arménienne du sermon de saint Ephrem sur Jonas." *Revue des études arméniennes* 6 (1969) 23–43.

Garsoïan, Nina G. *The Epic Histories attributed to P'awstos Buzand (Buzandaran Patmut'iwnk')*. Harvard Armenian Texts and Studies, 8. Cambridge: Harvard University Press, 1989.

Janda, Antonina, tr. *A Spiritual Psalter or Reflections on God excerpted by Bishop Theophan from the Works of our Holy Father Ephraim the Syrian arranged in the manner of the Psalms of David, together with the Life of St. Ephraim translated by I.E. Lambertsen*. Liberty: St. John of Kronstadt, 1997.

Kostanean, Karapet, ed. *Grigor Magistrosi T'ght'erě* [*The Epistles of Grigor Magistros*; in Armenian]. Alexandrapōl: Gēorg Sanoyeants', 1910.

Leloir, Louis, ed. *Saint Ephrem, Commentaire de l'évangile concordant, version arménienne*. CSCO 137, 145. Louvain: Peeters, 1953, 1954.

Leloir, Louis, ed. *Saint Ephrem, Commentaire de l'évangile concordant*. Chester Beatty Monographs, 8. Dublin: Hodges Figgis, 1963.

Leloir, Louis, ed. *Saint Ephrem, Commentaire de l'évangile concordant texte syriaque (Manuscript Chester Beatty 709) Folios Additionnels*. Chester Beatty Monographs 8. Louvain: Peeters, 1990.

Mariès, Louis and Charles Mercier, eds. *Hymnes de S. Ephrem conservées en version arménienne*. Patrologia Orientalis 30. Turnhout: Brepols, 1961.

Mathews, Edward G., Jr., ed. and tr. *The Armenian Commentary on the Book of Genesis attributed to Ephrem the Syrian*. CSCO 572–573. Louvain: Peeters, 1998.

Mathews, Edward G., Jr., ed. and tr. *The Armenian Commentaries on Exodus-Deuteronomy attributed to Ephrem the Syrian*. CSCO 587–588. Louvain: Peeters, 2001.

Meyer, Robert T. *Palladius: The Lausiac History*. Ancient Christian Writers, 34. New York: Paulist, 1964.

Mitchell, Charles, Anthony A. Bevan, and Francis C. Burkitt. *S. Ephraim's Prose Refutations of Mani, Marcion and Bardaisan*. 2 volumes. London: Text and Translation Society, 1912, 1921.

Outtier, Bernard. "Un discours sur les ruses de Satan attribué à Ephrem: texte arménien inédit." *REA* 13 (1978–1979) 165–174.

Renoux, Charles, ed. *Ephrem de Nisibe Mêmrê sur Nicomedie*. Patrologia Orientalis 37. Turnhout: Brepols, 1975.

Rolfe, John C. *Ammianus Marcellinus*. Loeb Classical Library. London: Heinemann, 1935.

Srjuni, A.Y. "Srboyn Ep'remi i Yusēp' ewt'n Vahangi [S. Ephrem on the Seven Vahangs of Joseph; in Armenian]." *Sion* 47 (1973) 26–37, 137–144.

Ter-Pétrossian, Lévon, ed., and Bernard Outtier, tr. *Textes arméniens relatifs à S. Ephrem*. CSCO 473–474. Louvain: Peeters, 1985.

Tonneau, Raymond M., ed. *Sancti Ephraem Syri in Genesim et in Exodum commentarii*. CSCO 152–53. Louvain: Peeters, 1955.

SECONDARY STUDIES

Baumstark, Anton. *Geschichte der syrischen Literatur*. Bonn: A. Marcus und E. Weber, 1922.

Beck, Edmund, Democratie Hemmerdinger-Iliadou, and Joseph Kirchmeyer, "Ephrem le Syrien." *Dictionnaire de Spiritualité* 4. Paris: G. Beauchesne, 1960. Pp. 788–822.

Bou Mansour, Tanios. *La pensée symbolique de Saint Ephrem le Syrien*. Bibliothèque de l'Université Saint Esprit, 16. Kaslik: Université Saint Esprit, 1988.

Brock, Sebastian P. "A Brief Guide to the Main Editions and Translations of the Works of St. Ephrem." *The Harp* 3 (1990) 7–29.

Brock, Sebastian P. *The Harp of the Spirit*. Studies Supplementary to Sobornost, no. 4. 2d ed. London: St. Alban and St. Sergius, 1985.

Brock, Sebastian P. *The Luminous Eye: The Spiritual World Vision of St. Ephrem*. Rome, 1985. 2d ed., Cistercian Studies Series 124; Kalamazoo: Cistercian Press, 1992.

Brock, Sebastian P. *St. Ephrem the Syrian: Hymns on Paradise*. Crestwood: St. Vladimir's Seminary Press, 1990.

Brock, Sebastian P. and George A. Kiraz. *Ephrem the Syrian: Select Poems*. Eastern Christian Texts, 2. Provo: Brigham Young University Press, 2006.

Buchan, Thomas. *"Blessed is He who has brought Adam from Sheol": Christ's Descent to the Dead in the Theology of Saint Ephrem the Syrian*. Gorgias Dissertations 13, Early Christian Studies 2. Piscataway: Gorgias Press, 2004.

Bundy, David. "The Sources of the Isaiah Commentary of Georg Skewŕacʻi." In Thomas Samuelian and Michael E. Stone, eds. *Medieval Armenian Culture*. University of Pennsylvania Armenian Texts and Studies, 6. Chico: Scholars Press, 1984. Pp. 401–402.

Clément, Oliver. *Three Prayers: The Lord's Prayer, O Heavenly King, Prayer of St. Ephrem*. Crestwood: St. Vladimir's Seminary Press, 2000.

Conybeare, Frederick C. *A Catalogue of the Armenian Manuscripts in the British Museum*. London: British Museum, 1913.

Conybeare, Frederick C. "The Commentary of Ephrem on Acts." In F.J. Foakes Jackson and Kirsopp Lake, eds., *The Beginnings of Christianity*. Volume III: The Text of Acts. London: Macmillan, 1926. Pp. 373–453.

de Halleux, André. "Ephrem le Syrien." *Revue Théologique de Louvain* 14 (1983) 338–343.

de Halleux, André. "Mar Ephrem théologien." *Parole de l'Orient* 4 (1973) 35–54.

den Biesen, Kees. *Annotated Bibliography of Ephrem the Syrian*. 2nd revised ed. Raleigh: Lulu, 2002.

den Biesen, Kees. *Simple and Bold: Ephrem's Art of Symbolic Thought*. Gorgias Dissertations 26, Early Christian Studies 6. Piscataway: Gorgias Press, 2006.

Djanachian, Mesrop. "Les Arménistes et les Mékhitaristes," in *Armeniaca: Mélanges d'études arméniennes*. Venice: S. Ghazar Press, 1969.

Fěntěglean, Garnik. "Epʻrem Xori kam Xuri'" ["Ephrem 'Xori' or 'Xuri'"; in Armenian]. *Sion* 1 (1927) 252–253.

Froidevaux, Louis. "Sur un recueil arménien d'hymnes de Saint Éphrem." *Recherches de Science Religieuse* 50 (1963) 558–578.

Geerard, Maurice. *Clavis Patrum Graecorum*. Vol. II. Turnhout: Brepols, 1974.

Hallier, Ludwig. *Untersuchungen über die Edessenische Chronik*. Texte und Untersuchungen IX.1. Leipzig: J.C. Hinrichs, 1892.

Hambye, Edward R. "St. Ephrem and his Prayers." *The Harp* 1 (1988) 47–52.

Hatityan, Artun. "Surb Ep'rem Xurin Asori (306?–379)" ["Saint Ephrem the Syrian Priest (306?–379)"; in Armenian]. *Ejmiacin* 36.1 (1979) 46–55; 36.2 (1979) 25–34.

Hemmerdinger-Iliadou, Democratie. "Ephrem: versions grecque, latine et slave. Addenda et corrigenda." *Epeteris Hetairaias Buzantinon Spoudon* 42 (1975/1976) 320–373.

Kéchichian, Isaac. "Saint Ephrem (†373) dans la littérature arménienne." *Haigazian Armenological Review* 13 (1993) 101–106.

Leloir, Louis, tr. *Éphrem de Nisibe: Commentaire sur l'Évangile Concordant ou le Diatessaron*. Sources Chrétiennes, 121. Paris: Cerf, 1966.

McVey, Kathleen E. *Ephrem the Syrian Hymns*. Classics of Western Spirituality. New York: Paulist Press, 1989.

Mathews, Edward G., Jr. "Armenian Hymn IX, ON MARRIAGE by Saint Ephrem the Syrian." *Journal of the Society for Armenian Studies* 9 (1996, 1997 [1999]), 55–63.

Mathews, Edward G., Jr. "The Armenian Literary Corpus Attributed to St. Ephrem the Syrian: Prolegomena to a Project." *St. Nersess Theological Review* 1 (1996) 145–168.

Mathews, Edward G., Jr. "A First Glance at the Armenian Prayers attributed to Sourb Ep'rem Xorin Asorwoy." In Roberta R. Ervine, ed., *Worship Traditions in Armenia and the Neighboring Christian East*. Crestwood: St. Vladimir's Seminary Press, 2006. Pp. 161–174.

Mathews, Edward G., Jr. "St. Ephrem, *Madrâšê On Faith*, 81–85: *Hymns on the Pearl*, I–V." *St. Vladimir's Theological Quarterly* 38 (1994) 45–72.

Mathews, Edward G., Jr. "Saint Ephrem the Syrian: Armenian Dispute Hymns between Virginity and Chastity." *Revue des études arméniennes* 28 (2001–2002) 143–169.

Mathews, Edward G., Jr. "Syriac into Armenian: The Translations and their Translators." *Journal of the Canadian Society for Syriac Studies* 10 (2010) 20–44.

Mathews, Edward G., Jr. "The *Vita* Tradition of Ephrem the Syrian, the Deacon of Edessa." *Diakonia* 22 (1988–89) 15–42.

Mathews, Edward G., Jr. and Joseph P. Amar. *St. Ephrem the Syrian: Selected Prose Works*. FOTC 91; Washington: Catholic University of America, 1994.

Mathews, Thomas F. and Avedis K. Sanjian. *Armenian Gospel Iconography: The Tradition of the Glajor Gospel*. Dumbarton Oaks Studies, 29. Washington: Dumbarton Oaks, 1991.

Mills, William C. *The Prayer of St. Ephrem the Syrian: A Biblical Commentary*. Rollinsford: Orthodox Research Institute, 2009.

Murat, Frederic J. "Vestasan asacuack' abbaj Efremi vasn Nikomedeaj kalak'i" ["Sixteen Sermons of Abba Ephrem on the town of Nicomedia"; in Armenian]. *Huschardzan: Festschrift aus Anlaß des 100 Jährigen Bestandes der Mechitaristen-Kongregation in Wien*. Vienna: Mkhitarean Tparan, 1911. Pp. 203–208.

Murray, Robert. *Symbols of Church and Kingdom*. Cambridge: Cambridge University Press, 1975. Revised ed. Piscataway: Gorgias Press, 2004.

Murray, Robert. "The Theory of Symbolism in St. Ephrem's Theology." *Parole de l'Orient* 6/7 (1975/1976) 1–20.

Nedungatt, George. "The Covenanters of the Syriac speaking Church." *Orientalia Christiana Periodica* 39 (1973) 191–215, 419–444.

Outtier, Bernard. "Les recueils arméniens et géorgiens d'oeuvres attribuées à S. Ephrem le Syrien." *Actes 29ᵉ congrès international des Orientalistes: Orient Chrétien*, 53–58, Paris: L'Asiathèque, 1975. Pp. 53–58.

Outtier, Bernard. "Saint Ephrem d'après ses biographies et ses oeuvres." *Parole de l'Orient* 4 (1973) 11–33.

Peeters, Paul. *Bibliotheca Hagiographica Orientalis*. Subsidia Hagiographica, 10. Brussels: Societé des bollandistes, 1910.

Renoux, Charles. "Vers le commentaire de Job d'Ephrem de Nisibe." *Parole de l'Orient* 6/7 (1975/1976) 63–68.

Russell, James R. "On St. Grigor Narekatsi, His Sources and His Contemporaries." *Armenian Review* 41 (1988) 62–63.

Schmemann, Alexander. *Great Lent*. Crestwood: St. Vladimir's Seminary Press, 1969.

Shirinian, Manea E. "Reflections on the 'Sons and Daughters of the Covenant' in the Armenian Sources." *Revue des études arméniennes* 28 (2001–2002) 261–285.

Stone, Michael. *Adam's Contract with Satan: The Legend of the Cheirograph of Adam*. Bloomington/Indianapolis: Indiana University Press, 2002.

Ter Petrossian, Levon. *Ancient Armenian Translations*. New York: St. Vartan Press, 1992.

Tēr-Petrosyan, Levon H. "Ktsʻurdkʻ S. Epʻremi Khorin Asorwoy (bnagrakan chshgrtumner)" ["Hymns of S. Ephrem the Syrian (Textual Emendations)"; in Armenian]. *Handēs Amsorya* 92 (1978) 15–48.

Terian, Abraham. *The Armenian Gospel of the Infancy*. Oxford: Oxford University Press, 2008.

Thomson, Robert W. *A Bibliography of Classical Armenian Literature to 1500 AD*. Turnhout: Brepols, 1995.

Thomson, Robert. "Literary Interactions between Syriac and Armenian." *Journal of the Canadian Society for Syriac Studies* 10 (2010) 3–19.

Thomson, Robert W. "Vardapet in the Early Armenian Church." *Le Muséon* 75 (1962) 367–384.

Tisserant, Eugene. *Codices Armeni Bibliothecae Vaticanae Borgiani Vaticani Barberiniani Chisiani*. Rome, 1927.

Tʻorosean, Yovhannēs. "Aknark mē S. Epʻremi Hin Ktakaranin Meknutʻeantsʻ Hay tʻargmanutʻean vray [A Glance at the Armenian Translation of the Old Testament Commentaries of St. Ephrem; in Armenian]." *Bazmavep* 82 (1925) 3–9; 84 (1927) 33–37.

Vardanean, Aristakēs. "Srboyn Epʻremi Meknutʻiwn ew skizbn Yobay [The Commentary of Saint Ephrem and the Beginning of Job; in Armenian]." *Handēs Amsorya* 26 (1912) 617–626, 666–674.

Weitenberg, Jos J.S. "Armeno-Syrian Cultural Relations in the Cilician Period (12th – 14th c.). In Herman Teule et al., *The Syriac Renaissance*. Eastern Christian Studies 9; Louvain: Peeters, 2010. Pp. 341–352.

Zarbhanalean, Garegin. *Matenadaran Haykakan T'argmanut'eants' Nakheats'* (Dar D-ZhG) [Catalogue of Early Armenian Translations; in Armenian]. Venice: Mkhit'arean Tparan, 1889.

INDEX

NAMES AND TERMS

Aaron	149	Ezekiel	151
Abraham	133	Father	47, 77, 89, 101, 109, 111, 117, 127, 129, 131, 147, 161, 163
Absalom	151		
Adam	47, 133		
Almighty	137	Font of Immortality	21
Amalek	149	Font of Life	21
Ananiah	151	Gabriel	83
Apostles	85, 89, 105	Gehenna	63, 71, 89, 113, 115, 117, 119
Baal	151		
Babylonians	153	God	41, 69, 91, 95, 99, 105, 107, 111, 115, 123, 129, 135, 139, 141, 143, 149, 155, 157, 163
Beneficent One	23, 33, 59, 63, 81, 91, 107, 113, 115, 117, 119, 121, 123, 125, 127, 137, 139, 141, 145		
Bridegroom	83	Goliath	133
Caiaphas	131	Good News	43, 67
Canaanite	121	Good Shepherd	23
Captain	23	Gregory the Illuminator	83
Christ	21, 25, 69, 89, 91, 95, 99, 105, 133, 159	Haman	151
		Hezekiah	133
Compassionate One	61, 77, 95, 119, 123, 145	Holy Spirit	23, 27, 29, 33, 43, 45, 51, 65, 69, 81, 97, 109, 117, 127, 131, 137, 141, 161, 163
Creator	35, 95, 97, 105, 111, 115, 117, 129, 161		
Cross	83, 99, 109, 121, 131, 135, 139	Hope	39, 49, 57, 75, 95, 99, 137, 139, 141, 147, 153, 157
		Husbandman	137
Daniel	133, 151	Image	25, 47, 125, 147, 159
David	79, 113, 133, 151	Isaac	133
Deliverer	25, 163	Isaiah	151
Divinity	81, 83, 87, 139, 141	Jacob	133
Egypt	129	Jehosaphat	151
Egyptians	43	Jeremiah	79, 133, 153
Elijah	133, 151	Jerusalem	103
Elisha	133, 151	Jesus	23, 25, 57, 65, 69, 89, 91, 105, 133
Esau	133		
Esther	151	Jezebel	133

John (the Fore-runner) 83		Pharaoh	43, 133, 149, 155
Jonah	133, 151	Phinehas	149
Joseph (patriarch) 133		Prince	99
Joshua	149, 151	Prophets	85
Judah	155	Protector of soul 59	
Judge	87, 95, 97	Radiance	159
King	97, 121, 141, 149, 155, 157	Refuge	137
Life	67	Restorer	161
Life-giver	95, 117, 127	Ruler	95
Light of the World 135		Samson	151
Lord of life	59	Samuel	151
Lot	133	Satan	35, 41, 43, 45, 111, 113, 115, 121, 163
Lover of mankind 23, 59, 87, 91, 99, 111, 113, 115, 117, 119, 121, 123, 125, 127, 145, 159, 161		Saul	151
		Savior	25, 89, 95, 105, 107, 111, 113, 117, 123, 135, 137, 141, 143, 159, 161
Maker	117		
Malchus	129	Sennacherib	151, 155
Martyrs	85	Siloam	39
Mattathias	155	Simeon	129, 155
Merciful One	33, 61, 91, 99, 117, 121, 123, 125, 127, 143	Sodom	119
		Sodomites	133
Micah	151	Son of God	99, 105, 133, 147, 161, 163
Mordechai	151	Stephen	83
Moses	133, 149	Sun of Righteousness 25	
Mother of God 83, 129		Susanna	133
Ninevites	119	Tartarus	73
Noah	119, 133, 163	Thekla	135
Nun	149	Treasury of all Goodness 21	
Only-Begotten	99, 105	Trinity	93, 103, 127
Patriarchs	85	True Light	21
Paul	133	Vardapets	81, 85
Peter	19, 79, 129, 131		

BIBLICAL CITATIONS AND ALLUSIONS

Genesis
	1:26	125, 147	3:24	133
	1:26–28	77	7:17–24	119
	2:7	125, 147	7:21–23	119
	2:8	47	7:23	133
	2:17	125	8:15–18	133
	3:1–15	145	14:13–24	133
	3:1–19	125	19:24–28	119
	3:15	35	19:1–29	133
	3:21	21, 37	19:26	73
			21:8–14	133

26:1–11	133	20:1–11	133
32:6–33:17	133	Tobit	
37:17–36	133	10:13	95
38	43	Judith	
39:1–6	133	9:12	95

Exodus
- 5:2 — 155
- 8:30–32 — 149
- 12:40–42 — 129
- 12:50–15:21 — 133
- 14:26–31 — 43, 149, 155
- 14:28 — 43
- 17:6 — 21
- 17:8–16 — 149

Numbers
- 11:2 — 149
- 12:9–15 — 149
- 20:2–13 — 21
- 21:7 — 149
- 25:6–15 — 149

Deuteronomy
- 2:27 — 45
- 6:7 — 83
- 11:19 — 83

Joshua
- 1–12 — 151
- 1:2–21 — 155
- 16:28–31 — 151
- 18 — 151

1 Samuel
- 8:4–22 — 151
- 17:21–54 — 133
- 31:1–13 — 151

2 Samuel
- 7:8–16 — 151
- 12:21 — 79
- 18:15 — 151

1 Kings
- 18:13–19:37 — 155
- 18:17–40 — 151
- 21:17–24 — 133

2 Kings
- 6:30–8:15 — 133
- 9:4–37 — 133
- 13:14–23 — 151
- 19:35–36 — 151

Esther
- 4:8–18 — 151
- 7:1–10 — 151
- 14:1–19 — 151

1 Maccabees
- 2:1–70 — 155

4 Maccabees
- 17:4 — 49

Job
- 10:8 — 61
- 19:9 — 61
- 30:17 — 57

Psalms
- 5:8 — 59
- 5:11 — 45
- 6:1 — 95
- 6:6 — 113
- 17:6 — 135
- 17:13 — 85
- 18:14 — 107
- 18:48 — 85
- 25:4 — 33, 39
- 27:9 — 97
- 34:13 — 57
- 36:7 — 35
- 41:4 — 71
- 43:1 — 85
- 46:6 — 87
- 51:1 — 95
- 51:4 — 59
- 51:11 — 69
- 52:3 — 45
- 55:6 — 43
- 57:1 — 35
- 59:2 — 85
- 63:4 — 113
- 67:1 — 95
- 69:16–17 — 95
- 69:28 — 55
- 74:16 — 153
- 77:12 — 29

79:5	95
79:8	95
80:2	107
82:4	85
85:5	95
88:2	135, 141
88:14	97
89:11	153
92:13	41
95:11	51
103:10	97
107:14	39
107:25–30	43
109:25	41
116:16	39
118:73	61
119:15	97
119:23	97
119:27	29
119:48	97
119:78	97
130:3	105
132:10	95
139:2	83
140:1	85
141:2	139
143:2	105
143:5	29
145:5	29
148:8	153

Proverbs
8:29	153
12:28	47

Sirach
11:14	95

Isaiah
6:3	131
6:6	33
41:10	135
41:15	87
55:3	137
58:6	39

Jeremiah
5:22	153
25:14	105
38:5–13	133
38:7–13	153

Lamentations
2:11	57

Ezekiel
11:19	21, 23
18:23	99
28:3	135
33:11	99
36:26–27	141

Daniel
1:8–16	25
3:13–22	151
3:13–30	133
3:40	153
3:42–43	153
6:16–23	133
6:16–28	151
9:4	71
12:3	45
13:7–62	133

Joel
2:31	71

Jonah
1:17–2:10	133
2:1–10	151
3:10	119

Micah
4:2	33, 107

Zechariah
1:3	19

Malachi
4:2	25
4:5	71

Matthew
2:13–15	129
3:3	59
3:7	133
3:16	43
5:22	63
5:26	45
5:45	155
7:7	101, 123
7:8	35
7:13	41
7:14	31
7:23	71

8:12	73, 91	14:32–42	129
9:2–8	41	14:65	121
9:5	67	14:71–72	131
9:6	47	15:17	121
9:13	101, 121	16:18	35
11:25	95	Luke	
11:28	35	1:30–37	83
13:3–23	51	1:75	47
13:18–23	79	2:7	129
13:37	29	2:25–35	129
13:42	73, 91	2:30	39
13:50	91	3:4	59
14:22–27	129	3:7	133
14:31	19, 129	5:24	47
15:21–28	121	5:32	121
15:27	23	7:38	79
16:27	87	7:44	79
17:21	49	10:19	35
22:10	19	10:21	95
22:13	73	10:29–37	37
24:48–51	77	11:9	123
25:1–13	39, 101	13:11	39
25:10	131	13:27	71
25:10–12	89	15:11–32	37, 97
25:12	107	15:13	53
25:24–30	101	15:18	127
25:32–33	21	15:18–19	37, 101
25:33	91, 107	15:20	117
25:34	89	15:20–24	121
25:41	45, 71	15:21	101, 127
25:41–46	89, 101	16:20	43
25:26	73	18:1	145
26:36–46	129	18:1–6	121
26:74–75	131	18:9–14	19
26:75	79	18:13–14	121
27:30	163	19:9	67
27:48	163	22:30	37
27:62–66	131	22:40	145
28:1	131	22:40–46	129
Mark		22:46	145
1:3	59	22:61–62	131
2:9	47	23:39–43	19, 85
2:17	121	23:42	95
6:45–51	129	23:43	161
9:43	71	24:1–3	131
12:42	21	24:26	55

John
- 1:9 — 21
- 1:14 — 99, 105
- 1:18 — 99, 105
- 1:23 — 59
- 4:10 — 27
- 5:8 — 47
- 6:16–21 — 129
- 6:65 — 77
- 8:12 — 21, 135
- 9:1–12 — 39
- 10:1–18 — 47
- 10:3–5 — 47
- 10:16 — 47
- 13:1–11 — 129
- 14:6 — 19
- 14:15 — 21
- 14:21 — 21
- 15:10 — 21
- 15:11 — 23
- 16:23 — 145
- 18:10 — 129
- 19:1–3 — 131
- 19:34 — 121
- 20:1 — 131
- 20:28 — 69

Acts
- 3:15 — 95
- 9:3–7 — 121
- 10:42 — 95
- 17:24 — 95

Romans
- 8:22–23 — 87

1 Corinthians
- 2:9 — 61
- 6:19 — 29, 51, 97
- 13:1 — 63

2 Corinthians
- 6:16 — 29
- 11:3 — 145

Ephesians
- 5:8–10 — 29
- 6:11–16 — 49, 53
- 6:14–16 — 49

Philippians
- 1:11 — 29
- 2:7 — 99, 121, 163
- 2:7–8 — 99
- 3:19 — 31

Colossians
- 2:14 — 89

1 Thessalonians
- 4:16 — 87
- 5:2 — 131
- 5:17 — 75

2 Timothy
- 4:1 — 95

Hebrews
- 2:13 — 81
- 3:11 — 51
- 3:18 — 51
- 4:1–11 — 51
- 4:13 — 135
- 12:11 — 25, 29

James
- 5:7 — 137
- 5:11 — 95

1 Peter
- 1:18–19 — 87
- 1:19 — 89
- 3:10 — 57
- 3:20 — 119
- 4:5 — 95
- 5:8 — 85, 107, 163

2 Peter
- 1:2 — 27
- 2:4 — 73
- 2:5 — 119, 163

1 John
- 2:3–4 — 21
- 3:22 — 21
- 3:24 — 21
- 4:9 — 99, 105
- 5:2–3 — 21

Revelation
- 1:8 — 157
- 1:17 — 157
- 2:10 — 55
- 6:12–14 — 87
- 14:13 — 49, 95
- 21:6 — 157
- 21:14 — 89

21:23–25   103
22:5   103

22:13   157

www.ingramcontent.com/pod-product-compliance
Lightning Source LLC
Chambersburg PA
CBHW080806300426
44114CB00020B/2849